even the rhinos
were nymphos

bruce jay FRIEDMAN

even the rhinos
were nymphos

BEST NONFICTION

the university of chicago press

chicago and london

BRUCE JAY FRIEDMAN is the author of seven novels (including *The Dick*, *Stern*, and *A Mother's Kisses*), four collections of short stories, and a number of full-length plays—among them *Scuba Duba* and *Steambath*. His screenplay credits include *Splash* and *Stir Crazy*.

The University of Chicago Press, Chicago 60637
The University of Chicago Press, Ltd., London
© 2000 by Bruce Jay Friedman
Al rights reserved. Published 2000
Printed in the United States of America

09 08 07 06 05 04 03 02 01 00   1 2 3 4 5

ISBN: 0-226-26350-9 CLOTH

Library of Congress Cataloging-in-Publication Data

Friedman, Bruce Jay, 1930–
    Even the rhinos were nymphos : best nonfiction / Bruce Jay Friedman.
    p. cm.
    ISBN 0-226-26350-9 (cloth : alk. paper)
    I. Title.
PS3556.R5 E94 2000
814'.54—dc21   00-029896

⊗ The paper used in this publication meets the minimum requirements of the American National Standard for Information Sciences—Permanence of Paper for Printed Library Materials, ANSI Z39.48–1992.

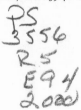

FOR

Dollie

AND

Irving

Contents

Introduction, 1
Some Notes on the Contents, 5

PART ONE: THE LITERARY LIFE

"Don't Dare Put Me in Your Play!" (or Story, Novel, Etc.), 11
Even the Rhinos Were Nymphos, 15
Algren and Shaw, 27
Tales from the Darkside, 30
Don of a New Age, 37

PART TWO: CELEBRITIES AND OTHERS

Some Thoughts on Clint Eastwood and Heidegger, 49
The Imposing Proportions of Jean Shrimpton, 54
To Cigars, with Love and Devotion, 66
Yank Paparazzo, 73
Frozen Guys, 78
Requiem for a Heavy, 86
School for Butlers, 97
A Champion for Bismarck, 107

PART THREE: LESSONS OF THE STREET

Charge: Murder, 127
Lessons of the Street, 145
Who's Watching the Border? 158
Tom Noguchi, 171

PART FOUR: ELSEWHERE

My Life among the Stars, 185
My Jerusalem, 193
Dark Watercolors from Port-au-Prince, 204
Tokyo, 216
Prague—the Gray Enchantress, 222
Little Rock, 230

Acknowledgments, 237

This moment of "truth" in novels, as opposed to the "truth" attempted by reportage, is an interesting and controversial subject. I am not at all sure that reportage always wins.

Anthony Powell, *Miscellaneous Verdicts*

Introduction

There is the life we lead and the one we touch up a bit, if not actually fabricate, to help along a frail ego and perhaps to impress grandchildren. In the romantic version I've concocted of my life, I received "training" as a journalist. Though no record of my stay there exists, I did indeed attend the University of Missouri and was awarded—without applause—a Bachelor of Journalism degree, which has always sounded suspiciously like something that can be snapped up through the mail.

But what exactly was that vaunted "training" of mine?

For my four years of effort, I can recall only that someone named Fenno was caned in public by George Washington for reporting that the president was a "rascal." Or it may have been Fenno who caned Washington. And for a brief period I was able to recite the names of editors who headed up turn-of-the-century farming weeklies, the ubiquitous Fenno being among them.

Armed with these credentials, I set out in the early fifties to find a job as a reporter, my first stop being the Associated Press. There to greet me was a large, expressionless man who showed me to a desk, then gathered up an armful, if not a bale, of wire service dispatches—having to do with troop movements in Taegu—which he tossed at me. Thinking this was some sort of journalistic beach ball, I playfully tossed it back, causing him to frown and to walk away without comment. Decades later, I still have no idea of what he was getting at.

Jobs were scarce in the early fifties, or so it appeared to me. Unless you were shooting for a career as an advertising space salesman, the Old School Tie of the University of Missouri Journalism Division was not especially useful. All journalism seemed a great, walled-off fortress (with Dartmouth graduates guarding the ramparts) that I could only stare at with longing. In the hope that any experience would be useful, I filled in for a time as a warehouse inspector, my job being to scrutinize ceramic umbrella stands that were made in Sweden and to send the defective ones back to Malmö with a cross note. Concerned about the effect on me of warehouse dampness, my mother took over at this point; a pioneer networker, her headquarters being the bar at the House of Chan restaurant in Manhattan, she arranged to have me given a tryout as an assistant editor at the Magazine Management Company (see "Even the Rhinos Were Nymphos"). Though my rise was far from meteoric, I was soon shipping writers to exotic locations and envying them as I saw them off. My solution was to steal away in the dead of night and to begin a full-time writer's life—later to be described unappealingly by a certain doyenne at a cocktail party in Southampton ("My, we've had a spotty career, haven't we?").

Spotty it may have been, but it has been consistently spotty. Without my mother's intervention (to the best of my knowledge) I have been able to wangle assignments from such diverse publications as *Esquire*, the *Saturday Evening Post, Harper's, Rolling Stone, Playboy*, and others even more diverse—*Saga, Wigway, Playbill*—in short, any magazine with a decent notion and the willingness to throw a few pennies in my direction. Along the way, I have published novels and short stories, done some screen work, and written for the theater, but I have always drifted back to a journalistic "base"—or at least my version of one—and especially when invited to do so.

When I began as a writer, an alarming number of years ago, it was fashionable to think that Hollywood "corrupted" literary types. In my— once again—spotty career as a screenwriter, I've always felt that I was the one who did the corrupting. Take the money, scribble a bit, and enjoy the room service. In much the same way, I think of myself as having "used" magazine journalism, as a means of getting out of the house, making an occasional mortgage payment—and shoring up a shaky education. (A knowledge of the editor Fenno's various activities can take you only so far.)

The only rule I've had—to the extent that anyone in this tenuous profession can afford to have a rule—is that each assignment be different from the previous ones. And having established that rule, I've cheerfully broken it, particularly in the case of Hollywood, where it is not so much the films but the "players" who continue to fascinate me (see "Tales from the Darkside" and "My Life among the Stars"). The only ones who express themselves more vividly than agents and producers are dentists ("I'm afraid there's no light at the end of the tunnel on that wisdom tooth").

An unintended but welcome result of my efforts in magazine journalism has been a pollinating effect on the fiction I've written. After spending several weeks in a Chicago homicide bureau (see "Charge: Murder"), the violent atmosphere lingers and suggests a novel, eventually published as *The Dick*. In Jerusalem, an Israeli Arab room service waiter singles me out as someone who can help him escape from Israel to attend the wedding of a brother in Queens. Though not reported in the piece that has brought me to this hotel ("My Jerusalem"), the incident, seemingly extraneous at the time, becomes a central plot point in a short novel in progress (if not retreat). A sharp-eyed reader once wrote to me, complaining that a detail in a travel article I'd written turned up in one of my novels. Is this an indictable offense? Should I be packed off to Rikers Island? Or, more favorably, is it a rallying cry for lonely writers around the globe: we can be as synergistic as corporate America.

I am not the first to have doubts as to whether objective journalism exists (who *was* the first?) any more than does "pure" fiction. My speculations on the social life of the Olympian gods (I have none at the moment) are bound to be different from any other, since each writer has a distinctive set of fingerprints. Much the same way, the journalist who interviews Hillary Clinton, as an example, no matter how cloaked in integrity, will show up with a baggage of personal prejudices—and be well on the way, before the first question is asked, to a report that is skewed favorably or otherwise.

Have I been less objective than most? (Does anyone care?) While keeping the door closed to the question of my overall sanity, I confess to having some mild difficulty distinguishing between actual events—and my imagined version of them. I am not the one to describe accurately the proceedings at the city council, or, for that matter, to infiltrate the Gambino family. Nor would I dispatch myself to report on bombing trajectories over Kosovo. If there is a need (continuing along with the job interview) for an impression of a circumstance, a sense of what some person or locale is like, an "enhanced" picture of events, I might give myself a call.

Let me try to justify, or at least explain, what is turning out to be a "tilted" approach to journalism—and life. Isn't a need to "shape existence" one of the forces that drives someone to become a writer, and to remain one? A need to manage events, harness them . . . on a more grandiose level, to bend and control the uncontrollable? Look into the lives of admired writers and you will often, if not always, find early family chaos . . . and an attendant need to restore order—at least on paper.

Look into those same lives and you will also find boundless curiosity. In the course of a long writing career, wretched comments are likely to be made about your work, and appealing ones as well. In the latter category, each writer has his favorite. Mine came from William Emerson of the *Saturday Evening Post* during what, I am now told, was the Golden Age of Magazine Journalism. In an introductory note to a piece I had written, he described me as "a Huck Finn off on his raft for a bright-eyed look at the world . . . and soaking it up like sunshine." Whether or not this was accurate (and I'm certainly not terribly bright-eyed these days), I enjoyed being perceived that way. Who, apart from Noel Coward, wouldn't?

And the check arrived on time.

Recently, and not untypically, I found myself pacing up and down, waiting for a reaction to something or other that I had written. Pacing and crumpling paper are both essentials in the life of a writer. My wife suggested that I find some other place to do my pacing. Acting upon her advice, I took a short trip to London. No sooner had I gotten off the plane than I began furiously to take down notes. It was not until dinner time that I realized I had no particular agenda, that I had not been sent there on an assignment of some kind. Was this a signal . . . an indication that the curtain was coming down?

Intrigued by that possibility, I began, once again, and furiously, to take notes.

BJF
New York City

Some Notes on the Contents

There is a temptation, in compiling a collection of pieces that span many decades, to update language, to bring past attitudes in line with current ones. My wife, who teaches social science and prefers "the raw files," has encouraged me for the most part to resist "improvements." Offering a stunningly presumptuous example, she asks: "Do we need an updated *On the Road*?"

EVEN THE RHINOS WERE NYMPHOS

I have often wondered what happened to some of my old colleagues at the Magazine Management Company. Recently, and after many years—I moved back to Manhattan, and there they were, appearing on the street, one by one—David Markson, Dorothy Gallagher, George Penty, John Bowers, James Collier, Melvin Shestack—the West Village apparently being the place that aging writers go, I would hope, to flourish.

TALES FROM THE DARKSIDE

There is no total escape from Hollywood, particularly the name-dropping so prominent in this piece. A friend, who is an actor, called recently from California and began to cough into the phone. When I asked if he was alright, he said he had caught Pierce Brosnan's cold.

DON OF A NEW AGE

I've written a postscript to the story of my friendship with Mario Puzo, who died last year at the age of seventy-eight. I recall him saying that after age seventy-five, "you are living on the casino's money." I hope my added remarks indicate, if only by indirection, how much I loved and now miss that man—and that it's not a case of too much indirection.

SOME THOUGHTS ON CLINT EASTWOOD AND HEIDEGGER

Eastwood sent a gracious note to me saying that he was a bit puzzled by the piece but that some friends he trusted assured him that it was flattering.

THE IMPOSING PROPORTIONS OF JEAN SHRIMPTON

The brilliantly quirky Harold Hayes of *Esquire* enjoyed odd pairings of subject and writer. It was his idea to put me together with Jean Shrimpton, the reigning fashion model of her time. Ali, the beautiful secretary who keeps popping up in the piece—and distracting me— "became," soon afterward, the actress Ali McGraw.

TO CIGARS, WITH LOVE AND DEVOTION

For the most part, I've given them up . . . but I did enjoy the romance.

YANK PAPARAZZO

In connection with this article, I was called upon to testify in an invasion-of-privacy suit brought against the "ambush" photographer Ron Galella. Following the trial, the *New York Times* reporter told me he admired my novels, but that I was the worst witness he'd ever come across in twenty years of covering the courtroom. Mrs. Onassis, however, thanked me for my support, as did Galella. To show his appreciation, he began to trail me around Manhattan, popping off pictures of me in different locations, causing his puzzled colleagues to do the same—as insurance against my turning out to be someone noteworthy.

A CHAMPION FOR BISMARCK

Virgil Hill continued to fight successfully for a time but, sadly enough, met his Waterloo in the ring against the great Roy Jones, Jr., who in 1998 knocked him out with a single body blow.

There may not have a University of Missouri Old School Tie, but Magazine Management made up for it. I had some trouble getting cooperation from the Border Patrol people in San Ysidro. My difficulties were brought to the attention of the public relations director of the agency, who turned out to be a former writer for my adventure magazines. His instruction to all parties was to "give this man anything he wants."

TOM NOGUCHI

A frustrating experience. I found it unusually difficult to pry information out of this seemingly courteous and outwardly cooperative gentleman. Later, I was told that he had an autobiography in the works—which may have been a factor. He did say I was welcome to witness an autopsy—an invitation I respectfully declined.

MY JERUSALEM

My usual style, in covering some new territory, is to simply wade in and let it all happen. This did not work too well in tightly knit Israel; it would have been wise to set up a few appointments in advance.

the literary life

"don't dare put me in your play!" (or story, novel, etc.)

A sk a writer if he bases his books or plays on existing people and he will invariably toss you an injured look that seems to say, "What kind of person do you think I am?" or "Anyone can do *that*." You might as well try getting him to admit that he colors his hair or take surreptitious tango lessons. "Well I sort of use them as a seed" is an answer that might come from a more forthright member of Our Little Tribe. "They're good as a jumping-off point and you go on from there." Writers are touchy when it comes to this subject; my feeling is that their sensitivity has little to do with the fact that live "characters" are capable of showing up with live attorneys. In a sense, fiction writers seem to feel that the use of flesh-and-blood references tends to tarnish and diminish their stature as storytellers. After all, the argument might go, if my sole accomplishment is to have gotten that bus driver down on paper, have I actually created a character? Wasn't it the Big Novelist in the Sky who did the creating, long before I turned up? And there is the Fiction-Is-Dead Crowd to contend with. If all you are doing is describing people you've encountered, aren't you merely a thinly disguised journalist after all.

It takes little in the way of courage to state that fiction writers do base their characters on actual people and not individuals in Norse myths. It might not be the only game in town, but it is one of the oldest—and would that it were all there was to storytelling. Writers make use of whole people, fragments of them, true versions of people, and distorted

Originally published in *Playbill*, October 1968.

ones, as well. They use glimpses of people, hallucinated versions of them, people they know, and people they have heard about from unreliable sources. The heart transplant technique that so astonished the world came as no surprise to storytellers, who are old hands at grafting sections of one person on to another in order to make up a single character. Writers may use characters in dreams, or even people dreamed about by the people in dreams, but there is always a flesh-and-blood dreamer at the source. When Tolstoy invades the sensibility of a dog, his model is either someone he knows and thinks of as having a doglike style—or more likely the novelist himself imagining how he would feel inhabiting the mind and body of such an animal. Many writers are most proud of their "totally imaginative" works. Yet even if the storytelling journey, so to speak, has been "pure fiction," the port from which the writer sets sail—and perhaps a passenger or two—will be one he has actually known.

I once heard a famed writer of political pieces say that he yearned above all else to write a novel about a tender and failed love affair of his middle years. "But she is still alive," he said, "and I could never do it to her." It may be that no man becomes a fiction writer until he makes a devil's bargain to "do it" to anyone on earth, be it wife, mother, mistress, best friend, or—if the work requires it—his beloved twelve-year-old daughter. Once made, the bargain need never be kept. In most cases, it is better not kept, since there is nothing automatically fascinating about one's teenage nephew meticulously and chronologically observed through six months of work and play. But it strikes me that the freedom to be a sonofabitch is absolutely vital. To write a story or play—and at the same time to be peering nervously over one shoulder wondering about a boyhood French teacher's reaction—is not only technically and psychologically impossible—it is an open invitation to asthma attacks. No question it is a feeble and cowardly defense that will stand up in no court of human relations, but it perhaps helps the writer to remember that he is the one— more than any character he might write about—who is likely to wind up exposed and skewered.

What about those real or imagined "victims" of fictional works, those who have sat—or imagined they have sat—as unwilling subjects for portraits they never realized were being painted. I once noticed a grim and sullen man who sat in a corner and gnashed his teeth through one of the liveliest parties of the year. It was explained to me that he had once been a friend of Thomas Wolfe and felt that he had come across himself one day in a Wolfe novel, portrayed unflatteringly and wearing only the thinnest of disguises. According to the story, he had allowed the real or fancied slight to filter into every chamber of his life and, somehow, to push him into multiple divorces.

Most writers have met people who are fascinated by the idea of being in books and plays and actually go about auditioning for parts in them. A fashion model who had been told I was a writer once dashed up to me and said, "My eyeliner tube exploded on a midnight flight to San Juan, but don't you dare put that in one of your books." In a slightly different category is the person who feels that though he himself is not quite up to carrying a book or play as a character, his job and daily surroundings no question are the stuff of best-sellers. "I just wish you could stand around my hardware store for a few days," he will tell the writer he's collared at a party. "If you saw the characters I have to deal with, you'd have enough material for a lifetime."

Many people have more or less ambivalent feelings about the idea of suddenly turning up in someone's book or play. In that way, they are very much like writers themselves, who on the one hand will sneer at critics' lists of Absurdists, Black Humorists, New Theater Writers—and on the other are fearful of being omitted from any such groupings. A cousin of mine read the galleys of my novel *A Mother's Kisses* and was certain he had been the model for one of the characters in the book. Somewhat hurt and upset, he called one night with more than a slight hint of litigation in his voice. After the book was published and reviewed, he called again, disturbed once more, but for a different reason. "How come the mother got all the attention?" he wanted to know. "How come no one said anything about me?"

Are people able to recognize themselves in fictional works? An editor I know is convinced she has been the subject of at least a dozen novels, each of the authors seeing her through a different prism. She claims to have spotted herself as a sex-mad agent, a cold suburban housewife, a junkie, starlet, lesbian schoolteacher, police officer, senator, and motorcycle slut. In each case, she insists, the evidence is irrefutable that she is the model for the character. She is an interesting woman and no doubt a many-sided one. Perhaps each of the characters actually represented a different side of her. But how sad it would be, really, if this were all illusory on her part and no one had actually found her vivid enough to write about in any role. I have written about people I have either known or brushed up against and have never had one confront me point-blank and, so to speak, catch me in the act. Much more typical was the experience I had when my first novel was published and a strange woman kept sweeping up to me each day at Schrafft's and saying, "How could you have written those things about me," then waltzing off in another direction. To this day, I haven't the faintest idea of what she was talking about.

No doubt it would be unsettling to walk into a theater one day and find a real or imagined likeness of yourself prancing across the stage for all the world to see. Or to feel that your secrets—innocently confided to another—were stacked up in hundreds of copies at Barnes and Noble. Still, I can't help suspecting that few such literary "victims" are taken quite that much by surprise. Writers, charming rascals though they may be, are also for the most part a wretchedly unreliable lot; anyone foolish enough to be in the company of one for long must sense that turning up as a character in a book is the very least of the potential hazards in such an involvement.

Is there any consolation to the person who feels injured by an imaginative work in knowing that he has touched someone so deeply, struck some writer as being so unique, so fair or even so unlovely—but most particularly so *alive*—that he would want to spend a part of his life trying to capture that quality and perhaps to make a permanent record of it? Having never come across myself in a book or play (except unmistakably as Prince Andrey in *War and Peace*), I can't say. I do know that writers will continue to describe people they know and it us unlikely that this phenomenon is anything to be feared or concerned about. Good writing, be it forward looking or pessimistic, proceeds, with rare exception, from an open heart and a warmth of spirit. The writer who sets out to "do a job" on someone is at best a pamphleteer, is schackled from the start, and will inevitably end up injuring himself and his own work. Then, too, a serious writer can only have his victory when he makes not just one but each person in his audience say: "I recognize that character. I know that character. In so many ways, I am that character."

even the rhinos
were nymphos

I n 1954, after several rather pleasant, humdrum years of Korean War duty, I was employed as an assistant editor of *Focus* magazine, one of the many publications of a medium-vast company called Magazine Management. Editorial jobs were difficult to come by in the early fifties. (Have they ever been easy to come by?) A job at *F.Y.I.*, the house organ of *Time-Life*, had been dangled in my direction and then mysteriously withdrawn. I was quite nervous before the final interview series and trotted around the block several times, turning up in a heavy sweat which may have counted against me. My disappointment was great, since I had been assured that although I would not actually be working on any of the esteemed Luce publications, I would "get to visit every floor" of the building. I had tried *Collier's*, where I was instructed to start a file on myself and house it in the personnel department, tossing in items of interest that might come about in my everyday life. At the end of the year, "the three most interesting files" were to be called down and hired. I was given an upcoming issue of *Collier's* and instructed to study it in an attempt to worm out the secret of the magazine's prominence. The lead story was a photo essay on airports at night, transport planes slumbering peacefully in their hangars. The following piece offered readers a history of garlic. On my own initiative, I created a photo essay on Bronx playground bullies which failed to impress Dan Mich, the powerful editor of *Look* magazine. However, I was invited to a party at which male and female *Look* staffers went into a little room and then popped out, wearing each others' underwear.

Originally published in *Rolling Stone*, October 9, 1975.

I am not entirely clear on how I got to the Magazine Management Company, but somewhere in the picture is a chance encounter involving my mother and a furrier at the House of Chan restaurant. I believe the furrier's son-in-law·worked for the company and helped me to get a foot in the door. My editor at *Focus* was a towering fellow named James A. "Big Jim" Bryans, whose view it was that in order to succeed at newsstand publishing, one had to hammer away at what he called the Big Emotions— that is, Hunger, Sex, Death, Jobs, etc. This advice has held up. I was introduced to Martin Goodman, the owner of the company, a congenial silver-haired gentleman of indeterminate age who looked a bit like Hopalong Cassidy. Although I was under the impression that I had already been hired, he looked me over, nonetheless, and said, "Alright, let's give him a try." I worked for the company for eleven years, and I am still not quite certain I ever pinned down the job. Through the time of our association, I found Martin Goodman to be a supportive friend, but at no time was I unaware of a chilling side to him, one that had sent scores of editors writhing into clinics with colitis symptoms. He was at his most quietly fearsome when some unfortunate new editor made the mistake of showing him a photo layout on logrolling. Part of the Martin Goodman legend is that his brothers called him Mr. Goodman. It was said that he was called Mr. Goodman as a little boy. Once, flushed with confidence, having written a well-received novel, I attempted to call him Martin. I thought I had done well until I realized my voice had been an octave too high.

Focus was a peppier and saltier version of a magazine phenomenon called *Quick* which was virtually bite sized and flourished in the early fifties. Most of the Magazine Management publications were peppier and saltier versions of other successful publishing ventures. That might have served as a motto for the company: A bit late, but peppier and saltier. We played Jayne Mansfield to the various Marilyn Monroes of publishing.

New magazines were created and done away with as casually as dimes are popped into Vegas slot machines. No sooner had I settled in as a *Focus* staffer than I was switched off to another bite-sizer called *Picture Life*. I believe that Martin Goodman began this venture because of his affection for the word "life." A genius at divining the buying habits of magazine shoppers, he had great faith in the pulling power of key words. I always felt he came a cropper in the case of *True Action*. Both "true" and "action" are clearly splendid·words individually; when combined, however, they seemed to represent a ringing rebuke to a magazine called *False Action*, which, of course, did not exist.

Picture Life, alas, did not flourish. It predicted correctly that Floyd Patterson would win the heavyweight title and received exactly one letter—from a dying man who was confident he would be able to eke out an extra month of life if only we were to run a six-page picture layout featuring Mitzi Gaynor sniffing gloves. No matter. A series of waggish freelance captions I did for a Magazine Management cheesecaker called *Tab* attracted the attention of Martin Goodman. I was pried away from my position beneath the thumb of "Big Jim" Bryans, given a secretary, an assistant, and the reins of a new entry called *Swank*. My three-man team was considered a large staff in MM terms; years later, when I visited the *Saturday Evening Post* and saw entire floors of people thrown over to the publication of one (skinny) magazine, I felt like Lemuel Gulliver on some weird and wasteful new island. (We were terribly arrogant at Magazine Management and always felt—much in the style of late-night drinkers who are convinced they can take over Haiti—that a handful of us could have "saved" *Life, Look, Collier's*, etc.) *Swank* had once belonged to Arnold Gingrich of *Esquire* and had published Hemingway stories in the twenties—but had never quite caught fire. I was instructed to "take off after *Esquire* and be classy, but not too classy." The advertising people refused to drop their truss ads, which were a trademark of Martin Goodman publications; I argued that you could not kick off each issue with a giant truss ad and then turn around and be urbane and classy (I now feel otherwise) but I was voted down. My first call to a literary agent—heady stuff—was to the distinguished James Oliver Brown. My goal—acquisition of the rights to a Boileau-Narcejac suspense novel, for condensation in *Swank*.

"I don't like your price, Friedman," said Brown.

"I'm not too crazy about it either," I said.

Actually, the fee of one thousand dollars for a twenty-thousand-word selection may have been an all-time Martin Goodman record breaker. In declining my offer, Brown said he had accepted one from Alfred Hitchcock for $150,000. (The novel was turned into the film *Vertigo*.) To this day, I think of Brown's name as being James Oliver I-don't-like-your-price-Friedman Brown.

Swank published new stories by William Saroyan and Graham Greene, and God alone knows who read them. Truss ads and all, the magazine attempted to be classy and risqué. I assigned the late A. C. Spectorsky to do an article on girl pinching. He did one on girl bumping which I rejected. He did a second version on girl shoving; I sent it back. He countered with a third, on girl tickling. I returned it and paid him half his fee. Years later, he asked me to join him at *Playboy*.

"I am making you this offer," he said, "because of your quite proper refusal to accept anything but girl pinching."

Swank failed to set the world on fire. I could tell its sales were feeble because Martin Goodman would walk into my office each month, smack the current issue, and leave. *Playboy* and its legion of imitators in the lit-clit field were beginning to throw their weight around. Risqué was not enough. Though dismissed by some as an "armpit" publisher, Martin Goodman, tapping some strange vein of propriety, refused to "go all the way" and *Swank* faded out of the picture, eventually being sold to someone down the street. In an ironic rendezvous with destiny, the magazine was subsequently published by Martin Goodman's son, Charles, quite properly, as a class tits-and-asser.

In my early years at Magazine Management, I had shown some flashy moves in the backcourt, but my shots were simply not going in. I was Mr. Around the Rim and Out. Despite my disappointing stats, Martin Goodman decided I was the man to take over *Male*, which, along with *Stag*, was a cornerstone of the Goodman chain, a hot seller in the burgeoning men's adventure field. There was a clear-cut hierarchy in this chamber of publishing. High above all others, at a lonely, nosebleed-producing altitude, stood the mighty *True*, which had achieved its status through newsbreaking revelations about hanky-panky in the conduct of World War II. Several notches below, but sturdy nonetheless, was a slick-looking Western cuspidor of a magazine called *Argosy*. There followed, at least in terms of "classiness"—if not circulation—*Saga*; and then, after a bit of a leap and a bound, one reached the nether world of the Goodman books (as our magazines were referred to at the time), *Male, Stag, For Men Only, Man's World, Action for Men, True Action,* and so on. By no means did Magazine Management represent the end of the line. There were legions of other titles that generally featured Gestapo women prancing around captive Yanks in leg shackles. When the men's field met local opposition, the broom used was generally a large one and we were miffed at being swept off the newsstands along with the leg schacklers. Standing off to the side, refusing categorization, was a publication called *Man's* magazine, which both fascinated and disturbed Martin Goodman. It had a modest circulation, was quite unflashy, and seemed to be morosely going its own way. It was, nonetheless, the only competitive magazine that Martin Goodman would smack. I think he was peeved that despite its sluggish appearance it had any circulation at all. And it wasn't his.

A regular activity at Magazine Management was the examination of current issues of *True* and *Argosy*—and perhaps some renegade magazine that had shown a flurry of sales—and the attempt to ferret out the secret of their various achievements.

"Do you think they have our books spread out in front of them?" someone would ask. (Do girls like it, too?)

"You're damned right," would be someone's brave answer—although it seemed unlikely that Fawcett's lordly Ralph Daigh would invest time in cutting his way through the underbrush of our truss ads to peek at a *Male* lead story. This was an era of great snobbishness. A *Male* editor would grow pale at a cocktail party when confronted by a *True* staffer. A *True* person, on the other hand, would be unable to meet the eyes of a *Timer-Lifer*, who in turn was made uncomfortable by the presence of an Alfred Knopfer. There was no end to this, of course, and I'm sure that even Knopfers would feel one-upped by *Times Literary Supplement* people, and so on up to God—that is, until the era of camp and the put-on, when it became a strong social advantage to identify yourself as the managing editor of *Forced Enema*.

I became involved with *Male* at a time when both *Stag* and *Male* had built circulations in excess of a million copies on the strength of stories about people who had been nibbled half to death by ferocious little animals. The titles were terrifying cries of anguish. "A Grysbok Sucked My Bones"; "Give Me Back My Leg"; they seemed to have even more power when couched in the present continuous tense. "A Boar Is Grabbing My Brain."

Salted in among these animal nibblers were backup yarns about third-rail executions. All this, in the supposedly halcyon Eisenhower years. I would have been only too happy to sail in and begin cranking out more of these—but there had been a sudden, unexplainable cessation of interest in these accounts of leg-nibbling ordeals. The men's adventure books had been holding the line with Sintown, or what I always thought of as "scratch the surface" yarns. (Outwardly, Winkleton, Illinois, is a quiet, tree-lined little community. . . . But *scratch the surface* of this supposedly God-fearing little town and you will find that not since Sodom and Gomorrah and blah blah blah.) Any town with a bar and a hooker would do—but somehow the unmasking of fleshpots did not quite do as a total diet for "our guys." We never did find out with any precision exactly who "our guys" were. They seemed to be multiple men's magazine readers who would buy *Argosy* and *True* and then return, with a certain petulance, and buy one or two of ours. Much in the style of someone who has eaten dinner, but requires a cup of chile to be put properly over the top. We were reasonably sure our readers drank beer and had some affiliation with Iwo. There may have been some migrant workers mixed in among them. My brother-in-law was the only reader I was able to pinpoint with any certainty.

We failed, finally, to come up with a concise formula, one that could be as crisply stated as that of, say, the confession magazines: "Sin, confess, repent." With a bit of tap dancing and some Nielsen-type research, we discovered what "our guys", whoever they were, liked and didn't. There were some surprises. Sports, for example, were of little interest. Fiction was weak. Forget about Westerns. There seemed, at the time, to be no appetite whatever for nostalgia. Perhaps there was a realization that the fifties *were* the past, even while they were going in. The Civil War could be slipped through as a theme so long as the writer concentrated on life in a vermin-infested cell. What we did find was a ferocious craving for what was actual and real (although, ironically, *Real*, as a title, did not work, a trusted employee of Martin Goodman's treacherously slipping off to try it and, with great embarrassment, failing instantly). Our staple product became the verifiably true story of some fellow who had survived a Japanese "rat cage," made a record-breaking Death Trek though Borneo, raided Schveinfurt, or helped to storm the Remagen Bridge. Dutifully, we served these up to "our guys," who were appreciative. There were, however, just so many Borneo death trekkers to be gotten hold of. Rather swiftly, *Man's World, Men*, and inevitably, *True Action* had been assigned to my group. This meant I had to purchase some fifty stories each month, an awesome number of death treks. (Most magazine publishers feel that if an editor comes up with one or two strong stories per issue, he is in good shape; not so with Martin Goodman, who required no fewer than twelve. If the last story in *True Action* was a bit shaky, he would smack it.)

It was at this point that there arose the notion of simply making up "true" stories and providing them with full documentation. What a giddy and bracing sensation as we set about falsifying our first "true" jungle trek. No doubt Goebbels, W. R. Hearst, and various CIA operatives before us had experienced that same lift to the spirits. *Above left*: The wallet dropped by Howard "Copter" Gibbons as he was searched by Customs at Manila Airport in 1943; *top right*, Aita, the jungle girl who assisted Gibbons on the first 35-mile leg of his 1,000-mile Borneo "Trek to Glory." There was, of course, no Howard "Copter" Gibbons. His photograph was that of a Hungarian gymnast, provided to us by Sovfoto, under the impression that we were doing UNESCO coverage. The agency finally got wind of what we were up to and threatened to sue if we did not stop using their gymnasts as Yank death trekkers. Secretaries around the office pitched in and helped us along with photographs of their boyfriends.

Once we had made our little "adjustment," we began with great verve to make up entirely new bombing raids, indeed, to create new World War II battles, ones that had turned the tide against the Axis and brought

Hitler to his knees. The master of the latter technique was Mario Puzo, who would create giant mythical armies, lock them in combat in Central Europe, and have casualties coming in by the hundreds of thousands. Although our mail was heavy, I don't recall a single letter casting doubt on any of these epic conflicts. Many correspondents, however, scolded us for incorrectly identifying a tank tread or rifle designation in our documentation. It required minimal effort on our part to begin making up brilliant reviews for our Action Book Bonuses. These in turn were culled from mythical journals of criticism. "Absolutely stunning in its impact . . ."—*Record*. (Well, a few of us around the office loved it and we had sort of gone on record as feeling that way.) Since it was so simple and pure an idea, I would guess that the idea of inventing "true" stories first occurred to Martin Goodman. Nonetheless, a certain ritual had to be carried out—one in which he would appear in my office holding the layout of a fabricated GI landing "a bit north of Anzio, and hitherto unrevealed, but a thousand times more critical to the Allied fortunes."

"This one true?" he would ask.

"Well, sort of," I would say.

"Mm hmm."

He would then give the layout a light tap, not quite a smack, and disappear.

We were not so much altering tapes as creating new ones; monkeying around with existing tapes could be a tricky business. On one occasion, we ran a fully documented piece about a Canadian who died after a valiant death trek through Indochina. To spruce things up a bit, and to add a bit of salt to the illustration, we sent along a few jungle nymphos as companions for our man. When the magazine was on the stands, we learned that the heroic Canadian was alive, after all—the most popular minister in the Toronto area. A surefire lawsuit if ever there was one— once our Canadian edition crossed the border. With the entire staff gathered round, I called a reporter on a Toronto newspaper and casually inquired about the fellow, learning that he had, indeed, been a popular minister, but had gone off to hunt bear and was believed to have perished in the wilderness. Covering the receiver, I hollered out: "He went bear hunting and he's dead."

A great cheer rang out and everyone returned happily to work.

In preparing our fabricated true adventures, it was important to maintain a degree of geographical balance. One day I glanced at the dummy of an issue that had gone to press and noted, with horror, that no fewer than three of our Yank "rat cage" survivals took place in Japan-dominated territories. George Fox, who was to share the screen credit on *Earthquake* with Mario Puzo, was dispatched by limo (the only limo dispatch in MM history) to the printer with instructions to reset the type, putting one rat cage in Germany and another in contemporary Rio.

Along with death trek and survival stories, yarns about tough cops who had embarked on county cleanups were surefire; also guaranteed to please were pieces that had anything to do with islands—storming them, hiding out on them, buying them at bargain rates, becoming GI king of them. (My favorite, written by the great Walter Kaylin, had to do with a seaman who took charge of one and went about ruling it while sitting on the shoulders of a weird little chum with whom he had washed ashore.) "Breakouts" were another highly successful feature. Any story called "We Go at Dawn" or "No Prison Bars Can Hold Me" would be read with satisfaction. It was preferable that the escape be from some death camp or other, but San Quentin did nicely and our readers enjoyed it immensely when people had to burrow their way out of mile-long tunnels. Another source of delight was the account of some GI who had attacked the enemy with an ingeniously devised contraption. For years, Glenn Innfield heroes went after the enemy with everything from lethal flying scooters to grenade-bearing chickens. Also popular was the revenge or "trackdown" yarn, one in which the hero caught up with someone who had behaved unattractively to him in a hellcamp (Remember me, Kraus?) and gunned him down in a postwar Ankara cafe. Additionally, our readers had a fine time with any story in which the author was in a lather about something, be it Furnace Repair Vultures Who Are Cheating You Blind or those So-Called Soviet Tuna Boats off Fire Island Which Are Stealing All Our Secrets. Our best man in this department was Joseph Millard, who could get himself into a snit on any subject and, indeed, did so some ten times a month. If America wasted too many of our hard-earned dollars on missiles, it got him hot under the collar. If not enough was spent, it got his dander up all the same. There was no pleasing the fellow.

As to the physical makeup of the "books," our readers seemed to prefer illustrations in which each hair follicle shone through with brilliance. Attempts at nonrepresentational, Chagall-like drawings brought out the worst in Martin Goodman. Illustrations were generally gotten up before the true adventures were created. No writer has ever been left quite so shaken as Mario Puzo, his first week on the job, when the author-to-be of *The Godfather* was shown a finished illustration for a thirty-thousand-word nympho jungle trek yarn he had not yet begun to write. Martin Goodman considered the "feel" of each magazine to be terribly important to its success and, like a newsstand alchemist, would brew up a different paper mixture each month—pulp, slick, semislick, four-color, duotone—giving each new issue a certain pimpmobile look to it.

Although Magazine Management had the reputation of being something of a "sin pit," the Goodman magazines, at root, were outrageously pristine, almost conventlike. Never before has there been a case in which the name triumphed so resoundingly over the game. Although "nymphos" abounded in the pages of *Male* and *Stag* (even the rhinos were nymphos) and girls were mentioned frequently who would do "anything and everything," one would have to look elsewhere to discover exactly what that anything and everything was. Would-be masturbators were made to settle for a few lubricious crumbs. "Throw 'em a few hot words," was Martin Goodman's edict when a nervous editor suggested heating things up a bit for sales. These were along the lines of "heaving breasts," "long shapely legs," "a flash of pink panties." It may be that a "dark triangle" or two slipped by, but I rather doubt it. In the pictorial division, each magazine ran a set of pictures of young women in bathing suits throwing haughty looks over their shoulders. The famed Magazine Management retoucher was Murray Schapiro, whose coveted job it was to airbrush out nipple aureoles and pubic hair strands on photos of cheesecake models who had been careless during shooting sessions. There is no record that a single aureole or strand ever slipped past his eagle's eye and made its way to the newsstand. (From the look of the current heavily pubic issue of *Stag*, one gathers that Schapiro has undergone a wild career change, and now spends his hours dabbing back in strands quite similar to the ones he spent years erasing.)

Despite his essential innocence of heart, the Magazine Management editor tended to walk about with a heavy sense of insecurity and the feeling of being up to something a bit shady. The cocktail party could be an unnerving experience, loaded with booby traps. Inevitably, the question would be posed.

"What kind of work do you do?"

"I'm in publishing."

"That right. What type?"

"Magazines."

"Really. Which ones?"

"Men's adventure."

"You don't say." (And here the trap would start to close.) "That *True* magazine stuff?"

"Sort of."

"What do you mean 'sort of'?" (Rare was the Inquisitor who failed to pick up the scent at this point.) "What are the magazines *called*?"

"Well, they're sort of called *Male, Men,* you know . . ."

"Oh, *those.* Haw, haw, haw. What'd you just call them? *Men's adventure.* That's funny. Listen, tell me something truthfully, I've always wanted to know. . . . Do you get to screw those girls or not?"

Time has a way of adding a cosmetic touch to past love affairs, old marriages, uneasy situations. I think of my years at Magazine Management as being carefree ones spent in a happy environment. I can also recall that MM editors had, perhaps, the highest divorce rate in publishing. I believe we came in at 3.7 per editor at one point, nosing out *Newsweek.* Quite regularly, one of our people, beset by domestic woes, would run his head at full speed into the watercooler. I remember giving it a hard tap or two with my own forehead. Still, there were compensations— money seemed to fly around in small gusts if not great blizzards. While salaries were kept low, Christmas bonuses were often substantial and it was possible to supplement one's income by staying awake all night and doing freelance assignments for the legions of MM publications. Though I gave the impression of being skilled as a death trek writer, I never actually *wrote* one of them and remained the coach who had never actually played the game. I did, on the other hand, create a column of short newsy items called *Stag Confidential,* which told drivers how to rotate their tires effectively, encouraged job seekers to "hotfoot it" up to Vancouver, and advised rascally types on how to spot "joydolls" at a glance. This was a time of great and disciplined production for me. As editor of five magazines, and an annual or two, I was able to commute two and half hours each day, write three novels and dozens of short stories and magazine articles, work out at Vic Tanny's gym, play games with my sons, and, to a degree, continue on with my marriage. I don't recall actually working on the magazines. They seemed to come trotting out by themselves. This may have been attributable to my one useful insight as an administrator, which was to hire the gifted and the guilty. It got back to me that I was considered a decent fellow who hired people and bought material on a compassionate basis. Let me correct the record and state that not a single decision was made on the basis of anything but total self interest. The more brilliant the employee, the less I had to do. I recall spending most of my time ordering up cheese danishes and taking strolls through the MM corridors, looking in on Bessie Little of movie, confession, and TV; the great Stan Lee, whose empire of comic artists, which at first fanned out into the distance, was to shrink to a single desk (and no secretary), then blossom forth into an empire once again when college students made cult figures of the Fantastic Four. Afternoons, I might allow myself to be worked over by the legendary "gentle con artist," Melvin B. Shestack, whose ingenious cons never once redounded to his own enrichment. (On one occasion he had me convinced that J. D. Salinger had ended his retirement and was about to go entirely the other way, with appearances on the Johnny Carson show—and that his first planned visit was to meet the team of *Male*, a magazine he had admired while living in seclusion. Shestack managed his con by including that one perfect, seemingly unfakable detail. All his information had been passed along by Salinger's tree pruner.)

It took me a good year and a half to gather up the courage to say goodbye to MM, and about ten seconds to adjust to my new life as a gypsy. Magazine Management was great fun, but it was just one of those eleven-year things. I had occasion, recently, to look over the current men's adventure field only to find that there was no field left to speak of. The once mighty *True* had been purchased by a California company, whose policy, as enunciated in its first issue, seemed to be one of dealing with the New Sophistication by facing East and breaking wind. "What this country needs is . . . a magazine fearlessly dedicated to men, and men's pursuits. Without apologies to anyone . . . We're not anti-women, we're pro-men. And if that's male chauvinism, then snort! oink! snort." With cover stories on Bob Hope, Johnny Cash, and Woody Hayes, *Argosy*, that once sleek, dangerous gunfighter of a monthly, would seem to be pegged toward retired police chiefs. *Stag* and *Male* appear to be beating an orderly retreat in the face of the *Gallery-Oui-Genesis-Game* onslaught, begrudgingly giving ground in the form of four-color "beaver" photos and articles calming masturbatory fears.

What happened to the men's adventure field? In terms of reader interest, the Korean War proved to be a bore. Long before Abbie Hoffman and Daniel Ellsberg, the prescient Martin Goodman was able to point out that you could not "give Vietnam away" on the newsstands. World War II receded, finally, too far into the distance and became parodistic by its nature. "Iwo" somehow became a laugh line, a Brooklyn joke. Mix in the power of Colombo, the appeal of instant replay, *The Towering Inferno*, the stampede of chic newsstand porn and you begin to get some answers. There is also the elevation-of-Falstaff (Dustin Hoffman)-to-hero argument for those who care to fiddle with such notions.

Recently, I walked into a handsomely appointed Madison Avenue cigar and magazine store in search of some of my old adventure books. The stalls were lined with row upon row of paperbacks such as *Anal Hatcheck Girl*—and racks of chic British import magazines, featuring color photographs of the labia minora of Victorian factory wenches.

I asked for *Male* and *Men*. Looking me over carefully, the owner led me to a back shelf, glanced about furtively and slipped my two purchases into a brown paper bag. Taking my money quickly, he returned to the cash register and refused to meet my eyes.

We never did make it into the club, and I must say I was pleased to find that out.

algren and shaw

I met Nelson Algren in the midsixties. He had admired my early novels and said in a review that I was more interesting than some of the others because I didn't know what I was doing. I thought I did, at least half of the time, but I enjoyed reading that all the same. And he said I was dangerous. I loved reading that. Call a writer dangerous and he is in your pocket forever. My favorite book of his was *Never Come Morning*. Although I had never written a play, he thought I would be just the fellow to adapt it for the stage. Twelve producers and agents convened at a Manhattan restaurant to put this deal together. When the question was raised as to who was going to pay for the adaptation, all twelve got up and left. I forget who paid the check.

Algren visited my family on Fire Island one weekend and quickly advised my sons not to put pots on the stove with the handles sticking out. He accidentally stepped on a neighbor's dune, and the man shouted at him to get off. "Where I stand is where I live," he declared, and then asked if I would go over and rough up the man a little, a prospect I found unappealing. Pretending to be the Jewish Scott and Zelda, my wife and I gave a party that weekend at which half a dozen marriages broke up, including, for all I know, that of the host and hostess. Algren left in the morning and was heard to ask: "Why do people destroy themselves?"

In later years, he said of my book *The Lonely Guy* that I had become too interested in *things*, which was fair enough—I hadn't done too well with people—but I felt he should have taken me aside and scolded me instead of doing it in front of half the world. He probably felt that he had loved me in print, so it was appropriate for him to hate me in print as well. He was probably right about that, too, but I pouted for a while nonethe-

Originally published in *Smart*, January 1990.

less. We made up at a party given for his friend Studs Terkel at Sardi's in Manhattan. Algren picked up my date, propped her up on his lap and began to tickle her as if she were a little girl, which she wasn't. But I knew then that we were back on track. Every one of his novels was glorious; every sentence he wrote seemed chiseled out of rock. (Surprisingly, his one literary regret was that he had never published in the *New Yorker*.)

When I asked him, in the late years, why he wasn't working on a book, he said that it had always been difficult for him to write anything.

"Besides," he added, "no one is interested in me."

. . . . .

Irwin Shaw showed up in my life during the run of my play *Scuba Duba*—also in the sixties. He sent me a telegram asking me not to do anything about the French rights until I saw him for a drink. There was some interest in the play from abroad—I can't say it was spirited bidding—but this was Irwin Shaw. I remember sitting in my mother's kitchen in the Bronx after "Tip on a Dead Jockey" was published in the *New Yorker*. Shaw hadn't been heard from for a while, the talk was all J. D. Salinger and Roald Dahl—and then suddenly there he was with *his* kind of story—bold and clear and romantic, not a word out of place. He made it seem so adventurous to be a writer. He asked me if I would assign the rights to my play to his wife, Marian, who was producing theater in France, and I said it would be fine. And I would be happy to jump in the river, too, if it was useful to him. He said he wanted me to meet the producer, Sam Spiegel, and Anatole Litvak, the film director.

"They live like emperors," he said.

I met them and they *did* live like emperors, but I didn't know what to do about that. As it turned out, my play was not produced in France—and this hung in the air between us for awhile. We picked up our friendship nonetheless in Southampton in the late stages of his life. Shaw would introduce me as a member of the artistic community, and then add: "Although he doesn't look it."

He didn't say much to me, but everything he did say lingers.

"You don't need anyone," he said, which I took to mean that I knew enough about my own writing and that the help that came from others was beside the point. No doubt he was talking about himself as well.

If I didn't have the last dinner with him before he left the States forever, I had one of the last. I didn't know Shaw was dying, but I knew something was up. I asked him how he—whose life had brushed across so many people, so many worlds—felt about a memoir, but he waved that off. Was it because he would have to reveal the identities of his fictional characters? That was it, he said. Or maybe he said it because he was tired. After the dinner, I went over to Bobby Van's restaurant in Bridgehampton and had a little cry for myself. Not a planned cry, but a more or less spontaneous one. A character in Anthony Powell's great series of novels, "Dance to the Music of Time," says that "writers coexist uneasily," which seems accurate, but they also cry over one another. The worst thing I could say about Shaw's stories is that only thirty-five or forty were provably classics. But he didn't want to hear about his stories. To tell a novelist his stories are fine is tantamount to throwing a drink in his face. And there it is: my first *tantamount*.

Toward the end of his life, I asked this powerful and tremendously endearing American author about his writing and he said the same thing Algren had: "No one is interested in me."

tales from the darkside

All of a sudden, I became a producer—after all my jokes about them. I wasn't a real producer—they had one of those—but I was *some* kind of producer. I felt uneasy about this, having been an enlisted man all my life, but I could see the allure of it. One fellow on the set kept saluting me. People slipped me their cards. No one had ever slipped me anything as a writer. One day I lost my car. I was positive it had been stolen. A production person drove me home and told me to forget about it. The next day, it was returned to my hotel. I had gotten confused and parked in an adjoining lot. I was positive I'd get teased about this, but no one said a word to me. You don't tease a producer.

. . . . .

As soon as I arrived in Hollywood this time, I had dinner with an old friend. He picked me up in a magnificent car. We ate at his home, which took up virtually an entire city block in Beverly Hills. His wife was staggeringly beautiful. Irritatingly, her manner was warm and self-effacing. The next day, I was having lunch with an agent when my friend entered the restaurant. The agent shook his head and said, "Poor bastard. He used to be one of the most powerful men in the industry. Now, he's finished." I told this story to Mario Puzo, who said, "There's finished and there's finished."

. . . . .

Originally published in *Smart*, Fall 1988.

I once got a call from Lindsay Wagner's agent asking if I would be interested in writing a series for her. I said I liked Lindsay Wagner, and, yes, it was certainly a possibility. The agent said that was great and that Lindsay would now go off and think creatively. That was the last I heard from either of them. I've since gone on to other things—was there any point to just sitting around?—but I wonder every now and then if Lindsay is still off somewhere, still thinking creatively.

. . . . .

As a producer, I got to talk to another producer as an equal. He told me his daughter had just been graduated from college with a degree in producing. I hadn't realized there was one. "Oh, yes," he said, his eyes watering with pride. "And someday that girl is going to own eight o'clock."

. . . . .

Yet another producer called to tell me he had to break our lunch date in New York City. Dustin Hoffman had expressed interest in one of this producer's projects. As a result, the producer had flown in with six writers to work with the great film star. Surely, I would understand. I did, and wondered if I wanted to be one of the six writers.

. . . . .

I keep changing my feelings about Hollywood. At one time, I thought of it as a place you go to die, but I don't feel that way anymore. I like it now. It helps, of course, to have something going. But possibly it's because I started to shake up the dice, to say at different hotels and try out some of the wonderful new restaurants. I stayed at the Four Seasons, where they can't do enough for you. They practically press your pants while you're still in them. I promised to thank the owner for the great job he was doing, and I didn't, so I'm doing it now. But for the first time, I found the Asian and European visitors irritating. A young man from Singapore was there, buying up bars and restaurants. He told a series of jokes, each one featuring a little Jewish guy: a little Jewish guy did this; a little Jewish guy did that. But the fact of his being a little Jewish guy had nothing to do with the stories. An American with gray curls sat beside the man from Singapore and may have served as his ethnic coach. Some

Germans laughed at a man who was about to step into a lowly Chevrolet Beretta. And a Japanese family didn't feel that the pool area was clean enough for them. Why was this so upsetting to me? Possibly because it was Hollywood. It's one thing to buy up Fresno or St. Louis, but this was the land of Linda Darnell and Errol Flynn, the very soul of America. By the time I was finished with my trip, I was a real Yahoo. I made a little speech on the set about how the country was being nibbled away. It was time to take it back. A stunt man agreed with me.

. . . . .

I ran into a director with whom I'd had a disagreement some years back. He said he was delighted to see me and had always wanted to get things straightened out between us. It's true, he conceded, that he had messed up my picture. But there were certain things going on at the time that he couldn't tell me about. I asked him what they were, and he said he was sorry, but he still couldn't tell me about them.

. . . . .

Credits continue to be essential in Hollywood. I was scheduled to have dinner with a director who called at the last minute. "Can I bring a friend along?" he asked, then quickly added, "He did *Conan*." A producer crippled with lower back pain told me he was not concerned, since he was on his way to see John Wayne's chiropractor. On the set, an extra offered me an excellent cigar and said he had gotten it from someone who was close to Cher. A pretty model at Le Dome announced that she had once been the third-biggest money earner in Milan. At the Four Seasons, a man staggered out of the bar, insisting he was the pilot for several Oscar winners. A stranger invited me to a picnic being given by Arthur Hailey's niece.

It's catching. During a break in an evenly matched set of tennis, I slipped my opponent a few credits. It wasn't as if I had given him *Star Wars*, but he was not in the film business, and I'm convinced his game went off a bit as a result. I won the match, but it was not my finest moment.

. . . . .

At the Beverly Hills Hotel, a writer approached a group of three producers and began telling them stories. They laughed until tears came out of their eyes. After he'd left, one turned to the others, made a face, and said, "Not funny on the page."

. . . . .

From time to time, I've run into a certain friend from New York City in the lobby of the Beverly Hills Hotel. The last time this happened, he asked if I was staying at the hotel and, if so, would I mind if he kept his bags in my room for a while. I couldn't help him—I was about to check out—but it occurred to me that he never actually registers at the hotel. He just keeps switching his bags from one friend's room to another. Nor does this state of affairs seem to bother him.

. . . . .

Yet another producer called me on a Friday and told me we had a deal on a picture in which I had expressed interest. He had the reputation of being an intelligent man who had never quite been able to get anything going. But he seemed to have something going this time. I celebrated that weekend, since it meant my income was secure for a while. The producer called on Monday to say the deal was off. It had never been that firm to begin with. I confronted him in the lobby of a hotel and suggested he never should have said we had a deal unless he was sure it was secure. That's what a deal meant, didn't it? He could not follow my line of thinking. Additionally, he was upset that I would bring this up in front of his female companion. "In front of my *girl*," he said. Then he sat down on a lobby sofa, buried his head in his hands, and began to cry. Months later, he called and tried to interest me in a picture about suicide.

. . . . .

I discovered a place called Kate Mantilini's on Wilshire and Doheny. Just driving by, late at night, I knew I would like it, and I was right. People with green hair sit opposite old Jewish grandmothers. The menu is LA Revisionist, featuring such dishes as meat loaf and mashed potatoes and thick slices of ham with gravy, which most people are now thought to crave after years of nouvelle cuisine. There is a movement afoot to call the place Kate's, which I feel would be a mistake.

At the bar, an attorney told his date that he could not make a commitment to her because he was still evolving. A young man said he was staying with Dean Martin's ex-wife until he got a toehold in the music business. Someone spoke derisively of a television director who did not have the balls to fill up a big screen.

At reliable Dan Tana's, a director said he was sick and tired of taking shit. When his producer asked him what he thought of the picture they were working on, he shot back that he wasn't sure. Two men were involved in a "go to the floor" deal. I'm not sure what that is, but I felt I'd like to be in on one. When asked what he was up to, another man at the bar said that he was agenting his tush off. At Nicky Blair's, a girl visiting from Queens said that she had just come from a party at which the host greeted her at the door and asked her to suck his dick. She left because she hadn't arrived at his level of partying.

. . . . .

Rare is the show-business individual who is not creative in one way or another. The very word once upset me, but it no longer does. A producer congratulated his director in the trades on being both creative *and* brilliant, and even that didn't bother me.

I was upset when someone first suggested I pitch an idea. What was I, some sort of pitch man? Now I happily pitch ideas at the drop of a hat. I may have to draw the line at "writerly," though. I hear about people being paid a great deal of money to think "writerly" thoughts. Perhaps I'll be offered that kind of deal—and change my mind—but for the moment I'm not going with "writerly."

. . . . .

A writer was about to be fired from a project. Such was his passion for the work that he offered to do another complete version, free of charge. The producers were stunned.

How could they resist such a magnanimous offer? They agreed to let the writer proceed. He finished the work, handed it in—and was fired again.

. . . . .

Back when I was just a writer, a producer told me he liked the first draft of a screenplay I had delivered. "Great," he said. "If this were a house, you would have the first two stories built." Encouraged, I did a second draft to which he responded, "Great. We can now see the tip of the iceberg." I suggested that this seemed like a step back, but he didn't see it that way.

An Italian producer was forced to abandon a film of mine when a pet project of his, after many years, fell into place. He delivered the news by bursting into my hotel room, bowing deeply, and with tears in his eyes, saying, "I have the great honor to announce that I have just signed Bobby De Niro."

. . . . .

About this same time, I seem to recall finding a down-and-out director in an alley outside a disco, dusting him off, and recommending him for a picture I was working on. Normally, I don't get listened to in this situation, but on this occasion I did. Several months later, the director called to tell me that I'd been fired. He'd stayed on, but he assured me that before making this decision, he had gone to the brink of quitting.

. . . . .

During my last trip to Hollywood, everyone was hunkered down because of the writers' strike, so it was difficult to spot trends. But I did notice a great concern with MOWs—movies of the week. It's one thing for Raquel Welch to be doing them, but what about everyone else? Should you do one? And if you did, could you go back and do a feature film? Or were you marked for life? A veteran writer pounded the table at Chasen's and said, "I'll *never* do one." But they certainly were on his mind. Then I met a fellow who has been enormously successful at producing them, but even he seems to be worrying about whether he's been doing the right thing.

My own particular experience with an MOW was bumpy. It was designed to be a rip-off (albeit a fun one) of a nineteenth-century classic. A director was signed on who felt it should be shored up with a rip-off of a Shakespeare comedy. The executive in charge, famed for knowing the mind of the TV-viewing public, suggested that the way to put it over the top was to salt in a rip-off of *The Godfather*. It was at this point that I withdrew from the project. I did not feel I was the man to rip off quite that many classics in one clip.

. . . . .

No matter where I stay and what I do, I always have the feeling that

I'm not seeing the real LA. But one night, I felt I actually had it in my grasp. I'd started out at Tommy Tang's, then taken a stroll along Melrose, and wound up at the Nuclear Nuance. This led, somehow, to a Fatburger's that was awash with *Less Than Zero* people. Suddenly, I was at the Comedy Club; there was Bruce Willis, with an MTV-style chorus crowding in close while he beat invisible drums at the bar. You could sit right next to him. That's when I thought that I had it. But then the closing lights came up, Willis vanished, and I was out on the street, the real LA having slipped through my fingers once again. Perhaps I'll catch it next time.

Before leaving, I was assured that my show, sluggish in getting out of the gate, had proved in the editing process to be a strong finisher. On the plane back, I had a long conversation with a Japanese businessman in which I thought we were discussing Kawabata and he thought we were dealing with Kurosawa. It was only when I expressed regret at the great author's suicide—and he insisted he'd met him recently at a cocktail party—that we realized our mistake. He read my palm and pumped me for tips on film investing.

Physically, this fellow reminded me of a man I'd met briefly at the *Playboy* mansion who called me soon afterward in the middle of the night. He sounded frightened and said he owed the producer Frank Yablans a comedy. Could I help him out? I said I was sorry, but I tended not to have any extras around. I wished him luck and wondered how he had gotten into that situation.

don of a new age

N oel Coward is said to have sent the following telegram to Marlene Dietrich on the occasion of her seventieth birthday. "It just occurred to me that I've loved you all my life." I don't know if my thirty-five-year friendship with Mario Puzo qualifies as a love affair, but it has been more rewarding than several of the actual ones I've had to endure. It began in the early sixties when I hired Puzo as an assistant editor at the Magazine Management Company, which published four monthly adventure magazines: *Male, Men, Man's World*, and—my favorite—*True Action*. (See "Even the Rhinos Were Nymphos.") I offered him the princely sum of $150 a week, with an opportunity to enhance his income by writing as many freelance pieces as he could handle. This was what Puzo described as his first "straight" job, and he misguidedly took my hiring him as an act of generosity.

Actually, I'd read his first novel, *The Dark Arena*, and saw in him someone capable of single-handedly writing half of our editorial content. In the five years that followed, he produced several million words for the magazines while also moonlighting a new novel called *The Godfather*.

Many of the stories were dramatized versions of great World War II battles—Anzio, Corregidor, the Bulge. When we ran out of battles, Puzo was only too happy to concoct new ones. Puzzled at first, readers who were veterans wrote us, hungry for details of these great conflicts that they had somehow missed. Among the many other stories he tossed off were a substantial number of mini-*Godfathers*, still there in the archives, waiting to be mined by some entrepreneurial film producer.

Originally published in *Los Angeles Magazine*, August 1996.

My memories of Puzo at this time all have to do with size—the size of his appetite, for one, especially when he would arrange to meet you for a Chinese dinner; if you were five minutes late he would slip around the corner and wolf down an entire pizza as an appetizer, then calmly "take in," as he put it, a seven-course Cantonese meal. Or the size of his appetite for books: I have a picture in my mind of him sitting in a chair with not one but six volumes in his lap, wetting his finger and taking "tastes" of each one. Then there was the size of his cigars and the enormity of his laugh: always filled with amazement at some quirk of human behavior. Above all, there was his great generosity. Even as a struggling assistant editor, he would fight you tooth and nail for the check at a restaurant.

I don't know if Puzo is the most intelligent man I know, but I always think of him as the wisest. On one occasion, three words from him may have saved my life. Years ago, after "Crazy Joey" Gallo had been released from prison, the mobster and his buddies had taken to staging Friday-night soirees at the Chelsea home of Jerry Orbach, the actor. Along with my wife and three children, I attended several of these fascinating and lavishly catered get-togethers, which featured an impressive list of writers, actors, socialites, and barons of industry. With great delight, I told Puzo about it. He listened carefully, thought for a moment, and said: "It's not intelligent." I never showed up again, and later, when I was invited to join Gallo and friends at Umberto's Clam House for a late-night meal, I declined. Had it not been for Puzo's three-word advisory, I might very well have been in the line of fire that fateful night when "Crazy Joey" was gunned down at that very restaurant.

.....

These thoughts travel through my mind as I drive to Puzo's house on Long Island to congratulate him on the publication this month of his new novel, *The Last Don*. It deals with the all-controlling Clericuzio clan, the most powerful Mafia family in America, as the Don prepares to relinquish power and ease his family into mainstream and legitimate America—the movie business, in particular. The Clericuzios are very much a modern-day version of *The Godfather*'s Corleone family, but Puzo's knowledge of that world has only deepened with the passage of time. (Puzo had wanted to call the book *The Clericuzios* and was disappointed when the publisher was unenthusiastic. Reluctantly, he now concedes that *The Last Don* is a superior title.)

Beginning with *The Godfather*, Puzo's triumph has been to combine a literary sensibility and a steamrolling narrative in almost mathematically equal measures—the dream of every writer. Once again, he has joined these two poles in the new novel—and with great power (a favorite Puzo word, incidentally.)

The Godfather dealt with Hollywood and Vegas only in passing, but in *The Last Don*, the real action takes place in those locations. Even as the old Don is wrapping up the family's illicit businesses back east, a new generation of Clericuzios is making its way west. One cousin has become a prominent screenwriter, while another runs one of the great Vegas casinos. At first they try to keep the family business at arm's length, but naturally that doesn't last.

There is always a slight downside to reading a Puzo novel. His seigneurial style is infectious. The night before our meeting I found myself admonishing my wife, suggesting that she "betrayed" me by not picking up the mail. My twelve-year-old daughter had "dishonored" me and failed to show proper "respect" by not putting her dishes in the sink. Then, too, there is the sharpening effect on the appetite, stimulated by the mouthwatering descriptions of banquets and the parade of lovingly described dishes. At midnight, before my visit, I became ravenously hungry for pasta and had to prowl the streets of Southampton in search of an Italian restaurant that hadn't closed its kitchen.

. . . . .

When I arrive at his house, I recall that it was once considerably more modest in size. Wings have been added on, as have a tennis court and well-tended garden paths, so that it's becoming something of an estate worthy of Don Clericuzio himself.

Puzo comes out to greet me, looking better and more relaxed than he has in years. Still moving gracefully, he wears a green country-club-style jacket and rich off-white slacks, which cause me to wonder about his tailor.

"They're old pants," he says. "I forget where I got 'em."

For some time, Puzo has been taken with the idea that he resembles Marlon Brando. I'd always been dismissive of this, but amazingly—now that he's in his seventies—he *has* started to resemble Brando. In truth, he looks better than the legendary actor.

He leads me into his huge, airy studio, which might easily exist in Malibu. It is lined with various translations of his books and cassettes of his movies. The new book and the various "trophies," including several Oscars, have the effect of making me feel a bit unsettled in his presence.

"Relax," he tells me. "You were the boss, and you're still the boss."

"Patrick Ewing never forgets his old coach at Georgetown, is that it?"

"Something like that."

When I suggest that *The Last Don* is awfully good, he is not entirely convinced.

"What about the ending?"

I have to laugh. The book was bought by CBS Television for $2.1 million (after a bidding war with Francis Ford Coppola); it's been sold to a long list of foreign countries; it's already received several enthusiastic reviews—and he's worried about the ending.

"It works, Mario."

I knew that he had put in years of research on the Borgias, and I was curious to know why he'd set it all aside to work on *The Last Don.*

"I had my notes assembled, I had digested the research, and I was probably the world's top expert on the Borgias. Then I wrote a few pages on my old Royal typewriter and realized that if I proceeded with the novel I would have to say 'M'lord' a thousand times."

"So you switched to Vegas, Hollywood, and the Mob?"

"Which is not to say that I won't return to the Borgias. Many of the ideas in my novel—having to do with deceit and corruption—were suggested by the Borgias. But it would never sell to the movies; the pope is a villain, although I do treat him sympathetically."

The Last Don is a return to the three subjects he knows best: the film business, gambling, and, of course, the Mafia. I've never spoken about Puzo to anyone who didn't suspect that he was in some way "connected," and it's no secret that Mafia figures have actually modeled their behavior—and speech—on characters in *The Godfather.* Did that amuse him?

"It works both ways. I've actually caught myself using some of the facial expressions and bodily gestures of Brando in *The Godfather.* And there was one chilling moment in Gary Crosby's house in Vegas. Two hard-looking men surrounded me and poked me in the ribs, saying, 'Admit it, Puzo, you're one of the guys.' I denied it, of course, then Crosby told me that one of my new friends was John Roselli, whose name I recognized from the literature and whose body was later found in a dumpster. The other guy was present at Bugsy Siegel's ambush and execution. He was unharmed, so you can figure out what his role was."

I recall that Joey Gallo had once asked Mario—through his publisher—

to write the mobster's life story.

"I declined—and told the publisher not to tell Gallo that we'd even had the conversation. My feeling was that, with all the contracts out on his life, he would be dead in six months. And of course that's what happened, and then my *publisher* thought I was connected."

In fact, Puzo's knowledge of the mob derives from tales he heard as a boy, extensive reading, and a rich imagination. He is a first-generation American who resists strenuously being called *Italian*-American. His parents were born in Naples, and he grew up poor in Manhattan's Hell's Kitchen. Later, he moved to Long Island and, except for extended visits to Hollywood and the great casinos of the world, has never left.

Puzo once told Nick Pileggi, the cowriter of *Goodfellas* and *Casino*, that there was an elderly man in his old neighborhood who became one of the models for Don Corleone in *The Godfather*. That's as close a connection as he's ever admitted. The ultimate irony would be if he really *is* connected and has been fooling his old friend all these years. (Puzo is generally affable, but his eyes tend to narrow a bit when asked the wrong question, and there's an ominous silence before he answers. I confess, this *has* always concerned me.)

· · · · ·

We stop to eat. Once a month, I have lunch in Southampton with Puzo, Joe Heller, Speed Vogel, and screenwriter David Z. Goodman, so I'm used to Puzo's tastes. But this time he has promised me "a good one."

"I don't eat much at this hour," he tells me, but obviously *somebody* does. The table is groaning with Italian delicacies—tender artichokes, paper-thin prosciutto, savory chunks of pepperoni, and, I'm happy to note, the mozzarella of my dreams. In the novel, Don Clericuzio refuses to eat mozzarella if it's more than twenty minutes old. His creator follows suit.

A mountain of cigars is on a table nearby. Puzo offers me one the size of a small baseball bat, the finest produced by J&R in America.

"You smoke these?" I ask.

"I chew them."

"Where do you find the willpower not to light up?"

"Actually, I do sneak in a few puffs once in a while."

At our "literary" lunches in Southampton, the discussions tend to be about women and money, but this time our conversation drifts to Hollywood and screenwriting. I recall that Mario had spent many enjoyable summers next door to Burgess Meredith in Malibu, and I wonder if he misses Hollywood.

"Not really. I had some wonderful times out there, but I'm content now to stay at home and work on my novels."

Doe he write his novels with a film sale in mind?

"Who knows what sells to the movies. I'm no expert. I was totally convinced that *The Fourth K* would produce an automatic film sale—and I was wrong." *The Sicilian* became a film, of course, but *Fool's Die*, which may be his personal favorite, was never produced.

As a screenwriter, he's had nine screenplays produced and he's won two Academy Awards, yet he remains curiously ambivalent about the form.

"I respect screenwriters, but I wish they'd come up with another name for what they do. It just isn't 'writing,' as I understand it. There's access to the eyes, the emotions, but they don't have the novelist's direct access to the brain. And though screenwriters are well compensated, the worst part of it is that they have absolutely no power. I was paid a million dollars to write *The Cotton Club*, and not a word of mine appeared on the screen. It's as if the screenwriter is the guy you put in right field as a kid because you were sure no balls would come his way. There isn't a producer I know who doesn't think he could write a screenplay if he just had the time."

Puzo is obsessed—and amused—by the unwillingness of studios to give even the best writers gross points of a film's profits. I remember that around the time he was having his first experience with the movie business, he called me about a deal he was being offered that contained something called a "rolling gross." I said, "Mario, I don't know much about grosses, but I can assure you that if it is a rolling gross, it will be rolling away from you. What you want is a *stationary* gross."

For all of his success as a writer for the screen, I recall a certain self-consciousness on his part about his skills at the craft.

"It's true. I never actually studied the form. One day I decided to take dead aim and read a guide to successful screenwriting. In the first chapter, the writer declares that one of the finest screenplays ever written was the one for *The Godfather*, which I had written. So that was the end of my studying."

We agree that an emblematic Hollywood moment came about when producer Robert Evans, during a *Cotton Club* script conference with Puzo, insisted that a city sidewalk blow up. There had been no buildup to the scene. No explanation for it.

"Why does the sidewalk blow up?" Puzo asked, genuinely confused.

"Because it just does," said Evans.

"And who knows?" Puzo says. "Considering it was a movie, maybe he was right. A novelist who did that would have been destroyed by the critics."

The Last Don contains his most scathing portrait of Hollywood to date, but when I ask if he would still rather be a novelist, even if he were twenty-six years old and just starting out, he surprises me.

"Absolutely not. I'd take the first plane to California and become a screenwriter. It's a cheerful life, it's fun, you're well paid—and the weather's great. Writing serious novels is simply too hard. It takes years to get recognition. You have to lead a monk's life. In eight weeks of work on *The Cotton Club*, I made more money than I did putting in four years on a novel. They criticized Nathanael West for abandoning the novel in favor of Hollywood. His four novels together earned six thousand dollars."

"It always comes down to money."

"It's in my book. A man's basic concern, his basic responsibility, is to put bread on the table."

"Or croissants?"

"That, too."

In speaking to writers, I always want to know which moment in their careers they found most satisfying. The sale of a first story? The great review? In Puzo's case, I assume his magic moment would have to do with the publication of *The Godfather*—which went on to become the biggest selling novel in publishing history—or the subsequent movies derived from it.

"It wasn't *The Godfather*," Puzo says. "My essential feeling was one of relief, obviously because of the economics. Actually, I was thinking in terms of fifty thousand or one hundred thousand dollars. I had no idea it would produce millions. But there was no real joy; there had been too many defeats, too many terrible times. My second novel, *The Fortunate Pilgrim*, was called a minor classic by the *New York Times*, and nobody bought it. Success came, but it was too late. It was like a girl you've been trying to date for four years. Finally, she says yes, and your feeling is, 'Who cares?' And there was a certain sadness about the experience. On rereading it I think it's a strong novel—better than I thought when I wrote it—but it was the first time I'd ever considered the reader, *catered* to the reader. Before that, I wrote exactly what I wanted and never gave the reader a second thought."

. . . . .

The hours slip by without notice. We talk of women, those who'd delighted us, puzzled us and, on occasion, betrayed us. A surprising feature of *The Last Don* is that the women, for the most part, are cheerfully predatory in their sexual behavior, seducing men, discarding them, moving on to the next conquest—a style that would have made a younger Puzo uneasy, if not terrified.

"That was Carol's doing," he says, shifting the blame—if that's what it was—to his longtime companion. "She enlightened me. Overall, I think feminism is a terrific deal for men, sparing them the tremendous expenditure of energy involved in caring for and protecting women. It strikes me, however, that women give up an important asset in not keeping up at least the pretence of fidelity. That lets men completely off the hook, and women lose their power."

Does Puzo, after a rich career, have any regrets?

"I wish I had worked harder," he answers ruefully. "All I can remember is goofing off. And I wish I'd been able to get out a book a year, like Clancy and Crichton."

I bring up Chekhov, who in his brief writing life produced five thousand pages of short stories.

"I'm not impressed by those guys," says Puzo. "They had no distractions. No television, no movies, no Super Bowl. What else did they have to do but write?"

And finally, we speak of advancing age.

"There are many advantages," says Puzo. "Chief among them is that I can now look at a beautiful young woman and know that she has no power over me."

We part several hours later, and I realize that the fuel that runs our long and satisfying friendship—apart from pure affection—is the exchange of stories. My last thought as I say good-bye is of one story Puzo told me that dealt with his mother's reaction when he announced that he wanted to become a writer.

"*Why*, Mario?" she cried out in horror. "*Why* must you do such a foolish thing?"

"I can't help myself, Mom," he explained. "It's like a hunchback. Can a hunchback lose his hump?"

POSTSCRIPT, 1999

I spent an afternoon with Mario a week before he died in July of 1999. He was quite frail but cheerful nonetheless and amused by "the things that happen when you're on the way out." A favorite was to fall asleep, then wake up and find "five sets of eyes, staring down at me, everyone wondering if I was still around." His major concern was that his new novel was going to come in at a "mere" 380 pages or so. Alluding to the legendary passage in *The Godfather*, he consoled himself by saying: "I have given them (the publisher) half a dozen 'horse's head' scenes, which should make them happy."

Along with many others, I had been caught up in *The Sopranos*—the cable television phenomenon—episodes of which contain more than one homage to *The Godfather*. I was anxious for him to share my enthusiasm, and asked—with some trepidation—how he felt about the series.

"I absolutely love it," he said. "And to have a character named 'Uncle Junior' is brilliant."

We spoke, as we had so often, of literature, which had sustained him through his long debilitating illness.

"Books," he said, reverentially, "are the only thing that has never let me down."

I said that I had reread *Gatsby* and *Catcher in the Rye*, both of which, for me, had remained formidable—*The Sun Also Rises* less so. The style had been parodied so often that the book *itself* seemed to be parody.

"Wait till you try reading *Anna Kar-a-nee-na-na*," he said, mispronouncing—deliberately I felt—poor Anna's last name. I recalled that he enjoyed doing the same to the famed Pavillon restaurant (it became Pavillyun), thereby showing his disdain for French food, if not all matters French.

We had a light lunch. He took a few stealthy bites of his beloved mozzarella, said he thanked God every day that he would not be alive for the Internet, then whispered to me his conclusion that "women are crazy."

As weak as he was, his handshake was firm as we said goodbye.

"I will get better," he assured me.

I spoke to him one last time on the phone. He asked what I thought of the ending of *Hannibal*. I said I had enjoyed what I had read, but hadn't quite gotten to the final pages.

"He does something daring," said Puzo. "Tell me if you agree."

I finished reading the book, and I did agree, but I was a day late in reporting back to him.

At the funeral service, the minister assured friends and family that Mario had not actually died, but was in "transition."

I'm convinced my old friend would have been delighted by that finding . . . and imagined him saying, like the boy full of wonder he'd remained all his life: "Hey, that's great. *Transition*. . . . And all I thought I did was drop dead."

PART TWO

celebrities and others

some thoughts on clint eastwood and heidegger

I'm crazy about Clint Eastwood, and if that automatically sounds chic, it's just going to have to sound that way. There's something intrinsically fair about him. He's no intellectual, but he's willing to learn. For example, I have a feeling that if you met him and Heidegger crept into the conversation, he wouldn't come up with one of those dumb Hollywood remarks along the lines of "Heidi-*who*?" He would, with quiet intelligence, say, "What's that name?" and scribble it down on a little piece of paper. Not a memo either, or one of those "From the Desk Of" things, just a little piece of scratch paper. Maybe he'd borrow it from somebody. And he wouldn't hand that scratch paper to any secretary, either. The next day, he would go down to the library—a small library out there where he's got all those acres—and check out a volume of Heidegger and read it himself. And he would get something out of it, too, maybe not *all* of what Heidegger was driving at, but something. And I'm not talking about remarks to drop at some William Morris agency party. Something he could really use. Out there where he's got those acres. And incidentally, with regard to those acres, he didn't just pick them up in that Ronald Reagan free enterprise frontier spirit either. I don't even think ecology is at the top of his list of concerns either. He just wanted a little room. And if someone trespassed on his property, he wouldn't just blow the guy's head off. Maybe he's got a gun

Originally published as "Could Dirty Harry Take Rooster Cogburn?" in *Esquire*, September 1976.

or two, but he doesn't have a whole collection. He'd invite the trespasser in, offer him a bite to eat. It wouldn't necessarily be a simple sandwich either, a ham and cheese. He'd serve him a salad. Why? Because he has enough confidence to feed the fellow some artichoke hearts and not see it as some kind of threat to his masculinity. Who knows, maybe he and the trespasser would get to talking about what Eastwood had just gotten out of Heidegger. The trespasser might just know a little about Heidegger. Those are the kind of fellows who do. Eastwood realizes that.

Eastwood sees that life isn't so simple, that it isn't just good and bad, but that there are a lot of grays in between. They talk about the squint. Boy, does he take a lot of heat on that. The squint this, the squint that. Take away the squint and the electronic music and what have you got? I happen to think you've got plenty. A complex individual, for openers. Let me throw a hot potato into this: I've come to the conclusion that he got that squint by trying to make difficult moral choices. Which is why he would gravitate toward someone like Heidegger. Heidegger might very well lead him in the direction of Wittgenstein, but I don't necessarily think Eastwood would make a career out of either one of them. If he didn't respond to Wittgenstein, he would just set him aside and not even add some other dumb Hollywood remark like "A man's got a right to his opinion." That's what makes him so special. He would simply say Heidegger yes, Wittgenstein no and go on about his business. If, at some later date, he came around to Wittgenstein's way of thinking, back he goes to the library. No ad in *Variety* either, just a quiet trip to the stacks.

I don't know the circumstances of Eastwood's personal life, but I don't think sex is all that important to him, even though they reflexively throw a scene or two into each of his pictures. I can't help but feel that he just goes through the motions—and not because he once got hurt and it was traumatic for him. There just wasn't ever that much to it for him. Oh, he'll *do* it, let a woman use him, maybe even throw in an animal cry or two. He has a great body and he's probably the cleanest one out there— not just that manly kind of clean, but the kind you have to have a lot of soap for. So he'll let himself be used, but the woman, if she has any intelligence, will see there's a part of him she hasn't touched. (Unless it's an Asian woman—an Asian woman would definitely have an edge.) And she would be right. Maybe he would even *like* it to be touched, but he doesn't know how to make this happen. That's what he's looking for in Heidegger and with all those acres out there, a way to be touched, even though he senses in some Kierkegaardian way that it's not in the cards for him and he'll probably go right on through that way. Never being touched. He doesn't just *play* those mythic fellows who suddenly loom out of nowhere with a murky past. He *is* one. And one thing those mythic fellows don't do is get touched.

That's where I give the Italians credit. They took one look at him, they saw mythic, and they grabbed it. And incidentally, I hope he has the good sense to stay with mythic. The second I saw him turn up as an art professor in *The Eiger Sanction*, I knew he was in big trouble. We were all in big trouble. Not that he can't make just about anything mythic. (Witness the otherworldly dimension he single-handedly got into *Play Misty for Me*. He was a disc jockey and he *still* got mythic in there.) But that one time, in *The Eiger Sanction*, he put too big a burden on himself. They couldn't even make the mountain mythic, so what did they expect from an actor who is more or less flesh and blood? (He didn't give up on that one, either, incidentally. He was mythic in fits and starts, and then he finally got disgusted.) In any case, I wish he'd stick with straight mythic and not try to broaden himself (on screen, that is). Let Al Pacino broaden himself. I'd love to see him just continue riding into Lagos out of some primordial past, go around doing mythic things, and get the hell out of there with the whistling sound. In other words, broaden himself within mythic. Pacino wants to play Beethoven, that's his business. Let Eastwood keep on refining mythic, although how on God's earth he's going to refine what he did in *High Plains Drifter* is a question I'd rather not have to answer.

Which brings me to another question, one that's been crying out to be asked since I got into this. The Duke or Eastwood? In a fight, forget it. A good big man against a good little man. Sugar Ray versus Ali. The Duke with those big, good-natured ham hands would eventually win. Eastwood would hit him with some vicious, nasty, small man's punches and the Duke probably wouldn't even feel most of them. It's as if they'd be coming from one of his spitfires. And the ones he did feel, he'd fall back, shake the grogginess out of his head, rub his slightly stubbled check, say "I'll be darned"—and then he'd start using the good-natured hands and that would be all she wrote. The end of Eastwood. Or would it? Let's not get too cocky on this point, us *or* the Duke. Because this is where I'd like to introduce a thought, something for the Duke to ponder. All along, we've been presupposing a fair fight. One of those saloon things where people get thrown over bars and the mirror breaks. What the Duke has to realize is that Eastwood has spent a lot of time abroad. And he might just come up with something crazy. Something the Duke has never seen. Something they didn't do in Laredo. Something out of Naples. Eastwood doesn't fight American, doesn't see any reason to. He'll pull the Duke's ear off. What would the Duke do then? Probably mumble something about gooks and walk off the set. Or for argument's sake, let's say Eastwood *didn't* pull the Duke's ear off. What if he pulled something metaphysical, something no one ever tried on the Duke? All of a sudden the Duke would be punching thin air. He'd have to stop after a while and ask a rancher, "Listen, neighbor, wasn't I just fighting a tough little skinny fella or was it my imagination?" With all of this, I'd still probably bet on the Duke because of his good-natured ham hands and Iwo. But there'd always be the possibility of an upset, particularly if Eastwood was cornered and went over to metaphysical.

As to whose company I'd enjoy the most, however, no contest. Eastwood all the way. Well, maybe not all the way. If we're talking about *enjoyment*, how can you casually dismiss the Duke? Most of that American stuff is good PR, and although I'm sure certain friends of mine will accuse me of falling into the old Eichman-was-a-great-guy-away-from-the-compound trap, I think the Duke would be fun to hang around with. He's simplistic, sure, but fun simplistic. Alright, charming simplistic. And in hanging around with Wayne, you'd be able to find him. There would never be that part of him you couldn't touch. You could touch all of him, and of course, right there is where you run into your problem. He's *too* available. I can just hear myself saying, "For crying out loud, Duke, could you be a little elusive for a change?"

What you would want, of course, is to have the Duke and Eastwood as a team, but of course that's impossible. It might be alright with Wayne to have Eastwood as a sidekick, albeit one he would have to keep an eye on at all times. But one thing you can bet on is Eastwood's no sidekick. Not that he's beyond entertaining the thought on some metaphysical level. I haven't the slightest doubt that he would comprehend my sidekick theory of literature (one I hope to get around to doing some day for the *Partisan Review*) which sets out to demonstrate that sidekicks (Maggio, Ratso Rizzo, that guy in *The Ginger Man*) are much deeper, richer than main characters because there was less pressure on the author when he thought them up. They were written relaxed. Like throwaway lines, which any stand-up comic will tell you are always funnier than the ones everybody slaves over. Eastwood understands all this, and he would probably go for the sidekick thing on a metaphysical level, but even *he* has to live in the real world—so the sidekick thing is out, if only on the basis of career stuff and percentages of the gross, which he needs as much as the next man. I don't see any reason to hold that against him. If there has to be a sidekick, let Wayne go be one. Or else drop the whole thing.

So on the basis of company alone, I'd go with Eastwood and it would always come back to that remote thing of his. That alienated thing that Beckett and Ionesco are supposed to have a lock on. For awhile, Antonioni had a lock on it, too, but I understand he's not so alienated these days. The point is, you're allowed to say Pinter and alienated all you want. You practically get a trip to Bermuda out of it. But mention Eastwood and alienated in the same breath and they look at you like you're an idiot. And are they wrong! As far as I'm concerned, he's more alienated than the whole pack of them. In think he's every bit as alienated as Beckett himself; what do you think of that?

I think it's only fair to point out that I fell in love with Stockholm, too, and found it a relief after Italy, where everyone was showering me with love. They don't blow kisses in Stockholm and, Lord knows, Eastwood doesn't. What he does is hold himself out of reach; and if you ever did get to him, sitting around with him on those acres, it would be on some high windy metaphysical plain, which as far as I'm concerned, is the only way you'd ever want to reach someone. That's what it's all about, and if it isn't, I might as well cash in my chips right now. We *all* might as well cash in our chips. It's a long shot, but I have a feeling I'd have a shot at reaching him up there on that plain. It certainly would be worth striving for. If you must know, I believe Clint Eastwood's remote, alienated style is a goddamned metaphor for our time. Which is why I salute him—as a man, as an artist, as a professional (and I understand he's an outrageous stickler for detail on the set, even though the net effect emerges as being casual), and as a complex human being.

the imposing proportions
of jean shrimpton

Write about Jean Shrimpton? Easy enough. I knew all about her. Meeting her would only confuse me. I had seen her face in the fashion magazines; she comes leaping out of that blizzard of Ban-Lon and Guerlain and Mojud pages and you know she is everything that's young and nonpolitical, all tossed together in one girl—the lines outside Truffaut movies, disco dancing, the Stones, underground film, those crazy stockings, the English rebellion—Sally Bowles brought up to date.

Or maybe not. Maybe she's a grmmmph . . . or more correctly, a grum-mmphlett (explanation to follow).

To prepare for our meeting, I watched a short, British-made film called *The Face on the Cover* (produced by the Maysles brothers). It was my first private screening, and in the small projection room I became a CIA man watching stills of the Commie spy apparatus, a small clapboard house in East Berlin, a notorious sidewalk café in Prague. The film kept describing Jean as a goddess, but when she first showed up and began to lope around I got that grmmphlett notion. Have you ever seen those documentaries about Africa in which a group of tall, spindly, F.A.O. Schwarz rag-doll things are bending all the way down to lap up water from a spring. Then suddenly a jeep shows up with cameras that begin to grind out at them; they look up, make a sound you would rather not hear and then begin a terrible feather-scattered gangling trot into the bush, the first clumsy thing they have ever done, and, of course, they are never quite the same again. They are a combination of baby giraffes and okapis

Originally published in *Esquire*, April 1965

and grysbok all mixed up into one gracefully scattered Disney–Dr. Seuss thing. Grmmphletts. Sometimes they simply push on to other springs, deeper parts of the jungle; other times they show up in blinking captivity as the highest-paid fashion model in the world.

There was much more to the film, Jean arriving from the country at a London modeling agency and being told she "had it," then doing hours of tush exercises to get the required slimness; a Beatle-topped photographer named David Bailey swarming all over her with his camera, saying there had to be this thing between the photographer and the model, although, God knows, don't get him wrong, you didn't actually have to sleep with the girl; an interview with Jean's mom and her builder dad in the London suburbs, stolid, square-jawed tabloid parents. For the most part, the tone was that of a titleholding fighter's camp. The pretty, bewildered young thing who had started with Jean and was doing all right now but had been kayoed by her in one round of an early fight ("Jean just sort of stepped right out in front of me"); the older, retired champ, acknowledging that Jean had "an enchanting little face" and might even last for a few more years; some teasing about the new young challengers who might be coming up fast out of town. There was not really much Jean in the film. Shadowy, wraithlike, she flicked in and out like a tongue. She was in it and yet she was not. A portrait of no one had begun to emerge.

In a drenching rain, a mournful art director took me over to meet Jean at the studio of Mel Sokolsky, a fashion photographer many feel is top rank, the new Avedon. The rain was prophetic. Later I was to feel I had been interviewing a raindrop, showering questions at the dawn. Jean is a great retractor. She retracted pauses, silences, a dozen sighs. She wanted to retract me, herself; she seemed to be out to retract the world. Speeding downtown on a bus, the art director, to get me rolling, told me a story about a long-distance operator who had recognized Jean's name, asked her if it was true you had to sleep with photographers to become great. Jean had told her you didn't have to be a fashion model to get sharvered and the operator had refused to put through the call. "And be prepared for craziness the second you step in the door," the art director told me.

At the studio I met Sokolsky, a short, blond, cigar muncher I thought I recognized as an old schoolyard basketball-playing chum from the West Bronx, furious dribbler, good set shot, easily wiped out under the boards. Could this be the same playground Sokolsky of my youth, now appearing in a mantle of fashion greatness? I felt like spotting him four points in a quick game of one-on-one, just to see. A beautiful woman named Ali, Sokolsky's secretary, flashed by on long, galloping legs, wearing a fashion-world outfit, a tiny skirt and thickly webbed stockings, boots, too. It is supposed to be an innocent, little-girl, rag-doll affair, but don't be fooled for a second. It is the horniest outfit in the history of the Western world. Off in the distance, I saw Jean Shrimpton, nude, startled, a cellophane mask over her face. Was this to be my introduction to the fashion game? As it turned out, it was a Shrimpton mannequin, to be shown in store windows across the nation. The real Jean Shrimpton sat coiled in a chair, legs braided, a girl and a half in one of those treacherous skirts, flicking looks at me, then kind of scampering away with her eyes. She had come a long way since her grmmphlett days, seemed resigned to her captivity. Perhaps she would recognize me as someone who had once taken a thorn out of her paw. "Hi, there," I said.

"Hi," she answered.

"That did it," said Sokolsky. "It'll never work out. A great wall exists between you two. You're the wrong fellow for the job. I can see you're not used to the world of gorgeous models and are all tensed up. Jean's a child of nature, a kind of girl-woman, and will do anything at all if it's put to her right. I'm the one who understands her. I can tell it, but of course I can't write it. *You'll* never get through, though."

"People are always asking me, 'What's the matter, Jean?' " she said. "There isn't anything the matter at all. Does that help you any?"

"Here we never ask her what's the matter," said Sokolsky. "That's why she loves it here. But you're from outside her world."

She seemed to feel sorry for me and said, "I'd love to eat scoops and scoops of butter-pecan ice cream, but it would affect my cheeks and that would be the end of me. Is that the sort of thing you'll be wanting?"

Sokolsky took me aside and said, "All right, I'll fill you in. The deal is it's all sex. Many of the girls in the business are like bitches in heat and this is a city of a million studs. Jean understands that if I were to come on with her it would be for real. There has got to be seduction in the photography."

"Well, it's not really sex," said Jean. "That is, you don't have to imagine being in bed with the fellow. But then there'll be a breeze coming through a window and it will be vaguely sexual."

Another Sokolsky, Stanley, flashed by like a Marx brother and said, "Hi, Pecky. We found out she had a pet chicken and called her Pecky, one more reason she prefers it at this studio."

"Another nickname for me is 'The Shrimp,' " she said, "which was inevitable."

The mannequin man, Larry Bartscher, showed up and said: "The mannequin business is a touchy game. This one came out great, the flesh is fine and the jawbone is under control. We had one major model, known for her big smile and a lot of teeth. Well, in *her* mannequin, the smile kept going on and on like the Mississippi."

The idea was that Sokolsky was to take pictures of Jean as the world had never known her. He danced by with the mannequin and said, "The only way would have been for us to disappear in the country for two weeks, Jean soon beginning to do natural, spontaneous things." I had to use the men's room, and Ali, who was showing me the way, announced, "I am taking him to the men's room," to a squadron of fashion-world goddesses. The mannequin man hollered after me: "Get it in that we're exclusive with Arnold Constable."

It was decided that the mood was all wrong for taking pictures that evening and I spirited Jean off to the most remote section of the studio. She settled into a chair, doing twisty front-of-fireplace, ten-year-old things with her legs, totally unaware of the tremendous havoc she was causing. Do grmmphletts ever know? "You're right, it is better down here. They're paying me and paying me, the poor dears, and they haven't taken any pictures yet. I like almost anything thin and sad and lonely, thin, drawn men, thin hands, anything lost and small and skinny. Anything with cheekbones. Waiflike things. And it's quite clear I'm not beautiful but merely happened along at the right time for me. I am really rather shaky and if four other models are in a store I will not try on hats around them."

I asked her if she had any fantasies and she seemed stricken, as though the jeep and grinding cameras had caught her at the water hole again. She poked around in her purse; were there several in there? "Oh, my. I don't really think I have any. I'd love to have some, but they won't come. If someone I love is two hours late for an appointment I often fear he's had an accident. Is that one?"

I said it was sort of one. Whereupon she made me her fantasy man; each time I saw her during the next week, she was to try some on me to see if they were real ones.

Her talk was streaked with sadness, impermanence—and she'd been disturbed by the situation of Christine Keeler, who'd had a notorious affair with a member of Parliament.

"How sad for her, how lonely. What a sad and marvelous body she had. It could never have happened to me, too moral, but thank God I've had a few affairs. I've bought a cottage in some hills near London. It is called Stepping Stones, Turnip End, Flower's Bottom. When it collapses, when it all goes down the drain, at least I'll have that."

"It all went so well for me, dad a builder, me with a pony and school so easy. My sister's engaged to a Rolling Stone. Other things? I'm twenty-two, five feet nine and a half, and get along with homosexuals." Small Negro street ones were always running up to her for autographs. "I so miss having a girl friend. Homosexuals are like having a spy in the enemy camp and are helpful in telling me how to get on with men."

A great black dog appeared at the door, a Trojan dog actually for Sokolsky, who leaped out from behind it. "You don't want me in here, right?" he asked.

"Right."

Jean said she lived in Greenwich Village and was curious about drugs, but only as an observer. There were books she had read, *The Great Gatsby* and *East of Eden*. "I loved *The Collector* because I understood every word of it, but the others I liked because it was right to. You see, I've got to be shown, got to be pushed, got to be led. And don't say the world 'leases' to me. I'd rather live where I am till I'm a hundred than have to deal with them." The photographers were like lovers and she did well with the ones who counted on her to pull them through. She knew, of course, the moment she set foot in the door. "I do so like clothes, but I never seem to have *got* any. And I must run now.

"I think," she said, scampering up the stairs, "that when it's all over, I'd rather like to be in antiques; they sound sad and lonely, although I don't know very much about them."

A handsome young studio man named Jordan Kalfus stopped me on the way out and said: "She's the whole British bag, her looks, her attitude, a winning combo, liked by one and all. You're a writer and probably have to stoop to these things, but the trouble with these articles is that it drags the whole level down. You know who says it all for me? That sculptor who works with big pieces of feces."

A fellow with long hair stopped by and said: "Little ones, too."

"That feces guy sums it all up," said Kalfus. "Anyway, Jean cuts through. She can sell anything from cheap dresses to gold pubic hair."

. . . . .

I came around several nights later to see Jean being photographed by Sokolsky. He stopped me at the door and said: "Oh, my God, I didn't know you were going to be here. It has to just happen. How is it going to just happen now. And it isn't going to be any good if you leave, either. You *were* here. And she *knows* you were here."

Jean was perched on a shelf reading a European fashion magazine. "Look at this word 'crepey' on the cover. I'm positive people will read it as 'creepy.' I've been off in the country riding foals, and oh yes, I think I had a fantasy. I was one of a great herd of little children, all of us flying through the woods. Ponies, donkeys, and rabbits were involved too. Does that do?"

"Well, we're finished for tonight, all right," Sokolsky said to me. "It's the same as if you were picking your nose. If you were all by yourself, you'd do it easily, nonchalantly. If a room full of people were there you'd tighten up."

I told Jean she smelled nice and she said: "I'm not a perfume person, if that's what you mean. Just a little after-bath. And look here in this magazine. All the girls say they are a hundred ten pounds. I said a hundred twenty-six, the only one who didn't lie." She said she was starting to like my questions and I should not get the idea she was condescending. "One friend of mine calls me that and it was only because I said he was fat and bloated and drunk when he was trying on a burgundy suit." She said she had had only one complete relationship, with an English photographer, total, terribly straight. They had found each other, come along together. But she had been too young for it. Now it might be different. A certain theater person was in the picture these days. "But with the theater ones there are those games you must play, and they know exactly where they have got you. He is always teasing me on buses, blowing out his cheeks to show how fat I am. Of course, he worries so about his weight, too, which helps me see how silly I must be when I carry on so." Once he had come in unexpectedly from New Haven to find Jean out, the apartment all smelly and dirty, and nothing in the fridge. "But I'm very faithful in my head, a faithful little creature."

"The proper place for me and my camera is all sealed up in the goddamned wall," said Sokolsky. "But oh, well, we'll risk it. Up you go, Jean, beddy by."

Another photographer named William Helburn came by with a famous model, Angela Howard. Helburn had matted down curlicued hair and snatched Jean down on his lap, giving her neck kisses. "He embarrasses me," she said. "Get him to stop."

Sokolsky flung himself across a desk, landing on his stomach alongside Miss Howard. "You're losing her to me," he said to Helburn. "I'm much sexier."

"All you Jewish guys are sexier," said Miss Howard. "Someone put crazy eyebrows on me today, lots of pokey pieces." She asked Jean if she had ever done any TV. "You just find a big check in the mailbox all the time."

"There is some sort of green card I don't have," said Jean. Ali had rounded up nightgowns and a thick flannel robe for the pictures Jean was to have taken in the Sokolsky family apartment. Jean started upstairs and Sokolsky hollered, "I have a camera that photographs naked no matter what you're wearing."

I went off with Ali, who said she had been booking models for three and a half years. "Jean's the most beautiful creature I've ever seen, a combination of little girl and animal. A thousand people I know have found her sexy, not hard sexy, nor obvious sexy, but real sexy. Other models come in and do a planned thing and it doesn't work. Jean traipses in wearing her funny boots and any old *schmatta*, and the contest is over. She doesn't even have to do her British tricks anymore, for instance, that Raggedy Ann one she has with her legs. Another model tried it and almost cracked her knees. One more lovely thing. She knows perfectly well that some of the people who take her out do it just to be seen with Jean Shrimpton. Fine. But for her to just *admit* it and say, 'He wants to be seen with me, that's all,' is very lovely."

Back at the office, Sokolsky and Helburn were talking about nose jobs. "I got one so my nose could look like your nose," said Helburn.

"It was a total failure," said Sokolsky.

Helburn said he had heard Sokolsky was grossing a million a year and that it was all wisely invested.

"We don't have nothing," said Sokolsky's brother. "We have thirty shares of something."

"Probably Xerox," said Angela Howard.

Sokolsky said he didn't see how anyone could gross a million. "God knows I'm not the lowest-paid man in the game. Yet I work day and night till the cows come home and I don't see any million." He excused himself to go upstairs and take pictures of Jean Shrimpton as the world had never seen her. "The proper place for you tonight," he told me, "and—don't get insulted—for anyone, would have been fourteen miles away from here."

. . . . .

I got to see Jean work at the studio of Bert Stern, who did not mind if I watched. He is a casual, soft-shouldered photographer, who operates with one hand, the other in his pocket, and who calls Jean "Bubbie." Jean was doing an emerald green rug for Callaway Mills, one of the Callaway people explaining to me that the idea was somehow "to build a bridge between the world of fashion and glamour on one shore and carpeting on the other." Jean was stretched out on a swatch of carpeting and seemed tied to it, a lovely fashion-world Gulliver, while an international team of Bert Stern assistants, a curly-headed Dutchman, a squat, lens-wise Japanese, flitted about her with tiny cameras, clicking off injection-like supporting shots. Stern himself worked high above, on a great catapult, calling for dogs to be used as props. A grey-haired woman stepped forth with two fashion puppies, selecting a Yorkshire terrier named Chowsie for the job and sending it across the carpet to Jean. "Say hello doggie to it," Stern hollered down to Jean, "and get it to look up here at the lens." Charlotte Barclay, the puppy woman, said that the dogs definitely knew they were fashion models. "When a job comes up they leap right into their modeling box and can hardly wait to get to work. I am convinced they live longer and happier lives than straight dogs. They get their bookings from Animal Talent Scouts, Inc." Miss Barclay said that Chowsie had been with Ethel Merman in *Gypsy*. "She went into the show as a puppy and still can't get the cues out of her system. I can't play Merman around the house. Let her but hear the last few bars of *Some People* and she starts to twitter and wants to run out onstage." A Callaway man spotted paw prints on the carpet and Miss Barclay went out to rub them off and to get Chowsie to look up at the lens. Stern lost his casualness and said, "It looks like an old sack. All right, get that goddamned hound the hell out of here." Jean sat up and hugged herself while other props were rounded up. She seemed to be tied to a stake. I imagined getting someone to distract the natives with feats of magic, then cutting her down; we would then escape into the jungle, incense-crazed, torch-bearing savages failing in their effort to track us down. I talked to a man with a brush who was standing by on the edge of the carpeting. He said he was Charles Simpson, a hair man, brought in on special projects. "Jean's hair is soft, natural, feminine, honey blonde. When they move her, I've got to keep an eye out and see that it doesn't get silly. If she lies down and has too much hair, it'll be all over for the poor rug."

Simpson said that Jean had pioneered big ears and made them chic. "Jean's ears are like lovely seashells. She just appeared on a cover one day, with her hair swept back and there they were, big as day, looking just fine, thank you. On anyone else they would have been disastrous. Jean has beautiful breasts. I'm surprised no one ever does anything with them."

French fries and hamburgers were brought in for the Callaway people. I crawled out for a moment to talk to Jean. She said she had worked late and was very tired and I was sorry I didn't have a French fry to slip her. I had heard she earned around sixty dollars an hour. It seemed very little for having to sit by yourself for long periods in the middle of carpets.

Jean was wearing a low-cut gown now and Simpson was right about her breasts. When new props arrived, Stern shouted down that she should lie back and when she did, she came out of her dress.

"They're out," she said. "You knew they'd come out."

"I did not," said Stern.

. . . . .

A call came through at noon the next day saying I should rush over to Sokolsky's studio, where a picture was to be taken of all the people who had created Jean Shrimpton. Since I was now one of the people, I got to stand in a corner of the picture. Sokolsky had arranged a giant mirror opposite us so that you were able to make the kind of face you wanted for the picture and be sure it got in that way. Music was played to establish the proper mood and a black Sokolsky dog named Eben sat in front of the group, baying at the electronic flashes. After the last shot, Sokolsky said, "Significantly, the writer was the only one who didn't look into the mirror." I talked to Jerry Ford, whose agency arranges Jean's bookings. "Oh, she'll last another ten days," he said. "Only kidding. Most models look alike. Jean's greatness is that she's different and looks like the reawakening of England, has the whole rebellion in her face. And, of course, the way her body hangs, the hips disjointed, a knee out of place, that's all hers, some of it studied, some natural. Oh, that long narrow body can do anything and has become a trend in our business. I knew she had it on instant appraisal." Ford said that Jean is bucking five hundred girls here, five hundred in Paris, and another five thousand who just brush up against the business and get lost. "I'd say she has ten more years in her, certainly not as *the* new look, but as a pretty high-priced model. Freedom of motion is the great thing this business gives her. If she's tired of New York, she can have six weeks in Paris and not miss a step. Let her want to work from 10:30 A.M. and quit at 3:30, we'll set that up, too. So put her down as kooky and new looking and you can *always* get her out of bed in the morning to work."

A small, nervous woman from Saks Fifth Avenue reluctantly confessed she was in fingernail mending. She said she had been doing nail work for a good many years, here and on the Coast. "I have the only nail bank in the world—it's like an eye or blood bank. If Jean were to break one, I'd be brought in and hopefully put the same nail back on. Saks wouldn't want me to say exactly what I use for the gluing. She has long, narrow, gentle hands, which makes it easy to see she's a gentle person.

If a person is nasty and claws and slashes at people, it shows up in their hands, and, yes, it gets into the nails, too. Jean has nails that are average sturdy and can go for ten days without nail work."

A short, dapper, no-nonsense Italian introduced himself as Enny of Italy and said he was involved with her hair. "She has a respect for people around her that you expect in a star. Her hair is good, of medium body, but it gets beat up. The top hair in the business gets sick when it is abused. So I get in there with my hands and tools. She has her hairpieces, I have mine. We work something out. How *I* like her hair is not the point. You must kill your own point of view, do a job." Halston, a jovial young hat man from Bergdorf-Goodman's, told me Jean could be anything. "Audrey Hepburn's younger sister or the vamp of all vamps. In doing her hats, I'm involved with her face, which you know about, and her bones, which are marvelous. What hits you is that she's always on time. She must lead a clean, healthy life." A girl from *Harper's Bazaar* said Jean was sexy and sweet like a Botticelli and that in doing the Paris shows she didn't break down like some of the other models. "Some are there only in body after several hours while Jean keeps rapport with the make-believe." A man from J. Walter Thompson said he had used her in a one-year campaign for Angel Face, a Pond's makeup, when she had first come to America. "Why? Because she literally had an angel face, although there was some sex, too. At that time, she was like a little girl who didn't care what you threw on her and was surprised at all the fuss. She wasn't sure America had really discovered her. Now she's sure."

A rumor spread that Jean's foot-massage man had shown, too late for the picture. Jean, who was sitting barefoot on a shelf, as though getting her feet ready, killed the rumor and said no, no, she wouldn't like a massage and wasn't really sure she liked being touched at all.

The pictures of Jean "as she had never been seen before" were all developed now and Sokolsky had them heaped up in boxed labeled "Shrimp." Jean went into his office to look at them and said, "Oh no, oh no, oh my God, no," near tears, a bird snatched in midflight by a great hand.

"You know why?" said Sokolsky, circling the room. "Because I caught her, I invaded her privacy. I'm in there. I'm *really* in there, the first fellow, and as a result the pictures are twenty times more exciting than her usuals."

I saw some of the pictures on a screen. They seemed fine, soft warm hued, casual, quite lovely. But Jean said her boyfriend would "do his knot" when he saw them.

"Then he's a jerk," said Sokolsky, "because they'll do you lots of good.

Jean's upset because she just expected ghost glimpses of herself and here you have the whole number, the way she really is. I've photographed the most beautiful women in the world and they're all afraid that one ugly pore in that one tiny blackhead still shows and that they're secretly homely."

Jean kept twisting her head around and around saying, oh no, oh no, oh no; grmmphletts are quite fragile and when they have their feet in traps about all you can do is calm them and wish them well. I told her I thought the pictures were quite nice and left.

. . . . .

Word was passed along to me that Jean traveled with a certain New York City crowd and there would be no real understanding of her unless I touched base with certain of its members. A representative one was Jane Holzer, a young, pretty girl who lives in a labyrinthian rich-girl apartment on Park Avenue and has been called a trend setter. I went to see her in the year's worst rainstorm and was greeted at the door by a maid and two rich-lady dogs. Jane came in after awhile, apologized for being late, and said she had taken a subway for the first time and wound up somewhere in Queens. "My thoughts on Jean? She has to put up with a lot of ickypoo people, but she is sweet, gentle, a kind of nice country bumpkin, really, except that watch out when someone comes along and unlocks what she's really got. I'm afraid you'll have to go off to London to really get the pictures. Jean comes out of that Cockney gang, Terence Stamp, David Bailey, Lionel Bart, the Rolling Stones, poor people breaking out of their class and not in a big race to grow old like jaded Americans."

I reminded Jane that Jean was not really ever poor and she said yes, she knew, but that it all fitted together anyway. "And never mind about her not being smart. We played a word game after Thanksgiving dinner, one in which you must see how many things you can think up that start with a certain letter. Well, she just whipped us all, especially on D for diseases. I think she may become a Capucine or else just go back to the country. Other stories? Once in London, she had this minicar, everyone throwing pits and other junk in the back. There was a crackling sound and a mouse showed up, living back there. Jean was the only one not frightened and loved the mouse."

"Okay, you can come out now," Jane said to a door and a young Australian model with the record short skirt of the entire fashion world appeared and joined us. She said she had lived five doors away from Jean in London and that Jean was animal mad, her flat filled to brimming with birds and dogs that messed all over the floor. "Jean would just merrily go about cleaning up after them, not in the least bit bothered." Jane said she had a thought that summed up Jean. "Most girls look in the mirror and go like this, " she said, making a hollow-cheeked, sophisticated face. "Jean looks in the mirror and goes like this." She did a puzzled "wha-a-a?" face. We drank and talked and before long, as had happened so many times before, Shrimp was out of the picture, evaporated, up in smoke.

. . . . .

The last time I saw Jean she was off to Washington, D.C., for a visit. She seemed cheerful. No more sitting on carpets for awhile. She told me there were still no fantasies but she had remembered another book, one she loved most of all. It was called *Precious Bane*, by Mary Webb, and was about a girl with a harelip. "I loved it so," she said, "and read it over and over and over." Like a famished man I pounced on that little tidbit and whipped together my fanciest notion yet: Lonely, frightened, afraid, Jean was confident that even if ten million photographers said she was lovely, the fairest in the land, one would slip through finally, and prove she had a harelip after all. She was a person with a spiritual harelip, a harelip on her psyche. I was proud of that one for a while, but it is now on the shelf, and I have a hunch the grmmphlett idea is going right alongside it. Another one you can have is the one that says there is no one there at all, just someone who has been made up, pasted together by an industry for its own use. There is a person there all right, a gentle and lovely one, as at least four hundred people have testified. It may be that the owner of the truth about Jean Shrimpton is that young rich lady I talked to who asked me to give her a ringyding if I needed any more material. "Don't you see it, silly," she said. "It's staring you right in the face. Jean's a woman. Perfectly content and easy about it. It's a rare phenomenon in America and that may be what's confusing you."

to cigars, with
love and devotion

Several years back, having written a play he admired, I was not so much invited as "summoned" to dinner by the Emperor, his eminence in this case being the legendary Hollywood mogul Sam Spiegel, driving force behind such epics as *The Bridge on the River Kwai* and *Lawrence of Arabia*. My dinner companions, apart from Spiegel, were an attractive collection of individuals who might have been known in the long ago as "jet-setters." The Emperor had reserved the private room of a handsomely appointed French restaurant in Manhattan. The dinner was more than satisfactory. Had there been some cigars in evidence, I would have moved it into the "exceptional" category. No matter how good the food, a meal that isn't topped off by a first-rate cigar is about as complete to me as half a Super Bowl game. My wife felt fine. The Emperor, on meeting her, had bowed low, kissed her hand, and absolutely floored her with the remark, "You are a voomin and you are byootzful." So she was set for the month. But I wasn't. Demonstrating that I was not only an urbane man of the theater, but also a direct and earthy street type, I asked, "Are there any cigars in this joint?"

On my left sat a once-great Hollywood director whose career for the past decade had, to put it charitably, been petering out. On my right, in all of his rotund splendor, sat the Emperor. Almost as though the moment were choreographed, both the Emperor and the once-great director offered me a choice of cigars. Spiegel's were snapped open at me, nestled together in a sleek, richly leathered pocket case, half a dozen rich,

Originally published in *New York Magazine*, October 22, 1973.

fragrant Havanas—in my imagination, if not in fact, *puros*, rolled from the finest leaves of the fabled Vuelta-Abajo area, and flown in secretly that morning. Their aroma reached out and encircled me like the plump arms of a Universal starlet.

The faded director on my left offered me a single cigar, large and imperious, to be true, but one that had seen better days. Fine cigars age and improve in richness for at least seven years of their existence, but this one was past its peak, tattered, and enfeebled, in very much the same condition, sad to say, as the director's career. Crackled and peeling, its outer wrapper flaking out onto my lap, it was offered with two trembling fingers, the director's left hand clutching at his chest, no doubt to fend off a possible coronary. Rarely has a man been faced with a more clear-cut moral choice. Turn my back on the director's gnarled and wretched specimen and I might as well book space for him in the intensive care unit at Flower Hospital. Pass up the Emperor's vastly superior offering and I would appear to have a soft core, showing that I was ill equipped for the rigors of Hollywood screenwork, canceling myself out as a candidate for lush Spiegel-sponsored film contracts. What to do. What would my heroes have done? Who *were* my heroes? The great Winston Churchill, no doubt, would have brought along his own cigars. Faulkner was a pipe smoker. What if I were to take the director's bedraggled offering, and at the same time, stuff a few of the Emperor's prize winners in my pocket, to be enjoyed at a less charged moment? At the time, it seemed that such behavior would appear gluttonous and draw the contempt of all present.

With a certain grandness of gesture, while my heart sank, I accepted the director's frayed and corpselike specimen and, turning to the Emperor, said, "Thank you, Mr. Spiegel, I already have a cigar." The director took a long shaky breath. I may have added years to his life. I spent the next half hour sipping a brandy and trying to light and then to draw on his crumbling, fossilized excuse for a cigar. Finally, I excused myself and stole off to buy a furtive Don Diego corona at a nearby store, puffing on it furiously like an addict. In pursuit of that final, perfect cigar, I've smoked more than a thousand since that dinner, but the memory of those half-dozen fat, noble, aromatic beauties, snugly and sensually lying together in the Emperor's rich leather case, has followed me into my dreams.

There is much to my style of smoking that disqualifies me as a connoisseur of cigars. For one thing, I will bite off the end of an expensive Don Diego lonsdale and, if I'm alone, strolling along the street, spit out the tip, Dodge City style. The end should probably be clipped off with a cigar cutter. Handmade cigars generally have a little sealing cap at one end which can be flipped off with a sharp fingernail. A literary agent I know drills a hole in his Havanas with a tiny, Swiss-made mechanism in a ceremony that is at least as complex as your average circumcision. He wouldn't dream of taking a puff without first performing this minor surgery. The whole idea of strolling about in the open air with a lonsdale (the ideal after-dinner shape) would be considered "vulgar" by some cigar aficionados; so delicate a work of art as a fine cigar must never be exposed to the hazards of the out-of-doors, where much of its richness and flavor might be blown to the winds. If one is sorely pressed to do a little alfresco smoking, the recommended shape is the small panatela.

I do not, except under extreme pressure, chew on cigars, but I do tend to get them wet ("shocking") and to smoke them all the way down ("unconscionable"). On this last issue, I am supported by John E. Duffy, the urbane humidor manager of the great Dunhill's, who feels that the How-Far-Down-to-Smoke issue is a matter of personal preference, much of the strength and richness of cigars being concentrated in that second section. This is good or bad according to individual taste.

I do own a humidor, but only occasionally do I keep cigars in it. At the moment, it houses needles and thread, these items being kept at 67 degrees, the ideal temperature for storing fine Havanas. Were I, logically, to keep cigars in the humidor, I would tend to chain-smoke them, another vulgar trait, according to the tobacco connoisseur. At least an hour should go by between cigars.

In the view of Zino Davidoff, author of *The Connoisseur's Book of the Cigar*, the "average smoker" keeps a stock of four hundred to a thousand cigars, replacing them hundred by hundred. The oldest in his reserve are three years of age. When Batista was in power, Daryl Zanuck, another Hollywood legend, kept his own Cuban plantation and has kept as much as $20,000 worth of stock in his Dunhill's humidor. I store no more than half a dozen cigars at a time, fresh ones, which is an indication of where I stand on the connoisseur's ladder. I do this in order to hold my smoking at a moderate level. I am smoking one now, a Montecruz corona (incidentally, this is another treat that is considered gauche, smoking while at work), and I have five spares on hand. I've set it up so that if I go through the five, I'll have to hop in my car and drive five miles to a drugstore in East Hampton, which will be closed. Then I will have to drive ten miles back, cigarless and irritable, but I will have kept my smoking down to a dozen seventy-cent cigars a day and my children will be able to have nice clothing.

Recently I had access to unlimited supplies of Havana cigars. That's right, Castro cigars. Don't ask me how I was able to pull this off. Suffice it to say that my patriotism doesn't quite extend to the point of declining Havana tobacco. (The late billionaire Nubar Gulbenkian apparently shared this view. When asked why a legendary capitalist would continue to smoke the cigars of the Castro regime, he replied, "Even if the devil were to take possession of the Vuelta, I would keep smoking Havanas.") I ordered boxes of Por Larranagas and Monte Cristo coronas. There are those who say that the day of the Havana is over, among them Ted Cott of the Cigar Institute of America ("Castro laid waste to the fields, the great hand workers left the island, the soil is not what it was"); Duffy, the Dunhill's humidor man ("The Montecruz, made in the Canary Islands, is the finest cigar in the world today"); and Norman Stein, of the Stage Cigar Store ("Castro takes a handful of cigars and stamps one batch Upmann, another batch Punch, the next one Rey del Mundo, and so on—they're all the same").

Whatever the case, if the Havana has had it, you could have fooled me. I smoked box after box of my hoard, walking around in an affably drugged state for several weeks—and then I stopped. People told me my complexion changed and that I had turned a sort of *maduro colorado* color, in other words, the sort of reddish brown hue of a full-bodied, medium-strength, aromatic Havana. Back I went to my half-dozen-a-day Montecruz coronas, each one unhumidored, each one allowed to age about as long as it takes for me to get the wrapper removed, one end cleanly or sloppily bitten off, and the other end lit with a safety match.

Blindfolded, or even allowed to peek a little, I cannot tell the difference between a Havana, Cape de Vinales, tobacco of Palacios, and a second Havana, Cape d'Isabel Maria, tobacco of the Vuelta-Abajo. There are great smokers who can pull this off, making the wine experts seem like unlettered clods. Another insufficiency of mine is to stub out cigars instead of allowing them to go out by themselves. And perhaps the darkest of all my smoking transgressions is to allow cigar butts to accumulate in ashtrays, forming what an otherwise ladylike novelist friend referred to as "little rows of turds." (I am working at this last offense to the sensibilities.) I do not smoke "up" in the finest tradition, that is, following each cigar of the evening with one that is greater in strength. I smoke up, down, and sideways—that is, quite haphazardly—and very often, whatever I can get my hands on. On the other hand, I do not go along with a celebrated Broadway bookie named "Morrie" who insists that "any cigar is good."

Though my credentials as a cigar connoisseur are disgracefully lacking, I will match my actual love and devotion to a fine cigar with anyone's, almost including that of Churchill himself, who smoked several hundred thousand in his lifetime, growing healthier and more robust with each puff; Freud, who filled the room with cigar smoke while making sense of his patients' dreams (and ignoring his doctor's advice to give them up); Raoul Dufy, who exchanged masterpieces of art for cigars; and Franz Liszt, who entered a monastery at the end of his life after asking for and getting permission to smoke unlimited cigars (and dying with one between his lips). Samuel Gompers, founder of the American Federation of Labor, was limited by his physician to one cigar a day. Since he began his career as a cigar maker, he went back to rolling his own, cranking out a foot-long model each day. That was his "one cigar." We would have gotten along. Groucho Marx, or so goes the legend, was warned by his wife that it was either his cigars or the marriage. "Well, we can still be friends," he replied. Another reason I'm a Marx fan.

I smoke cigars when I'm happy, and I light one up when I'm less so. They do the trick as well—when I feel nothing. I celebrated with a cigar when I sold my first novel and bit into one when another novel was treated rudely by the critics. Although this confession probably spoils my chances for elective office, I recall smoking my way through a mild nervous breakdown. I was ill recently; all bad habits had to go—except cigar smoking, my bottom line. My father smoked Admiration Joys when I was a boy. No doubt this is where it all began. When he reached his seventies, I introduced him to Don Diego and Montecruz, and he claimed I spoiled him. We smoked cigars at Friday night fights when I was in my late teens, and we pulled at a couple of torpedoes during the first Ali-Frazier fight. While we were waiting for my mother to die, we smoked them in the outer lobby of the hospital floor. It made it a lot easier. When I was at college, my father gave a cigar to my roommate, Arthur Frommer, who later became a giant in the travel industry. Frommer turned green and may never have smoked again. The only tobacco that ever made me sick was a pipe mixture called Three Nuns.

Women are said (who *says* these things?) to find cigar smoke objectionable. But whenever a woman has professed to enjoy my company, she's had no complaint about my cigars. Several women have told me they associate cigar-smoking expertise with skill in the bedroom. Perhaps. And of interest. I recall a time when my father, upon meeting a friend, would stuff a cigar in the fellow's vest pocket. And more often than not, he would have one stuffed back in return. It seemed a nice and convivial custom.

One of my pleasures is to smoke a cigar while I'm driving. I have learned to clock highway distance in terms of cigars. The trip from my summer rental in Amagansett is a two-cigar drive (with a twenty-minute stop at McDonald's). A great treat is to play casino blackjack all night long, sipping brandy, and puffing away at a corona.

Cigars have been a lifeline for me. For the most part, they have intensified moments of pleasure, and most of my smoking associations fall into this department. Yet I am fascinated by the bizarre behavior they bring out in many people. In lieu of a raise or a key to the executive john, a former boss of mine offered me unlimited access to his cigar supply. "Just go in and take a handful anytime you like," he said, "and don't bother asking me about it." Several days later, while he was seated at his desk, I walked into his office and took one out of his humidor. "What the hell are you doing?" he asked. "You said it was all right, " I answered.

"Oh," he said, looking a bit puzzled. I tried this on several other occasions and each time I took one he gave me a dirty look. I went back to my own supply.

Mario Puzo, a colleague of mine and a man whose generosity is firmly established, admits to occasional and unaccountable streaks of cigar stinginess. "It happens late at night when I'm down to two cigars and a friend signals me that he wants one. I just won't give it to him." In his *Godfather Papers and Other Confessions*, Puzo, in turn, claims that Bob Evans, of Paramount Pictures, a multimillion-dollar empire, would hide his stock of choice Havanas, making it almost impossible for Puzo to get at them.

At a recent dinner party, as I was about to light up a Montecruz, the hostess, a woman I had always thought of as gentle and mild mannered, all but smacked it out of my hand and said: "Put that away. My husband will give you a good one." As it turned out, her husband did offer me a fine cigar, a silver-tinned Punch, smuggled in from Canada. But why the sudden ferocity on her part—totally out of character?

Recently I stood on the second floor of the famed Dunhill's on Fifth Avenue. The first humidor that caught my eye was lettered "John F. Kennedy." It had the look of a small casket. Kennedy had smoked a short slender Havana called Fior de Allones and kept a substantial stock of them at Dunhill's. Toward the end of his life, he had to declare an embargo on Cuban tobacco (a thousand tons of Cuban leaf were stockpiled at the time in Tampa warehouses, so it took a while for the supply to run out). When he came under pressure (from columnist Walter Winchell, for example) for continuing to smoke Havanas, several friends of the Kennedys began to stock Havanas under their own names for the president to tap. I looked at some pictures of the late president, youthful, ferociously handsome, a cigar stuck jauntily between his teeth. He was the last of the chief executives to smoke them openly and with such evident pleasure. According to Duffy, they had found a handful on his body after the assassination. Or somewhere in the presidential limousine. They didn't stop the bullets, but looking at the picture, I hoped, not particularly liking myself for the presumption of the thought, that they had given him some pleasure through the short and furious years of his life.

yank paparazzo

In an age of specialization, lives there a man more specialized than forty-year-old Ron Galella, who has thrown over the last five years of his life to leaping from behind hedges and vaulting out of Chinese restaurant coatracks to take almost five thousand unauthorized pictures of Jacqueline Onassis in "frightened-deer"-type poses? Undeterred by Secret Service men, high fences, bodyguards, and her own decoy techniques (sunglasses, flower bouquets, slipping away through restaurant kitchens), the tall, paunchy shutterbug has relentlessly tracked his lovely prey to at least two of the four corners of the earth, "nailing" her in Cyprus, Naples, Scorpios, Sardinia, midtown Manhattan bicycle paths, Peppach, New Jersey, Brooklyn Heights, and the depths of Chinatown. Curious to know more about this strange through-the-lens romance with the beauteous former first lady, we, or let's face it, *I*, did a little tracking down of my own, smoking out Galella in one of those neat, conspicuously inconspicuous two-family houses in Yonkers, New York, favored by gangland individuals who prefer to live with as little outward flash as possible. The sign above the studio door said, "Ron Galella—Photographer with the Paparazzo Approach." It was my idea that perhaps Galella's voyeuristic stubbornness had to do with a need to catch his parents in the act of connubial mischief, cathartically recreating that primal bedroom shocker in every youngster's life. Using a paparazzo technique of my own, I pounced on him with this notion as soon as I'd set foot in the door. "No, no, no," he said, dismissing the theory as being too fancy, "my father worked hard all his life for a casket company and my mother

Originally published as "Why Won't Jackie Onassis Leave Ron Galella Alone?" in *Esquire*, March 1972.

lives three houses down. That's not it at all." Then why the fierce need mercilessly to ferret out the former first lady and catch her in unguarded moments?

"One word," said Galella, "challenge. Take Sophia Loren. She says, 'I have no secrets, paparazzo me.' Or Natalie Wood. She opens her *own* front door in Hollywood. I introduce myself as the American paparazzo and in five minutes she's back in a miniskirt, any pose I want. What is *that*? Even Liz—her body's shot, her face is beautiful—puts up with me though she keeps hollering out 'Fuck off' a lot."

"But Jackie," he says, eyes narrowing, "always trying to outwit me. Snobbish, cool, turning up in black, which she knows perfectly well ruins my chances for a two-thousand-dollar color cover . . . But how she can dress . . . slim . . . nice. My beef is that she'll wear the same Valentino red dress three times in one week. Does that do me any good? And lately, it's pants, pants, pants. Also, Levis with stains on them, three times in one week. With whole rooms full of Valentino clothes. Oh, she's a bitch alright."

But surely, I suggested, in view of past history, she has a right to a reasonable amount of privacy.

"Now you see," said Galella, shaking his head in frustration, "you're taking the same position as Airy." Ari Onassis? "Right," said Galella. "He's different, a humble man who puts his arm around me—while Jackie lurks in the car—and talks softly, even though he keeps pointing to town houses and restaurants and saying, 'I should have bought that one.'

" 'I am surprised there is an American paparazzo,' Airy says to me, 'in a country so rich.'

" 'There is,' I say.

" 'Why do you do this?' he says.

" 'You have your job, I have mine.'

" 'She has had much tragedy in her life.'

" 'Yes,' I tell him, 'but life goes on. I'm not a sadist, giving her pain. This will help her forget. If not for me, people would kill themselves with curiosity about her and the kids. There is a big void for an American paparazzo with courage and I am filling it.'

" 'Don't do it anymore,' he says.

" 'Then give me a job with Olympia Airlines.'

" 'Yes,' he says, 'and for that I will pay you one dollar.' "

Though his relentless pursuit of Jacqueline Onassis is practically a full-time job, Galella owns up to doing other bread-and-butter jobs, however, halfheartedly. After her, there is simply no number two, but he does concede that Ali McGraw is slowly coming up on the outside rail.

"She's nice, cooperative, but she won't take a madonna picture with her child. She says it's because of crackpots. I respect that and say let's use it, the madonna protecting her child. It doesn't even have to be her baby. She can use any baby, just grab a baby and hold it, madonna style. It could be just the back of the goddamned baby's head, just to show her protecting the baby, madonna style, from crackpots. I've got to have that picture. I've told her nice. If she doesn't cooperate, I'll have to go paparazzo."

That is the style, generally, according to Galella; ask them nice, then go paparazzo. The latter often involves hippie disguises, Afro hairdos, Mexican sombrero outfits, holing up for seventy-six hours in a locked customs shack with foot-long rats and only cream soda to drink—all for an exclusive series on the Burtons aboard their yacht, *Kalizma*. Bribes, an army of low-ranking tipsters, maids, doormen, chauffeurs, fans, all slipping you informational tidbits on the whereabouts of the greats.

"Hangar men are terrific for Sinatra, and there's an American Airlines stew who lets me know every move Ali McGraw makes."

Ask nice, then go paparazzo. Galella once pursued this formula with Raquel Welch, and "this creature who was created by the pictorial media had the nerve to refuse me.

"I had no choice," says Galella, in the style of Clark Kent tearing off his business shirt in the newsroom john. "I had to go paparazzo."

Despite her concern about a crotch-revealing costume on an Ed Sullivan special, Galella barged onto the set, snapping away and asking questions later. Soon afterward, at the Madrid Hilton, he met Pat Curtis, the starlet's husband, who said, "Raquel don't like you."

Occasionally, there is a lucky haul. Once, miraculously, Greta Garbo materialized out of thin air at York and Sixty-Third in New York City. Dashing up to her, his motorized Nikon clicking away, Galella shouted, "I have found gold."

"Why do you bother me," said Garbo, popping on sunglasses and fending him off with an umbrella, "I have done nothing wrong."

"If you ask me," says Galella, "she was guilty about something."

When not working in disguise, Galella's style, particularly in crashing sealed-off functions, is to dress well, "a black suit, preferably, walk with authority, look like somebody, don't ask any stupid questions. And at all times have a lot of balls, which I have. I'll talk to anybody, even Warren Beatty. And you've got to go through lights. I passed ten red lights chasing Mia and Andre Previn when they were hot. The only one who ever shook me was Julie Christie, going ninety miles an hour along a cliff in Malibu, although I caught up with her the next day and shot her unguarded in a supermarket, a famous picture. Beatty confronted me and said are you the one that sneaked a picture of Julie Christie. I threw him off by saying it was an accident, that I was trying to get Doris Day in a bikini."

Galella does not pretend to speak for his brethren across the sea, but as far as he's concerned a paparazzo must have ethics.

"I will not go into anyone's home. They have glass windows, it's another ball game. And under no circumstances will I follow a famed person into the ladies' room."

The work is not without dangers. Ari's short, stocky bodyguard once twisted Galella's camera straps around his neck; outside the Dorchester in London, Richard Burton's bodyguard, Gaston, smacked the Yank paparazzo on the jaw for trying to get a picture of Liz and Michael Wilding, Jr. (Galella smacked him back.) The worst pummeling came at the hands of four crew members on the Cuernavaca set of "Hammer Smith Is Out"; yanking him out of a cave in a Mexican siesta costume, they (allegedly?) broke his teeth, split his lips, kicked him in the neck and ribs, and generally worked him over for a full five minutes. Galella ended up with one of the crew members in a Mexican prison, depressed not so much about his battered face as the thought of five hundred undeveloped shots that had been destroyed in his hotel room. After a weekend in jail, Galella summoned the police chief to his cell and said, "Mexico has left a bad taste in my mouth."

Oddly shaken by this statement, the south-of-the-border law enforcer let him go.

Always, despite flickers of interest in other legendary ladies, it is the elusive Onassis who haunts "the world's only American paparazzo." I looked at Galella's photographs of her and other celebs, half expecting to find shots of Duke Wayne picking his nose or Doris Duke yanking at a foundation garment. It wasn't that way at all. The pictures for the most part were quite prim, and in most cases flattering. Liz did not come off too well, but Sinatra never looked better, and the same for George C. Scott and Mia Farrow. I could not find a bad one of Onassis in the bunch, a tribute either to the charmed perfection of her profile or to some perverse gentleness in Galella's touch. Most of them did have a surprised-deer-in-the-forest quality. All of which prompted me to wonder why she didn't simply pull the rug from under Galella's feet by inviting him in for a formal shooting.

"Too smart," said Galella. "If she stopped ducking me, she knows the market on her would dry up overnight."

The idea persists that Galella's fascination with Onassis extends beyond a paparazzo's normal interest in an elusive subject. For example, he keeps a precise and vivid record of the number of times she has put her hands on him. Once, at JFK International Airport, it was an angry, red-faced shoulder grab and a shout to the police, "Arrest this man." On a slightly famous Madison Avenue bicycle path series involving John F. Kennedy, Jr., and Caroline, it involved a cry from Onassis to Secret Service men, "Smash his camera," a phrase the enterprising Galella quickly snapped up for the title of an autobiographical book he is preparing for Putnam's. Most vividly, however, Galella recalls a time, late at night, when the celebrated beauty emerged from "21," spotted him, gently pinned his wrists, and looked deep into his eyes, saying, "You've been hunting me for two months."

"She seemed fascinated," said Galella. "And why not? We have a lot in common. I'm persistent. I get what I want. So does she. She wants to dominate, to do things when *she* wants. I say no, I'm Italian. It's got to be when *I* want."

With each of his brothers and sisters married, I wondered if Galella had any marital plans of his own.

"Not on the immediate horizon. It would have to be a girl willing to vault out of bed in the middle of the night to catch Jackie coming out of the Carlyle. How many girls like that are there left?"

I wondered, finally, if Galella had in mind some ultimate coup de paparazzo, a pictorial corker he might consider the crowning sneak shot of his career. "That's easy," he said, seemingly amazed I hadn't come up with this one on my own. "Jackie in hotpants. No man alive has ever gotten such a shot. And I happen to know she has three pair, my information coming from a source at a Madison Avenue boutique.

"My God," he said, his eyes watering over at the prospect, "can you imagine something like that?"

"But no sunglasses."

frozen guys

I heard they had a frozen guy in Southern California. I tracked him down to a small factory that tests and makes thermal equipment for natural-gas companies. At the time, I didn't realize he was a famous frozen individual, the first fellow ever to have himself packed away in ice.

"Can I look at him?" I asked the company owner.

"Hold on there," he said. "I didn't say we've got him here. We don't want to be known as the body freezers. People would be showing up at all hours of the night with fresh cadavers, asking that we ice them up. Our insurance rates would go sky-high."

I had a feeling he wanted to show him off, despite his protestations. Why have a frozen fellow there if you don't want to give people a look at him?

"Let me just take a quick peek."

"All right."

He led me out back to a kind of airplane hanger. The frozen guy was in a vacuum bottle about nine feet long. Liquid nitrogen was being pumped into it. I heard they had been running around all morning trying to stash him somewhere, after they found out I was coming. The sign on the container said: Contents Nitrogen-Cooled Biological Specimen, Add Liquid Nitrogen as Needed to Keep Liquid Level above Three Inches and Temperature Below 150 Degrees Kelvin. You could not see him in there, which was all right with me. I had seen some frozen folks and they looked awful. Each one seemed to be trying to say, "For Christ's sake, thaw me out. Can't you see I'm freezing my ass off?"

This particular fellow had been hauled up in a van one night by his

Originally published in *Playboy*, August 1978.

son. He was in a container, but it had sprung a leak. At first, the son said he just had "a little tissue" in the container, but he didn't fool the company owner.

"I knew he had a frozen guy in there all along. He finally admitted it. The idea was to switch him from his old container into ours, but before I would do that, I insisted that the son join in. I didn't want the fellow to get dropped and then all of a sudden the boy would have four fathers."

I tapped the container a little to test it for coldness, and also to see if I could jiggle the fellow around in there. It was a little frosty on the outside, though not anywhere near as cold as it was on the inside. And the fellow was in there solid.

"What happens to him now?"

"Our main interest was to try out our container," said the owner, "and to prove it was better than the old one. In ours, for example, he gets to lie horizontal instead of being on his toes for all eternity. We gave him a home for a while. It's time for him to be pushing on."

. . . . .

The process is called cryonic suspension. Getting frozen down, right after death, and kept at a low temperature (minus 320 degrees Fahrenheit) until the thing that did you in is cured, and then getting thawed out. Say it was your heart. You might get thawed out at a time when all they have to do is pop in a new heart. And off you go. Or it might be your brain. According to the freezing crowd, the brain doesn't suffer much damage from the cold. And Dr. K. A. Hossmann of the Max Planck Institute for Brain Research showed that the brain nerve cells don't die when blood circulation stops; rather, the brain capillaries become constricted, choking off attempted recirculation. So they would replace a section of your brain. When you get thawed out, you don't necessarily have to go with the same body. Say you've been scattered all over the highway and they've been able to bury only a few sections of you. At the time you get thawed out, they may have perfected cloning, in which case all they will have to have is one of your cells to work with. With a DNA printout of that cell, they can come up with a new you. Or, with some tampering, they might mix up your style and bring you back as a combination of you and Willie Mays.

There are a few little hitches. For freezing to have any chance at all, you've got to catch the fellow at the moment of death (cessation of heartbeat, breathing, and/or brain waves). That way, freezing has a chance of stopping cellular death. It would be even better to start cooling the fellow down before he went out. But if you throw a sick person into dry ice, it's still called murder. If, on the other hand, you can get that sick person's cooperation and that of the hospital, you can start cooling him down before he makes his exit. People are signing up to have this done to them. Not many, but some.

Another significant hitch is that they have had no success whatever in doing this. They have been able to freeze people and put them in suspension, but they have not been able to thaw anybody out yet. All they have to show thus far is a revived cat's brain, some dog kidneys, and a couple of hamsters. There has been much excitement in the freezing community about that cat's brain. Professor Isamu Suda and two associates at Kobe University froze it for more than six months (to minus 20 degrees centigrade), thawed it out, and heard it give off almost normal brain-wave patterns. Dr. Frank M. Guttman of the University of Montreal and four associates froze some dog kidneys (to minus 80 degrees centigrade), thawed them out, hooked them back up to some dogs; some were able to trot right off, using the thawed-out kidneys. There has been good work done on beetles and rabbit and mouse embryos. I saw some hamsters that had been frozen and thawed out; they were walking a little funny, but they seemed to be getting on all right. Relatively simple stuff such as skin, corneas, blood, sperm, and bone marrow gets frozen and banked in liquid nitrogen all the time and later used. The only thing they haven't been able to freeze and bring back is a whole complex organism. The freezing community feels that once it can do that to a chimp, say, everyone will climb aboard the bandwagon and want to get frozen.

. . . . .

The fellow in the Southern California container was Dr. James Bedford. He became the subject of a book called *We Froze the First Man*, written by Robert F. Nelson, one of his freezers. The bible of people freezing is a book called *The Prospect of Immortality*, written by Robert C. W. Ettinger and published in 1964. Dr. Bedford, along with a lot of other Americans, came under its influence. But he was different, in that he decided to do something about it. When he saw that the end was near, he left his money to the Bedford Foundation, whose aim was to get its founder frozen and keep him that way. Bedford was frozen in 1967. (While the blood was drained from his body, cooled to two degrees centigrade, the arteries and lungs were perfused with DMSO and Ringer's solution. Bedford was then wrapped in aluminum foil, put into an insulated container, and packed with dry ice. There his temperature was reduced to minus 79 degrees centigrade. Later, he was put into his permanent capsule, that giant container filled with liquid nitrogen, and held at minus 196 degrees centigrade. A foil face covering allows him to be easily identified.) He wound up in a capsule made by Ed Hope of Arizona. Since then, he has been kicking around. The freezing crowd celebrates Bedford as American's first cryonaut, but he has not had much of an afterlife. After I came across him in Southern California, he was sent to the Bay Area of San Francisco and is currently back in Southern California. The truth seems to be that nobody is terribly interested in having a frozen fellow around.

Not too many others have followed in Bedford's footsteps. There have been about thirty known freezings in this country. There were fourteen stored in Chatsworth for a while. There are a handful in San Francisco and New York. Two lawyers with pistols showed up at the south Florida cryonics group and said they had seventy wealthy men frozen in Trenton, New Jersey, and wanted to know the correct way to freeze the seventy-first. No black people have ever gotten themselves frozen. Some of the early frozen people have been thawed out and buried old-fashioned style. Those in charge of them seem to have said the hell with it.

The people who have gotten frozen are spoken of in the freezing community with a certain superstar reverence. *Ann DeBlasio. Jim Bedford. Little Stevie Mandell. Genevieve de la Poterie.* It's as if they're talking about Janis Joplin and Jimi Hendrix. The freezing community tends to be tight and clannish. A romance sprang up between Steven Mandell's mother and Ann DeBlasio's policeman widower. Both were visiting their departed kins' containers and fell in love.

The idea of getting frozen has not caught fire. The people in people freezing feel it's because they haven't nailed a star. "If we could just get Raquel Welch" is what they say. Omar Bradley's wife looked into it on behalf of the general but then backed off. When Eisenhower was fading, the group fired off a letter to Mamie but got no response. They had heard he might go that way. A strong rumor persists that Walt Disney is in cold storage in Salt Lake City, but it can't be pinned down. They still feel they need a Telly Savalas to put them over with the public.

Most of the freezing community (often called the Immortality Crowd) lives in the Bay Area of San Francisco. The "action arm" of the group is called Trans Time, Inc. ("Life Extension through Cryonic Suspension"). Those are the people who actually freeze you. What you do is pay one thousand dollars to the Bay Area Cryonics Society, just to get on board. Then you take out at least a fifty-thousand dollar life-insurance policy, payable to the society. That covers the cost of getting you frozen and keeping you in a container until you are ready to get thawed out. Each person who signs up wears a bracelet that says: "Whole body donor. Resuscitate and cool. Do not embalm or autopsy." If you drop dead on the street, the hope is that someone will read your bracelet and phone the Trans Time hot-line number. A truck speeds over and starts freezing you as fast as possible.

All the members—and directors—of the Bay Area Cryonics Society and of Trans Time wear those bracelets and have signed up to get frozen. There don't seem to be any weirdos in the group. They are intelligent fellows, many of them distinguished scientists at Berkeley, biophysicists, gerontologists, futurists. They are an upbeat, optimistic group, and even though all have signed up to be encapsulated, none expects that that will happen. It is their feeling that by the time their number is up, breakthroughs in life extension, transplants, artificial organs, suspended animation, etc., will enable them to live forever. Each of them has a side research gig; at this point, there is not much money in people freezing.

Since there did not appear to be any great rush to jump on the freezing bandwagon, the people at Trans Time gave a kind of freezing cocktail party while I was in San Francisco. Folks who had already signed up were there to talk to people who were flirting with getting frozen but wanted to be convinced it was the right move. Again, no weirdos in the crowd. The cocktail party was given at the home of a professor of communications at San Francisco State. Many of the people at the party were older fellows with young wives. That may have been a factor in their wanting to get frozen. These fellows were marathon runners and pumped iron, but inevitably, they were losing the race. "Once you're thawed out, can you go back to sex?" one of them wanted to know. "If not, the hell with it."

It may have been my imagination, but all of the people there seemed to have chilly handshakes. Only half of the invited guests showed up. The host felt it was because they were scared stiff of living forever. There was a lot of diet talk. Sardines and asparagus. J. D. Rockefeller's diet of breast milk from recent mothers. And the usual bad jokes. People in the freezing community tell the world's worst jokes. Freeze a jolly good fellow. Many are cold, few are frozen. That kind of thing. There were some knocks at the government for its lack of interest in cryonics. "Only thing those guys ever freeze is wages." The talk switched to the Russians who were claiming to live to be 150. Paul Segall of Berkeley's Department of Physiology and Anatomy pooh-poohed these claims. He had heard the men had falsified their birth certificates to get out of army duty. People who lived in the Andes were another story. There was something about living high up and at an incline that made for longevity. Anyone who wanted to live in the mountains at a slant had a chance to lead a long life.

Several people took pot shots at a passage in Arthur Hailey's book *The Moneychangers* in which a character thinks that the cryonics people make a mockery of death.

"That's exactly what we want to do," said Saul Kent, a futurist and strong freezing advocate.

Segall took over and told of his experiments with a tryptophan-deficient diet in which he had gotten rats to live the equivalent of eighty-five years. And to give birth to little rats, late in life, as if they were having children at seventy. He also said it was his view that diet, marathon running, living at the right altitude, and not smoking were all fine— but that the key to long life was each person's "biological clock," which, barring a building collapse or a highway crash, determined how long each person would be around. And the only way to live indefinitely was to get in there and fiddle with the hands on that clock. Most of the cryonics people are gerontologists, but the "sexy" part of life extension is freezing and Segall always went back to that. His partner, Harold "Frosty" Waitz, a biophysicist at Berkeley, was freezing yeast under pressure. When water freezes, it can exert a pressure of thirty thousand pounds per square inch. Which is what makes steel pipes burst in the winter. Frosty was freezing his samples under an equivalent counterpressure, which, logically, would make for a nice, easygoing freeze. At best, we would learn how to freeze people without messing them up too badly, and we might finally learn how to freeze tomatoes.

Segall envisioned a time when a man who wanted to "get away for a while" would simply freeze himself for a decade, get thawed out, and pick up where he had left off. What about the social, educational, mind-boggling "reentry" problems a cryonaut would face after being frozen for a hundred years or so and waking up to an outrageously different world? Answer: At that time, we would hope to have an "education pill" that you would pop and be brought right up to date. Still, the complications were endless. A man has himself frozen; his son follows suit. The man thaws out before the son does and a situation arises in which the father is much younger than the son. More immediately, maybe even just around the corner, was a method of freezing people and laying them out in the vast permafrost, presumably saving all that cemetery space for high-rises.

An angry fat fellow suddenly stood up and declared that the freezing people were tampering with "the natural order of things."

Which, in turn, led the host to make a quite moving speech. "If I run seven miles before breakfast because I want to live longer, is someone going to tell me that I'm tampering with the natural order of things? If I eat a low-cholesterol diet and try to breathe clean air and take vitamins, is someone going to tell me . . . ?" It was a speech along the lines of Joseph Welch's famous "Have you no shame?" admonition to Joe McCarthy. It silenced the angry fat fellow and it rallied the cocktail party.

One fellow said, "If there's a chance that freezing works and the government doesn't freeze people, then the government is committing murder."

Everyone then ate a lot of cheese and went home.

. . . . .

There is something about the mere mention of people freezing that makes some people angry. Full of new insights, I went to the Washington Square Bar and Grill and tried to share my budding interest in cryonics with a vacationing waiter from Las Vegas. "You say that kind of thing to me," he said, "and I'll smack you in the mouth."

. . . . .

The next day, I meet Segall and Frosty Waitz at the Trans Time warehouse near Berkeley, where people are taken to get frozen. They talk, nostalgically, about great freezings of the past—the judge's mother, the rabbi who said a prayer over Steven Mandell's container, the Catholic priest who blessed Ann DeBlasio's capsule.

"What happened to some of those people?" I ask.

"Well, you're leaning on a liquor store salesman."

I am, too. There are a couple of frozen people in capsules on hand (it's two to a capsule at Trans Time, for economy's sake). But apart from them, the pickings are lean.

"People just aren't going for this," says Waitz, "and it's a shame."

"Do you really enjoy this work?"

"I can always get up for a freezing."

We wander over to Earth People's Park Commune to see the Trans Time freezing truck and to meet some people who have assisted Segall in his chilly work. The truck looks like the kind that sells ice cream. Segall lives at the commune, which is filled with leftover Ken Kesey people. There is much talk about Wavy Gravy and the Hog Farm and DMT and Abbie Hoffman. Moppet hippie girls pop in for a glass of wine. Segall calls these people "the Chinese Army." They are casually interested in freezing. "Can you get frozen with a hard-on?" one of the moppets wants to know. "Jesus," says another, "a hundred-year hard-on."

Segall and I wander off and his mind begins to soar in a manner that reminds me that scientists are the only remaining heroes. The humanists tell us that the heart is a reservoir of pity and courage and that man will endure. Stuff that we know. Segall tells of devices that will let you stand in Hoboken and look around in San Francisco. Each man his own CBS-TV network. Gadgets that will let you look around inside yourself. Take a brisk tour of your internal organs. ("I can't see you today, I'm visiting my pancreas.")

"But what about freezing? Are we really going to be able to do that? Bring people back?"

"Absolutely," Segall says. "It's just money. There is no reason why people have to die."

"Besides," he says, "I understand we're getting Timothy Leary. If Leary comes over to freezing, watch everybody get on board."

. . . . .

By this time, I've had enough freezing. I don't want to hear any more about Ann DeBlasio's being maintained at minus 196 degrees centigrade. I have visions of Segall and Kent and Waitz all throwing me into the Trans Time dry-ice container and sealing me in there, the first sensitive Jewish writer cryonaut. I'm sorry I ever heard of perfusion and Forever Flasks. I've got the secret minutes of past cryonics meetings that tell about the moment Steven Mandell's cryocapsule was welded tight. I just don't want to be frozen. Ben Franklin once said he wouldn't mind being preserved in madeira, but that's different. Every frozen person I've seen looks like he's sorry he ever got involved with the thing and wishes someone would please toss him a sweater. It's too goddamned cold. *That's* why they can't get themselves a Telly Savalas.

Still . . . if they ever actually froze a chimp stiff and brought it back to life. . . . The philosophy isn't all that bad. You get frozen and at least you have a shot. You get sealed up, forget about it.

On the way home, I have a dream in which I am reunited with all my dead uncles. I wake up and I have my first head cold in ten years.

requiem for a heavy

Charles Liston (a.k.a. "Sonny," as it says on the arrest sheets) is buried in South Las Vegas, and the visitor who would like a peek at the grave is advised not to keep the taxi meter running. Unless he has most of the day at his disposal and is willing to brave the thirty-five-mile-an-hour dust winds that race across Paradise Memorial Gardens, the odds are that he is not going to find the burial site. The Big Ugly Bear was a man of substance in Vegas, and the instinct is to look for a giant, flowered memorial, the biggest one at Paradise. Some one thousand Vegans and "prominent personages of the sporting and entertainment worlds" were there to see him off early this year, and even though many of the fight crowd, such as Sugar Ray, Jersey Joe, Ali, and Smokin' Joe Frazier, were criticized for "snobbing" Sonny, Ed Sullivan, Ella Fitzgerald, and Doris Day turned up and the Ink Spots stayed up all night reworking the lyrics of "Sunny" to be sung at the ceremony. Not the original Ink Spots. The funeral cortege made a full circle of the Strip, "the way Sonny wanted it," and as the procession entered the burial grounds one of the local fuzz saluted. When pallbearer Joe Louis saw that, the Bomber almost dropped his end of the silver-steel coffin. According to Louis, the Bear would have said, "Well, will you look at that sucker." Las Vegas was the one place in the country in which Sonny Liston felt completely at home, and the town went to a lot of trouble to see that he "went out good," except that nobody paid much attention to the gravestone itself. Not only is it not the biggest one at Memorial, it's the smallest. About the size of a passport wallet. He is in there between Cappie Leo Hennon and Orval D. Collings, and they've got bigger ones. Paradise Memorial does

Originally published in *Esquire*, January 1974.

not go in for giant gravestones, leaning instead toward giant plastic floral wreaths, which is nothing to be cynical about since these are terrific plastic flowers and you have to actually touch them to find out they are phonies. The stone says Charles "Sonny" Liston, 1932–1970, thereby answering if not silencing the smart money that fixed his age at around fifty and kept insisting, erroneously, that for Christ's sake there was a daughter out of Frisco who looked around forty-six herself. A tiny blue flower that might have been yanked out of a Puerto Rican wedding cake is affixed to the stone. In keeping with the Paradise Memorial motif, it is plastic and you can get your hands on ten for half a buck. The grave itself is lined up in almost geometric precision with the jets that take off and land at McCarran Airport, and one can almost imagine the Big Bear reaching up and catching one back east to see if his prediction of Ali over Frazier ever checked out. "Of course it depend on what happen in the dressing room," he told promoter Hank Bloomfield.

"It's a great symbol," says the cabbie, who has tripped over the grave quite accidentally after an hour of searching for it. "Suppose I run back and get my Polaroid and snap a picture of it."

"Don't bother," says the visitor. "Besides, it's not a symbol. It's just a small grave."

Sonny Liston first came to Las Vegas in 1960, looking for a fight with Howard King, but after a quick sample of the local conditions, he spun around on his heels and was gone. "I'm not staying in any big-assed hotels that segregate," he told Mel "Red" Greb, who was later to promote the second Patterson fight. In 1966, he came back to Vegas to stay, buying Kirk Kerkorian's house at 2058 Ottawa for $70,000. "In cash," says another promoter, Hank Bloomfield, "just in case you think he was worrying about money." He had an arrest record as long as the Strip itself, and there were not many towns left that were open to him. As an ex-felon, he registered with the chief of detectives and was told that he would be expected to behave himself and that even though your average Nevada citizen gets to carry a gun, unconcealed, he would not be able to. The gun part didn't bother him. He carried a holstered .38 anyway. The cops didn't bother him either and, conviction-wise at least, he more or less stayed out of trouble.

"He loved Vegas," said Hank Greenspun, publisher of the Las Vegas *Sun* and a casual friend of the Bear. "There were many of, shall we say, his element here." In 1966, with the cloud of the Lewiston fiasco hanging above his head (Ali had "phantom-punched" him out in one minute and forty-two seconds of the first round, the shortest heavyweight title bout on record), Liston, whether he knew it or not, was on his way to becoming an "opponent." Yesterday's story. Las Vegas is very kind to acts of this sort. At the Thunderbird Hotel, Julie London's name is printed in letters higher than the tallest building in Scranton. Tommy Leonetti is a big name in the "desert mecca," and so is Phyllis McGuire. They are just getting wind of the Beatles on the Strip, and the Grand Funk Railroad, with shrewd agenting, might get itself booked into a lounge. This is Myron Cohen and John Gary country, the only place in the world where you can hear Liz Renay and Lionel Stander paged in the lobby. Eight grown men can spend an entire dinner discussing not President Thieu but Bobby Vinton's career. The styles are a bit sluggish, too. Those fantastic high-rumped casino goddesses still wear ponytails and white Courrèges boots, and the mini has at least a decade to go. One has the feeling they are going to keep wearing those white boots until they catch the beginning of a new cycle. Just as the toughest of racketeers will give you a soft handshake, there is a weird kind of gentleness in tough Las Vegas toward the stale and the slightly repudiated. In 1966, as far as Vegas was concerned, Sonny Liston might still have been the heavyweight champ.

. . . . .

The democratic world of the casino is one of the few places where the two Americas really coexist, where Ben Dexter of Wyoming cattle country and divorced Mrs. Rosen of Lawrence, Long Island, sit charmingly and nonpolitically, side by side, while the freaks split pictures and blackjack dealers named Bunny and Randy grind them down and shoot them the inevitable one-liners ("If you didn't have bad luck, you wouldn't have any luck at all"). Everybody is welcome in Las Vegas, and that included Sony Liston, who was not a favored citizen of Denver or Philly and who was the only heavyweight champion not to be licensed in New York State. He moved easily, as they say in the suspense novels, in that wash of teased hair, old-lady waitresses in minis who actually turn certain guys on, big-bellied security guards, and hundred-dollar hookers who will take a quick Nixon Recession forty if it's a weekday and the hour is late. He loved the slots. In 1964, training for the first Clay fight, he had one installed in his cottage at the Thunderbird. In the late sixties, he played alongside Vegas's late-night "huddled masses," the midgets in white socks, hard-looking women in glasses who look as though they are mothers of mass murderers, and pieces of guys who used to be hidden in attics and are now whisked in on late-night wheelchairs. Not much of a blackjack player, he would grind out two or three hundred and then go back to practical jokes, using the still potent Liston glare to frighten a fellow next to him into pulling to twenty. Once, with the jailhouse strength that was not only legendary but real, he picked up a blackjack table and held it over his head a while.

Alligator shoes. Fast Cadillac rides with the desert roads chewing up your tires as you flash past the two-and-twenties (underage girls: two minutes with them gets you twenty years in stir). Not much of a place to train. No gyms, and you would have to bring sparring partners in from the Coast. But he kept in shape. There was always someone to shame the Bear into getting his big body up at four in the morning to do five miles around the golf course, the only way to beat the dust and the desert heat. "He didn't do too bad on the comeback, either," says Hank Bloomfield. "I estimate a quarter of a mill. He was shrewder than most people think and always knew ten grand up front and a piece. Also, he didn't pay anybody. He didn't pay trainers, he didn't pay hookers, nobody. I spent a fortune trying to get him a license in New York and I never once saw the man put his hands in his pockets."

There were two Liston crowds, one the easygoing Broadway–Vegas crew—Lem Banker, Ashe Resnick, Moe Dubilier, Jimmy "the Greek" Snyder, Lenny Kent, and B. S. Pully—and in the last years a "bad bunch," into drugs and from the West Side, which is hard to find and where only one cab company will go because of the stickups. There was faithful Geraldine, who kept house, kept the books and called him "Charles," and there was a certain "tall junkie girl" who, according to Red Greb, "ruined the last two years of his life." And there was the strange reverence for Joe Louis. Once Liston and the Bomber were partners at the crap tables and the issue of who would do the rolling came up. "I'm the idol around here," said Joe, taking the dice from an uncharacteristically submissive Liston.

They found him dead and alone on January 5 of this year, dead for about a week in his home. The Big Bear slumped over in an undershirt, swollen, discolored, lots of blood. Big story. Needle marks. Heroin. Grass. This has got to be good. Either he had OD'd or been "seen to" by some of that West Side crowd. Another week of waiting for the other shoe to drop. Then the toxicological report from a "private lab" in Los Angeles. "Natural causes." That got more laughs in Vegas than Jack E. Leonard's routine on Totie Fields's hot shorts.

. . . . .

One way of describing Las Vegas is a town full of people who were close to Sonny Liston. Everyone you meet was "the closest one to him," and if that isn't close enough he will give you the name of someone who was even closer. Lem Banker, former health-club owner, once proud bookmaker, a twelve-year escapee from Jersey, and pallbearer at the Liston send-off, was one of the Close Ones: "In the last years, no one was closer to Sonny than me. I'd like to see him go out good. He had one helluva smile and plenty of wives of hotel executives were sorry to see him check out. The chicks liked him, except for the hookers who got sore because he wouldn't pay them. He was Sonny Liston. He respected Gerry, though. She fed him when he got out of prison and she was strong. One night they had an intruder in the house. Gerry said, 'Charles, get the shotgun and see who that is.' He said, 'No, *you* get the shotgun.' And went back to sleep. The only person to outstare him was Eartha Kitt in the Cork Club in Houston. They put on some staring contest, like two death rays going at each other, anyone steps in the middle gets zapped. They were both rough cut, out of the same package. They didn't shake hands and wind up buddies, either."

Banker loved the way Sonny would order "Rocks Fort" cheese. Once, when their flight was about to leave for the East Coast, they held up the plane by rolling out to the airport in wheelchairs. They went to fights together, and whenever it was a black and white match, Liston would say, "The colored guy got to knock him out to get a draw." It would take World War III to get the easygoing Banker's blood up, but drugs are one subject that will turn the trick. Drugs can really injure a man's name. They are part of a baffling new culture, and of course there is no way for a man to "go out good" if he has been linked to them. He wouldn't care if they found a needle stuck right through his arm. There is no way Liston could have OD'd. "I don't care what they found on him. The needle marks were old army inoculations." Banker traces all the trouble back to an auto accident one month before Liston died. "He bent the steering wheel of a Fleetwood Caddie and took twenty stitches in the head when he went through the windshield. I told him not leave the hospital. I drove him back, and all the way home he was picking glass out of his head. He said he might need 'plaster surgery.' Anyway, the guy died of natural causes and don't tell me drugs." Was he *dealing* in drugs? There had been such rumors in Vegas. It was said that Liston had been under narcotics surveillance and the last man to see him alive was a local narc. Dealing, of course, is another story to Banker, totally different from using and, since it involves the quick turnover of a dollar, not really violative of the "playground" code. "I know the story about him and the guy out of Cleveland pushing stuff together and I don't rule it out. Sonny was a big hero on the West Side, and if they saw a way he could make a couple of bucks they would do that for him. But he didn't take anything in his arm. I was crazy about the guy and my interest is in seeing him go out as a sort of lovable Huck Finn of boxing."

Another local type (do they have to call them "Vegans"?) who can't see drugs is Davey Pearl, a referee who runs Davey's Locker behind the Sands. A small, cheery spaniel of a man, he seems to come marching right out of a Hollywood "sidekick" file and quickly assures you that he never made any money off Liston, not a dime. "I was known as the Conscience of Sonny Liston and he would never do a bad thing around me. What I did was run with him, every day, sometimes six miles. At first there were twenty guys on the road with us, each one trying to cut him up and get something out of him. One by one they dropped out and I stuck. He was suspicious of me, too, but one day I showed I was insulted and he started to trust me. He liked my quick little steps and figured if he matched them with his big steps he was really doing some running. We kidded around a lot on the phone. I would crack Sonny up by calling him in either a high soprano or a low bass and saying, 'This is the chief of police, get rid of your broads.' After the Wepner fight, they paid him $13,000 in twenties, and to show how much he trusted me, he said, 'Davey, go get the dough.' He had a good side that was never played up. I saw him give two twenties to a guy with a heart condition who needed scissor-sharpening equipment. Once he sent his old sweat suits and headgear to the boys at the state pen in Carson City. There's no way the man was a junkie. He had a deadly fear of needles and airplanes. He had too much pride in his strength. Once I filled a wheelbarrow with rocks and put it at the bottom of a ravine. George Foreman got it to the top once. Liston did it up and back three times. Another kid training with us ran away. I don't see him with junk. Besides, I was his conscience. He knew that if I heard he took heroin, if I heard he took a *drink*, I'd quit him in a second."

Natural causes. This is the official verdict in Vegas and it's the way the playground crowd prefers to see it and you are starting to buy it a little yourself until you are steered in the direction of an attractive hooker, a sidekick of Sonny Liston, who is perhaps best not studied in the cruel light of daytime. She may not even exist in the daytime. Fast approaching her midthirties, she is into gimmicks to stay ahead of the new talent. You can have this hooker and her girl friend for a bill and she assures you that two heads are better than one. At the moment she is hunting for a little bitch who has been bad-mouthing her around town as a girl who squeals to the fuzz. This girl needs to be straightened out. The hooker does not have that many years to go, and she can do without that kind of public relations. With little prompting she tells you of an evening during which she and Sonny and another white chick sat around and all fixed together. How he had gone from sniffing coke to shooting it and, when that didn't get him off, had moved on to skag and how sad it is. Of course, she is a hooker and used to making up crazy stories. Sometimes she gets big tips for them. But then she tells the story a second time, in immaculate detail, and you are almost sorry you asked.

"The man took an enormous belt and OD'd," says Hank Greenspun, who usually has the word "embattled" stuck in front of his name and has rarely been known to straddle a fence. "No question about it. This was a tailor-made story for us, but Liston was very involved with kids and when I heard about the drugs I was all for holding it back. I didn't. Still I don't see any reason for the big cover-up. Hell, I was taking my girl back from school when I heard about our move into Laos. I was so damned depressed I would have taken anything I could get my hands on, heroin, LSD, you name it."

A.D. Hopkins, who covered the story for the *Sun*, tends to back up his publisher in the drug department. Hopkins was surprised about the heroin in Liston's house and would have thought he ran with a classier bunch, a cocaine crowd. He had heard of a narcotics raid in which a narc barged into the room and Liston threw him right back through the door and that was the end of it. After the news broke on Liston's death, Hopkins went into one of the Bear's hangouts and was there when the announcement was made. The first one to speak was the bartender. "Drugs?" he asked.

The fortunes of both men and big hotels shift quickly in Las Vegas, and it is not uncommon for a man to protect himself by having two or three hats at the ready. People who become addicted to the desert town will go to any lengths to stay around. After Lem Banker closed his health club, he thought nothing of showing up at Caesars Palace as a "greeter," just to keep in touch. Without so much as a blush, "Red" Greb, who once promoted the second Liston-Patterson fight, now works the crap tables at the same hotel. During his break, he takes you aside and speaks furtively.

"Sonny never got along anywhere, but he came the closest in Vegas. He was loaning money to a guy who was going across the border and coming back with junk. That and a tall junkie cocktail waitress are the two things that messed him up. No, he had never been busted here, but he was running with some bad people and it was coming to that."

Another switcher-arounder is Vince Anselmo, once PR man for the Thunderbird, now managing editor of the *Sun*, who remains misty eyed over (1) Roland LaStarza and (2) the days when the T-Bird was the action hotel in Vegas. "Liston trained with us for the first Patterson fight and we put him in Bobby Kennedy's cottage. He was a huge man, I'm small, but I'm the one who put a slot machine in his room and he played that thing like an old lady in tennis shoes. I'd seen the guy all over town with users and when the report came over that he had died, I was praying it was a natural. But if you want to talk fighters, what about Roland LaStarza." He seems to feel that it he keeps boosting his man's stock, somehow he will get the forgotten LaStarza into the pantheon.

Another intimate of Sonny Liston who is not particularly knowledgeable about the drug scene but is well versed on the dark side of the ex-champion is Hank Bloomfield. He claims to have scaled the first Dempsey-Tunney fight, worked sixteen years under Mike Todd's thumb, and discovered Montgomery Clift. He is a small man with suspect teeth and of an age your sainted mother might have described as "two years younger than God." At present, he runs the Nevada Sports Palace, a gloomy five-thousand-seater which is set up for ice hockey but will go to rock concerts if Vegas doesn't take to the skaters. "*Esquire?*" says Bloomfield. "Thanks a lot. I had the artist Varga and they swiped him away from me. The thing to remember about Liston is that he was a convict at heart. He always carried a pistol. He was very rough with people and it would be nothing for him to pistol-whip someone.

"Liston was America's guest, and I never once saw him go to his pockets for a tab. His interest in me was that he saw me kibitzing with Governor Rockefeller and thought I could get him a New York license. That impressed him. We were going to open a car-wash valet service together, pick up and deliver, his idea. Liston had the films for the two Patterson fights which he liked to watch all the time, him beating up Patterson. Drugs? Not my department. Ask me about the two Clay fights. In the first one, he said he couldn't lift his arms and in Lewiston he blamed it on Walcott's count. My own opinion? He did business. He did business in the second Clay fight."

Geraldine Liston isn't talking, but on the other hand she isn't not talking either. She keeps you on the phone a long time, telling you that she isn't going to talk to you. She comes across as one of those strong black women who, according to government charts, keep so many black families together. She has moved out of the house now into an apartment because of her grief and the shock of finding Sonny dead in that place, although W. E. Bennett, the Nipsy Russell look-alike who runs *Golden*

West magazine, says that it is because Sonny was dead in the house a long time and they can't get the smell out. "No more press for me," she says. "They'd come out and wine and dine and sweet-talk Sonny and me and then go look at what they wrote." Geraldine met "Charles" when he was a munitions worker in Denver and she worked for S&W Foods. Two of her big piques are the allegations about Sonny's age and the sly remarks about the first Ali fight. It is very important to her that you know that Sonny was born in 1932 and that he suffered a painful shoulder injury before the Ali fight and failed to cancel only because he was afraid of a bad press. The most ridiculous thing she ever heard was that Sonny was on junk. When she heard that, she just laughed and laughed.

There is a crime scene report on Sonny Liston at sheriff's headquarters in Las Vegas and also a dead body report, number 204–236. They are finally handed over to you, but very tentatively and not until you've been given a long, clear-eyed once-over by Captain H. E. "Gene" Clark, Vegas's chief of detectives. Put this man in a TV series as either family doctor or hometown lawyer and you can sit back comfortably with forty percent of your prime-time audience assured. He holds the reports tenderly, like some freshly unearthed Thomas Mann novel, his main concern that there be nothing taken from them that will be "of embarrassment to my men." Then, after a final trusting look, he calls you by your first name and parts with them. What was he getting so excited about? Most writers of police reports, in an effort to be "classy" and show they are not unlettered, make syntactical boners, but there are none in the Liston material. It is written simply and the grammar is fine. They say that Charles Liston was found at his home at 2058 Ottawa, wearing only a white T-shirt, "the condition of his body abnormal and extremely swollen . . . had been hemorrhaging about the mouth and nose . . . the victim's body was lying faceup with the upper portion of the body resting on a dressing chair and the feet on the floor. The feet were pointing west and toward the east. Found at the scene were a small green balloon, partially open . . . and a white powdery substance visible on the counter . . . believed to be heroin . . . also a wax paper bag containing marijuana, removed from his pants pocket, and a clear gelatin capsule with a powdery substance within." Clark has nothing to be embarrassed about and neither do "his men." But what about Liston, his great hulk keeled over bare assed with all that white powder spread all over the place. Wearing an old-fashioned T-shirt. What about *his* embarrassment. You've been told by the deputy sheriff there is one hot potato, one "sensitive" area that the chief of detectives will not discuss, and you've been told right. "I can't get into anything in the drug department," says Clark. But he does point you in the direction of Richard R. Robinson, the head of the Federal Narcotics Division, which, and here one must use the word "allegedly," had Liston under surveillance. The last man to see Liston alive was a narcotics agent who won't say why he made the visit but does say he found Liston in good health at the time.

The Federal Narcotics office is at the end of a long, spare Antonioni-style corridor in the Federal Building. Sam Osborne, one of the four narcs assigned to the entire state of Nevada, works undercover and is so delighted that someone has taken an interest in his work that he loads you up with marijuana surveys and booklets about the evils of cocaine. "We've got something you'd like, if we can give it to you," he says of the Liston case. But his boss, Robinson, checks with higher-ups in Washington and it's nothing doing. "I've got no love for Sonny Liston, but he was never actually arrested for dealing and so I can't get into it with you." Long pause. Osborne is almost ready to jump out of his skin in his effort to let it all hang out. "Did Liston OD?" you ask. The coroner said it was "coronary insufficiency." Robinson tries to help. "When someone dies in an auto crash, you can say his heart stopped, too. Suppose you ask the coroner how that differs from a heroin overdose. That would be a good place for you to start." You start to leave and Osborne, who is really wild now, grabs your arm and says, "You see, we're in the position of trying to tell you something, except that we're not allowed to."

Dr. Herman, the Vegas coroner, is about to wind up his business for the day and is a little testy when asked about the death of Sonny Liston. He's been asked about it too many times. No, he can't show you the actual autopsy report. "It's in our special form, our style." But he can read your selected portions of it. Yes, there was a finding of morphine and codeine in the body. Yes, heroin breaks down into those substances. But they were only in trace amounts, not enough to kill. Yes, there were intravenous marks. But he won't be budged. Death was caused by "pulmonary congestion and edema . . . probable mild coronary insufficiency and myocardial fibrosis . . . pulmonary emphysema. . . . In Sum: Natural Causes." And that's the end of it.

Except that it isn't. The rumors are so thick in Vegas you're lucky if you don't trip over one. He OD'd. He was partners with a bad cat from Cleveland and when he didn't come up with his half on a big drug shipment he was wiped out. He "carried himself too mean" and someone on the West Side took care of him. After days of prowling around, the homicide story doesn't seem to wash. But the drug picture won't go away so easily. The gelatin capsules weren't cold tablets, the white powdery substance wasn't Ajax cleanser, and the morphine and codeine didn't get into his blood in candy bars. He didn't fall on all those needles, either. Still, there isn't a public official in all of Las Vegas who will say he OD'd. They may not have liked Sonny Liston, but they respect Tommy Sands and Tommy Leonetti and they give ceremonial dinners for Joe Louis, and "natural causes" may be the benefit they never gave for the Big Ugly Bear. The CIA doesn't kill people but it does "terminate" their lives "with extreme prejudice." Our invasion of Laos is a minor "incursion" and when we bomb another country's radar stations it is simply a "protective reaction." The South Vietnamese, dashing off in retreat, are "mobile-maneuvering." A Nixon man says the government is "moving the ball downfield" on poverty. So why not "natural causes" for the Big Bear, who did most, if not all, of his terminating and protective-reacting in the ring. There is another, darker side to the story, but why push it? Or in the words of a tired old blackjack dealer at the Sands who's seen them come and seen them go, "What's to accomplish?"

school for butlers

On a sweltering day in August, in the presidential suite of Houston's Lancaster hotel, nine individuals who aspired to become butlers in the "British style" were being drilled in the fundamentals by an expert in the field. Several members of the group, pretending to be guests, were seated at tables, while others circled them, pouring tea and coffee.

"Cover those thumbs," the man instructed one of the servers. "And no rocking back and forth on your heels."

"Turn your tray a bit, " he told another. "We don't want Mr. Lee having to lunge across to get at his creamer."

"Pretend you are serving the finest brandy," he said to the group at large. "Keep it all quiet, elegant. We're not waiters. There's no 'Hi, my name is Eddie' here. We're offering *ten*-star service, not five."

The slender, energetic, fifty-seven-year-old man who was putting the group through its paces was Ivor Spencer, who heads up the Ivor Spencer School for Butler Administrators and Personal Assistants, which has its main branch in London and other, occasional outposts in Palm Springs and Hong Kong. Spencer is a pleasant-looking man with warm eyes and a nose that, surprisingly, is flattened, as if he were an ex-fighter, which he isn't. For the last nine years, he has been coming to Houston to conduct a condensed and grueling three-week version (no days off) of a course that takes eight weeks to complete in London. Though there had been no plan to have this happen, the group this year was composed of nine trainees who were strikingly different in appearance and style. One could imagine them being herded into a living room by Hercule

Originally published in *Wigwag*, December 1989.

Poirot as suspects in an Agatha Christie novel. Among them were Pierre (referred to as "the major"), a twenty-four-year veteran of Special Forces, whose military evaluation—on his résumé—stated that if he remained in the army he was certain to become a general; Colin, who appeared to be the eldest member of the group, a shy man who had decided to make a career switch from poultry breeding; and Terry, a powerfully built good-old-boy type with a thirteen-year background in the explosives industry. Unexpectedly, three of the trainees were women. They included Jade, a Yugoslavian beauty with a femme fatale style who was seeking a career more challenging than the one she had in airline scheduling; Eva, a platinum blond twenty-two-year-old, whose aim it was to become Denmark's first woman butler; and Kathleen, an attractive housewife who did not want to be a butler at all, but was there to bone up on gracious living, her husband having decided to branch out from real estate into politics. Rounding out the group were Peter, a young Scotsman with experience on luxury liners; John, a veteran of self-realization courses in New Zealand, who thought it important to change career direction every fifteen years; and Julius, a soft-spoken American who was employed as a houseman in Minnesota. His story was somewhat representative. He had enrolled in the course to raise the level of his skills a notch and perhaps land in a situation that was more grand than his current one. Spencer had made it known that he considered Julius a "natural."

Before signing up for the course, each of the applicants had been put through extensive phone interviews by Spencer, and then had had to pay out four thousand dollars in tuition and set aside up to fifteen hundred dollars for living expenses. (Most of the students stayed at the YMCA or the Holiday Inn, where they were given special rates.) Spencer had been careful not to deposit their checks until the course was under way and he had gotten the feel of each of them. Fresh in his mind was his experience with one applicant who came in carrying on about the situation in Ethiopia and insisting that "these people" (his potential employers) had no right to their money. Spencer decided quickly that he would be a poor candidate for the work and returned his deposit. There was no guarantee that any of the trainees would wind up with jobs, although Spencer had pledged to do his utmost in this regard and had a reasonably good record of placing his butlers in wealthy households about the globe. One graduate was employed by Rupert Murdoch and another by Robert Maxwell ("You know who *he* is"). Others were working in the presidential suite of the Frankfurter Hof Hotel in Germany, and two young men who had been pulled out of a Liverpool slum and trained by Spencer were now with the royal family. Still another had worked for Linda Ronstadt.

The salary that got mentioned was in the $35,000–$55,000 range, which became more attractive when the add-ons—such as medical care, food, lodging, and automobile (except for New York City)—were considered. Then, too, Spencer was able to cite examples of wealthy individuals who had snubbed their families and left everything to their butlers. And there was an opportunity to invest along with canny employers, which could lead to small fortunes as well. Still, the emphasis in the course was on the pleasures of providing an elegant life for the employer rather than on personal enrichment, which was best left, in Spencer's view, to chefs and headwaiters.

. . . . .

On the day that they were fine-tuning their serving techniques at the Lancaster, the group was headed down the homestretch. There was some nervous anticipation of the graduation to come and the feared "assessment," in which Spencer would evaluate each individual's performance and give the trainees an idea of what he thought their chances were in the field. To help them get the feel of the work, the men wore suits and ties; the women had on no-nonsense tailored outfits. Only the hard-working Spencer was somewhat unbuttoned, giving him the look of a butler who's gone off to the pantry for a quick smoke. In the weeks that had passed, the class had learned how to select cigars, organize barbecues for a thousand guests, order shirts (from Prince Charles's tailor), book tickets on the Concorde, and hire and fire household staffs. On a more personal level, they had been drilled on drawing morning baths, pressing out wrinkles in the morning newspaper, serving wake-up drinks, laying out clothing for the day (two choices—and only topwear for madam), and giving discreet updates on their employers' shares ("With your permission, sir, Disney has gone rocketing up three points this morning"). Highly particularized tips had been passed along, such as how to chill champagne when refrigeration has broken down (wrap bottle in wet newspapers and hold out the window of a speeding limo) and what to put in the finger bowls (lemon for fish dishes, rose petals for all others). The group had worked on methods of foiling terrorists (gather your family in a safe enclosure *inside* the house) and been told what to do if a fire were to break out (gather up a Matisse or some equivalent valuable and run outside—after attending to human life, of course).

Now, in the closing sessions, Spencer had been taking the group back to basics, reminding them to be friendly but not familiar, to keep their voices pitched lower than their employers', to maintain a good carriage (they'd had drills in which they walked across the room with glasses on their heads), and to serve tea and coffee in a way that was quiet and unobtrusive. As to the importance of the last, Spencer asked the trainees to hold off on their pouring exercises for a moment and threw out a hypothetical situation in which a Mr. Lee is about to close a deal of some kind with a rich and widowed nymphomaniac. "You come along hollering out 'Black or white, what'll it be?' and before you know it, the poor man has lost the moment."

Throughout the course, the fictitious Mr. Lee, along with his family, had been put forth as the ideal employer. To tie on with the Lees would be a butler's dream. Predictably, they were enormously rich and were Americans. "Tough, tough, tough" is the way Spencer described them, "and they'll demand their pound of flesh." Nonetheless, they were desirable as employers, because they paid butlers three times as much as their English counterparts, and life around them would be much less restrictive than, for example, with a Saudi Arabian employer. (Several of the Spencer people had found life in Riyadh unappealing.) Mr. Lee, more often than not, was the CEO of a corporation with global interests and needed to have his bags packed and Concorde tickets booked at a moment's notice. Once he arrived at his overseas hotel, he expected to be registered in his room, not in the lobby. Though he was anxious to have his affairs dealt with in a seamless manner, he was quite frank about wanting a butler for reasons of status. The Lees were New Money, which was not to be sneered at, since Old Money, as Spencer reminded the class, had once been New. Additionally, New Money wanted, with almost a passion, to see to it that things were done correctly. It was important for the Lees to be among the first to see hot new Broadway shows and to be recognized in restaurants. Toward this latter end, butlers were encouraged to carry at least forty snapshots of the family, to be given to key maître d's in major cities so that the Lees could be picked out of crowds on their arrival and greeted with ceremony. It was less clear what Mrs. Lee did with her time, although she enjoyed throwing huge barbecues and learning about economies that had been achieved by the butler. If he was able to wangle a discount from the salmon supplier, it was likely to become the chief topic of conversation at one of her dinner parties.

Though the Lees did not insist that butlers keep household accounts, it was wise to do so, since they were capable of sudden "purges" in which they would want to know exactly what their four cars were costing them. The Lees were shaky when it came to matching up outfits and planning menus, but were to be advised in these areas with the utmost diplomacy ("If I may say so, the dress doesn't quite suit your figure, madam"). Often, butlers spoke as many as ten languages and were vastly more educated than the Lees, but it was essential that employers not have this thrown in their faces. "You are not," Spencer had reminded his students, "the greatest thing since sliced bread, either."

The Lees tended to take wide swerves when it came to personal moral-
ity. Though capable of leaving a table when "blue jokes" were introduced, they were not beyond some hanky-panky of their own. When Spencer had finished counseling the group on the pouring of tea and coffee, he moved along to the handling of situations in which, for example, Mr. Lee was discovered stretched out in a London hotel room with a woman beside him. The butler was advised to ignore her—unless he was addressed directly—and simply to place two orange juices to Mr. Lee's left and go about his business. If at some future point Mrs. Lee were to ask if her husband had looked up his old girlfriend while abroad, the butler was to make use of the most valuable response in the butler lexicon: "Not to my knowledge, madam." In so doing, the butler was in a position to save Mr. Lee millions in a divorce settlement. Butlers were not to get involved in family squabbles and were to occupy a safe middle ground, never taking sides, all of which would be comforting to the Lees. And they were to serve the Lees unstintingly, drawing the line only at the procurement of drugs and hookers. "Tell him to look in the yellow pages," said Spencer, taking an untypically firm line with the Lees.

Spencer next reviewed the tricky subject of tipping. The Lees did not want to be bothered with this function, and the job of passing out just the right tip fell to the butler. As a general rule, Spencer felt it was much better to be extravagant than to undertip. What you wanted to avoid was a nightmarish situation in which the headwaiter could fling a meager tip in Mr. Lee's face and call him a cheap bastard. Spencer next turned to Investment Tipping, a custom in which gifts of cash and merchandise were seeded about in restaurants and nightclubs, even if there was only a slender chance that the Lees would show up at them. If Mr. Lee did get one of his once-a-year cravings for Szechuan food, a warm welcome would be extended to him by the host, who had been favored with a tastefully selected scarf or pair of gloves.

Spencer called upon Peter, the young Scotsman who had worked on luxury liners, to help brief the group on shipboard tipping. Peter confirmed that it was important to tip just about everyone in sight. "Otherwise," he cautioned, "your bags might be thrown overboard."

"But don't you want to get in there quickly to the hairdresser and masseur?" asked Spencer, in a leading question.

"Yes, you do," said Peter, who further cautioned the group not to forget the cruise director, who could set up special treats such as visits to the bridge, and the all-important maître d', who would see to it that the Lees were given a fabulous table. Alerted to the fact that the Lees were great tippers, top waiters would ask to be assigned to their table.

"And how would they know the Lees were great tippers?" asked Spencer, whose questions tended to be medium speed and easy to hit.

"Because they *got* that table," said the class, in unison.

There was some puzzlement in the room as to how to know what a good shipboard tip was. Spencer advanced the fresh notion that it was perfectly acceptable to ask a purser, for example, what he expected to receive in a given situation. The butler would then be free to meet the figure if it seemed fair or to shave it a bit if it seemed excessive.

From time to time, in the area of tipping, the butler would find the shoe on the other foot, with a departing guest of the Lees' pressing a tip into *his* hand. Spencer demonstrated the style of receiving such a gift: clasping the guest's hand, looking straight ahead, and resisting the urge to take a peek at the bill's denomination. If this proved impossible—and the tip turned out to be one dollar from a difficult guest who had been waited on hand and foot for months—the butler was to grit his teeth, wish the offending guest a safe journey, and tell him to hurry back at all costs. While on the subject of difficult and prying guests, Spencer reminded the trainees that under no circumstances were they to tell such people the amount of money Mr. Lee had paid for his Corniche or the name of the perfume used by Mrs. Lee. Such questions were to be referred to the Lees themselves.

. . . . .

At a later session, Spencer tied together some loose ends in the handling of household staffs, stressing the need to be egalitarian: "The little Mexican in the kitchen who probably doesn't even have his green card and rarely gets to see the light of day—is there any need to kick his ass?"

"Absolutely not, sir," volunteered Colin, the former poultry breeder.

"And how do we handle him?" asked Spencer, tossing up one of his soft pitches.

"Encourage his strong points," put in John, the sharp-nosed New Zealander.

"Exactly," Spencer said, pleased that the group had grasped the thrust of his instruction.

Spencer emphasized that in the hiring of staff it was important to point out in advance that they could be searched at any given moment, since maids had been known to leave the premises with sticks of butter in their stockings and a chef might be tempted to disappear with a fillet of beef beneath his hat. Butlers were to see to it that staff members had proper haircuts, polished shoes, and a scrubbed look. "What's the good of opening a tin of the finest caviar if you've got the smell of socks hanging about?"

Spencer next demonstrated the proper position of butlers at garden parties, in the thick of the traffic, often wearing a two-way headset and radioing back to the kitchen to have the chef step up the pace on sausages and hold off on the chicken. No matter how conscientious the staff, the butler was to be ever on the alert for soiled plates that had been overlooked. If need be, he was to "crumb up" personally.

. . . . .

As the day drew to a close, Spencer's tone softened, and he regaled the group with inspirational tales of butlers such as Bryce, who would get up at three in the morning and drive into downtown Los Angeles in order to get bargains on floral arrangements, and a young man in Palm Springs, who at the age of twenty-two had salted away a quarter of a million dollars by making shrewd investments along with Mr. Lee. His greatest admiration was reserved for Ross Hallum, now an instructor in his London school, who had been the butler and valet to Earl Mountbatten of Burma, viceroy of India, the most decorated man of his time in England. Mountbatten, in his later years, had been required almost constantly to attend functions. "The job of sorting out his medals alone would have been enough to discourage a lesser man," said Spencer. "Yet Ross was up to it. Now there's a butler for you."

. . . . .

Late one evening, in one of his few idle moments during the course, Spencer pointed out that he was also England's leading toastmaster, having presided over more than 850 royal events. A toastmaster's job is to perform in the manner of a master of ceremonies at formal gatherings—introducing speakers; rattling off their titles, honors, and decorations; and "inadvertently" unplugging the microphone if they should use profane language. In 1962 Spencer was elected president of the Guild of Professional Toastmasters. The suggestion that George Jessel might have been an American counterpart drew a frown ("much higher level here"), although he quickly conceded that the late entertainer had ability. With his wife of forty years, Estella, looking on adoringly, Spencer produced a scrapbook of glossy photos in which he appeared in his toastmaster uniform, leaning in over the shoulders of members of the royal family. Spencer grew up as a poor boy in London's East End and went to work as a member of the kitchen staff at the Dorchester, which may explain his disdain for chefs ("all those grease spots on their whites"). Hiding behind a screen in the ballroom one evening, he had watched a banquet given in honor of Winston Churchill and was taken not so much by the great Allied leader as by his scarlet-coated toastmaster. It was then that he decided to become one himself and to involve himself with royalty in general. Recently, he organized a wedding party for Mark Thatcher, and feels it was a crime he wasn't called on to do Malcolm Forbes's much publicized (and criticized) gala in Tangier.

Spencer first got the idea for his schools in 1981, while he was organizing parties for a film producer in California.

"You need a butler," he told the man.

"Fine," the producer said. "Get me one."

Returning to London, he was unable to come up with a candidate he considered suited to the relaxed American style, and decided to train one of his own. When the fellow he selected, a disgruntled salesman, got high marks from the producer, Spencer decided to set up his schools there and then. He had trained more than a hundred butlers since that time, and is opening a new branch of his school this month in Sydney, Australia. He remains wary of Japan and is unforgiving of their pronunciation of the word they use for female butlers. "Buttresses. Can you imagine?" Nonetheless, a Spencer school for Japanese butlers has been set up for 1990.

Though he has achieved success as a toastmaster and as director of an expanding chain of butler schools, Spencer confessed to having an unachieved goal.

"The White House," he said, with his eyes agleam. "Getting one of my people in there would be something, wouldn't it?"

.....

A man named Robert Gourdin turned up at one of the closing sessions to instruct the class on the characteristics of wines and liquors. (Earlier on, the trainees had made field trips to Tiffany, Neiman Marcus, and Dunhill.) Attractive and world weary in his style, Gourdin had once been the head sommelier at "21" and was able to treat the group to anecdotes related to the drinking habits of Danny Kaye (he ordered only champagne and steak tartare) and John Jacob Astor (he drank some awful fruit mishmash, but tipped three hundred dollars). After establishing that it was impossible to cover his subject in the short time allotted, Gourdin, who is now the champagne expert for Moët & Chandon, nonetheless took the group on a verbal tour of the European vineyards. After saluting the great Dom Pérignon, he pointed out that anything to do with champagne was copied from the French, and that German wines carried a tremendous amount of information on their labels. Wine bottles of a great variety were set out on tables, and from time to time illustrative sips were taken by the trainees. Great fun was had with Colin, who had never tasted wine before and was caught adding Sweet 'n Low to a New Zealand chablis. As the session wore on, Gourdin, whose judgments had been reasoned and scholarly (the fermentation level of brandy is stopped at the 16-percent level), became sharper in his opinions ("Anyone who puts ice in a champagne glass should be shot"). Finally, after a joking announcement—"I don't know if I'm going or coming"—Gourdin brought the session to a close and was applauded warmly by the trainees, who agreed that he had been charming.

For the graduation ceremony, held in the familiar presidential suite, Gourdin had remained behind to help the class erect a cascade of five hundred Baccarat glasses, each of them valued at forty dollars. He had once held a spot in the *Guinness Book of World Records* for building the tallest champagne pyramid, having successfully piled up two thousand, but someone had come along and bested him with six thousand. It was his intention to seize back the record by going to fourteen thousand, but he had not yet found time to address himself to this. The butlers-to-be had made their own preparations for the graduation buffet, setting up trays of hors d'oeuvres and a silver service, using the activity as a final training exercise. A delegation had been dispatched to a local gourmet shop for a huge platter of rattlesnake canapés, which were to be a surprise gift for Spencer.

Among those on hand for the proceedings were representatives of Tiffany and Company, a lawyer who had obtained visas for trainees who needed them, a local NBC crew, and a successful alumnus of the school, who was probably the world's tallest butler. Peter, who resembled the young Laurence Olivier, and who is a former rugby star, had been placed with a wealthy widow in the Houston area, and the arrangement had worked out nicely. Along with his other functions, he had become a big brother to the widow's children. Now that the widow had remarried, it was expected that he would be kept on. He had only one suggestion for Spencer, which was that the training be made a bit more informal. He had begun his employment by working on the property in "black and stripes," only to be tapped on the shoulder and told that in this situation a short-sleeved shirt would be fine.

Diplomas were handed out by Spencer, who introduced each of the graduates with a familiar-sounding Vegas-style anecdote ("Peter here flew over from Scotland and his arms are tired"). After the presentations, Gourdin produced a saber, exchanged circumcision jokes with his old friend Spencer, and then sliced off the cork of a champagne bottle. He then poured champagne into the top glass of the cascade, which was to foam down and fill the glasses below. When this failed to happen, members of the graduating class came forward with open bottles of their own and filled the lower glasses. Spencer stepped aside for a moment to take a peek at the evening news, and applauded vigorously at Leona Helmsley's conviction for tax evasion. He pointed out that Mrs. Helmsley had hung up on him when he told her he expected a commission on butler placements.

There was sadness in the air as the group broke up, and some apprehension about job prospects. Jade could look forward to an interview with a wealthy European family who owned four homes, and Spencer felt she was a shoo-in to get it. The major, who had emerged clearly as the star of the group, seemed confident. (In a surprising development, he hopes to join forces with Spencer to provide a security *and* butlering service for CEOs.) For the others, the future seemed less certain, and there was concern on their parts, because in most cases the tuition money had been hard to come by. Several of the new graduates lingered behind as if expecting Spencer to impart some final wisdom.

Drawing himself up to his full height, and throwing off the *presence* he had told them to try to achieve, Spencer sent them off with these words: "Try to remember that being a butler is quite the most magnificent job in the world."

a champion for bismarck

O n an unseasonably balmy night late last October, a twenty-five-year-old athlete with a sculptured torso, the sullen good looks of a Latin film star, and legs that his trainer described as "the best in boxing" left his dressing room and made his way toward a ring that had been set up in the Civic Center of Bismarck, North Dakota. Accompanied by his cornermen, he carried in one hand the flag of North Dakota and in the other a banner that commemorated the state centennial. As he approached the center aisle, shuffling to the amplified beat of "The Final Countdown" by the rock group Europe, the crowd, which had sensed his arrival, caught sight of him and began to whoop and holler and scream and—in some cases—to weep with an almost religious fervor. Visitors had been promised a phenomenon that was unlike any they had ever experienced, and if this was not quite the case, it was impressive nonetheless. "Vir-gil! Vir-gil!" the crowd cried out, stomping their feet, literally rocking the rafters and bringing the decibel count to a painful level. They had come from Zap and Hebron and Hazen and from Lincoln and Max and Pick City and McClusky. They had arrived in vans and pickup trucks and even two-seat crop-duster planes. Broad-boned and generously built, they wore Stetsons and cowboy boots. An unusual-looking group of boxing fans, they might have been more at home at a rodeo—and indeed the Badlands Circuit Final had vacated the arena only two nights before. Among the honored guests at ringside was Brad Gjermundson, the shy, bespectacled four-time Saddle Bronc Champion of the Dakotas.

Originally published in *Wigwag*, May 1990.

The crowd, estimated at 7,700, was primarily from the Dakotas, and of late they had not had much to cheer about. Population was dwindling and a recent drought had been costly. The oil and gas boom that had been expected to revitalize both states in the early eighties never took place; this had demoralized the capital city of Bismarck, which had planned to "service" the hundreds of rigs in the area that were now inoperative. *Newsweek* had insultingly suggested that the Dakotas, proudly looking forward to their centennial, faced a future of social and economic blight and were doomed to become once again a silent and desolate prairie with only wild buffalo looking on as survivors. That North Dakota, according to a Northwestern National Life Insurance survey, was America's second healthiest state (after Utah)—and the least likely to experience an earthquake—was of little consolation. It was as if the young man who climbed through the ropes, and received yet another tumultuous ovation as he did so, carried on his muscular shoulders the hopes and aspirations—the very future—of the Dakotas.

. . . . .

On that evening, Virgil "Quicksilver" Hill, the center of the crowd's adulation, held the World Boxing Association light-heavyweight title, which he had defended successfully six times after taking it away—or "wresting it," as it's often put in boxing circles—from Leslie Stewart as an eight-to-one underdog in Atlantic City two years before. Though Hill, a 1984 Olympic silver medalist, had been born in Missouri, he had been raised in Grand Forks and had adopted North Dakota as his home—as it had adopted him. During his rise to boxing prominence and his travels about the country—and on one occasion to Paris—he had become a good-will ambassador for the state, always taking pains to point out that North Dakota people were singularly decent, generous, and hard working. From all evidence, he meant every word of it. As he looked out at the crowd, he could see that many of the spectators wore Virgil T-shirts and neon caps and carried Virgil Hill banners as well. He was aware, too, that Virgil had become the favored name for male infants born in the state. His portrait hung in the state capitol along with those of other luminaries born in North Dakota, such as Peggy Lee and Eric Sevareid; the gloves he wore in his victory over Bobby Czyz were mounted in the state's Heritage Center.

In preparation for his seventh title defense, Hill had trained for a period of six weeks at the Club Mirage Resort, in Arizona, during which time he had boxed one hundred and seventy rounds and run more than two hundred miles. Though his record as a professional was an unblemished

24–0, he had been unable to shake the reputation of being a "one-handed" fighter. That is to say, although his left hook was considered quick and effective, his right hand was thought tentative, if not ineffectual. An additional question that hung in the air was the hypoglycemia attack in August that had forced him to put off this title defense, originally scheduled for September. Had he fully recovered? Hill had been weaned away from his beloved junk foods and put on a sensible diet (his mother, at one time a boxing judge, had been brought in to cook for him), and he appeared as sleek and fit as a racehorse. Still, there was no doubt that his opponent would waste no time testing his endurance and would apply maximum pressure from the opening round on.

Much was a stake for both Hill and Bismarck. A swift and impressive victory would virtually force the "old man's club" of Hearns, Leonard, and Duran to take notice of Hill and would perhaps lead to a lucrative fight with one of its gentrified members. At minimum, there would be a call for a unification fight with Jeff Harding, the World Boxing Council champion, whose own title defense was being shown to the ESPN cable television audience as a special treat on the same night as the Hill fight. Still another possibility would be a fight with "Prince" Charles Williams, holder of yet another light-heavyweight title (the International Boxing Federation's), who had come to Bismarck to stake his claim for such a fight. At one time, and not too long ago, there was only one titleholder for each division. The splintering of titles in each division—and there are new divisions, too, such as *super*bantamweight and cruiserweight—has been criticized for confusing the public and watering down the legitimacy of any title. Advocates of this proliferation insist that the public enjoys having all these new champions—the more the merrier for boxing and for box-office receipts.

An irony for Bismarck is that a dazzling Hill victory would enhance the champion's marketability and make it more difficult for the city of fifty thousand to "hold" him for future fights. But, for the moment, the local businessmen who made up the nonprofit organization Civic Center Promotions, Inc., which had sponsored Hill's four previous title defenses in Bismarck, thought only of another triumph for their favorite. Somehow, when that bridge was crossed, they would find a way to convince Bob Arum, the chairman of Top Rank and the promoter of Hill's previous fights, that Virgil Hill *was* Bismarck—that the two were inseparable—and that even if they were unable to match Las Vegas and Atlantic City dollar for dollar on future promotions, they would always be able to provide a boxing rarity: a community (and paid audience) of men, women, and children who were united and almost frenzied in their devotion to their hometown hero.

Awaiting Hill in the ring, and seemingly unfazed by the pandemonium, was the number one contender for the WBA title, a well-seasoned (though unmarked) thirty-one-year-old Californian named James "The Heat" Kinchen, who was acknowledged to have fought on a much higher level of competition than his young opponent. His current reputation as a ferocious puncher had been enhanced by a one-point loss to the great Thomas "Hit Man" Hearns in a fight that many observers felt Kinchen had won handily. Unlike Hill, who had slept fitfully and eaten sparingly since his arrival in Bismarck four days before (no breakfast, no lunch, spaghetti with tomato sauce for dinner), Kinchen had dined on ribs and chicken-fried steak and whatever dish struck his fancy. And he had slept like a baby, enjoying a pleasant recurring dream in which he would take the championship belt away from Hill and put it around his own waist. Though Kinchen had been cast as the villain or "spoiler" in the match, it had been difficult for locals to work up much rancour for this agreeable man, who had publicly thanked Hill for giving him a chance at the title (he had never fought for one before) and whose rudest comment had been that he had "a few surprises" for the champion. His trainer, the white-bearded West Wambold ("I know, I know. I look like Kenny Rogers"), had taken on the bad cop role, suggesting that Hill would be quickly dismantled by his man, and that he would be well advised to take out advertising on the soles of his sneakers. "I don't know why Virgil even *accepted* this fight," he had said to local reporters. "James is going to tear his head off."

Still, for all his amiability, a great deal hung in the balance for Kinchen as well. A victory would open the door to major purses that had been denied him throughout his career. His record was forty-four wins (thirty-one kockouts), two draws, and, significantly, six losses, including a recent one at the hands of the obscure Christophe Tiozzo, in Issy-les-Moulineaux, France. Another defeat would have to start him thinking about retirement and would mean that although he had been a "bridesmaid" (number one contender) on four different occasions, he would never get to wear the coveted belt he kept stripping from Hill in his dreams.

. . . . .

On the Friday before the fight, the Virgil Hill entourage checked into the Kirkwood Motor Inn, a labyrinthian three-story structure that was undergoing renovation and appears always to have been doing so. It is situated opposite a large shopping mall that is the focus for most of the commercial activity in Bismarck and has replaced in importance the old Main Street downtown area (which looks down upon the mall from one of Bismarck's few hills, as if in disappointment and confusion). Bismarck, by any measure, has more than enough shopping centers, parks, hospitals, and schools for its small population—it has four Chinese restaurants— but the city does not appear to have come together aesthetically. Most of the city's energy has been thrown into commercial "events," such as the Women's International Bowling Congress, the Gitchi Gumi Riverboat Competition, the United Tribes Pow-Wow, and a Bill Cosby concert, which was scheduled for November at the Civic Center.

The city was incorporated in 1875 and even then could be caught attempting to call attention to itself. It had changed its name two years before from Edwinton to Bismarck, hoping to flatter Germany's Otto von Bismarck into investing capital in its railroad, but there is no evidence that the Iron Chancellor paid the slightest bit of attention to this ploy. Bismarck nonetheless slogged along with its exotic name, gaining a questionable prominence with its regular appearances on weather charts as having the most frigid winter temperatures in the nation. Though the city cannot be said to lie at a crossroads of history, the Lewis and Clark expedition did pass through at one point, as did General Custer, who set out from nearby Fort Lincoln for his unfortunate rendezvous with Sitting Bull. Both events are duly recorded at well-kept sites along the Missouri River. For all Bismarck's attempts to present itself as a well-placed hub of commerce, its main resource would seem to be the unforced friendliness of its residents. Organizers of the Women's International Bowling Congress pronounced the host city "friendly to a fault."

. . . . .

A man who exudes such small-town conviviality from every pore is Marlan "Hawk" Haakenson, the tall, shambling mayor of the capital city and one of Hill's early boosters. As the champion prepared to sign in at the Kirkwood, Haakenson, true to his nickname, swooped down upon the startled fighter and said, "Thank you, Virgil, for not turning your back on Bismarck." He then told arriving guests that he and his wife had been the only locals to attend the Atlantic City fight at which Hill had won his title. Though Bismarck had actually outbid Atlantic City for the rights to host the fight, the champion, Leslie Stewart, had insisted that the event be held at the flashier and more prestigious resort center. When Haakenson learned that his city had been passed over for the fight, he said to his wife, "Let's go, Barb." Off the two of them went in their mobile home (the mayor is terrified of flying), driving until they reached the Trump Plaza Hotel. Parking their car on the street, they remained where they were for the duration of their visit, taking time out only to watch the fight. "When people ask where we stayed," said the mayor, "I tell them, 'The Trump Plaza,' and then add, in a muffled voice, 'parking lot.'"

Sharing rooms with Hill at the Kirkwood was Freddie Roach, his twenty-nine-year-old trainer and a key player on the team. Though Roach is small and angelic looking and might easily pass for a young minister, he is, in actuality, an ex-fighter, and a good one, who had risen to the eighth-ranked position in the WBA superbantamweight division before breaking his hand. Though he continued to compete for a while ("We'd freeze the hand, but it would wear off after a few rounds"), Roach soon had to face the inevitable and retire. Hill had been his stablemate in the Las Vegas camp of Eddie Futch, and when it appeared that the North Dakota prospect was being ignored, Roach took him aside and began to give him some pointers. He soon became Hill's trainer (he also trains Marlon Starling, the current WBC welterweight champion), and the two became fast friends as well, a situation Roach found an impediment once serious training began. It had been Roach's feeling (and continued to be so) that Hill, though a champion, was not a fully formed fighter—which did not dismay him. "A complete fighter," he explained, "is a shot fighter." It was his frank intention not only to sharpen Hill's boxing skills but also to alter his style along "crowd-pleasing" lines—to have him plant himself and punch more—so that he would escape his reputation of being a "runner" and in the process attract larger purses. Inevitably, in conversations between the two men, the name Mike Tyson would come up. "I can handle him," Hill would say. "Just make sure I have a good pair of track shoes."

Roach's plan for Hill in Bismarck was to have him come down slowly from the vigorous training he had completed in Arizona, doing only the lightest of workouts. It was thought to be a bad sign—and one of insecurity—for a fighter to be caught sparring just before a match. But keeping the high-strung Hill relaxed and quiet did not turn out to be an easy matter. Horror movies at night were tried unsuccessfully, and on the day after his arrival the champion could be found in a recreation center in Mandan, Bismarck's sister city across the Missouri River, sparring one-minute rounds with his trainer. As Hill whistled punches into the over-size catcher's-mitt-style gloves worn by Roach, the two men whispered to each other confidentially, as if they were ballroom dancers. Though the champion's combinations were crisp and well timed, he seemed to be off balance when he threw his suspect right hand. "He *has* a right hand,"

Roach assured onlookers. "He just has to develop confidence in it."

Looking on, and seemingly unperturbed, was Hill's father, Bob, a retired French Canadian plumber with the sad eyes and hangdog look of a bloodhound. The senior Hill, who had run amateur boxing clubs in Grand Forks, said that Virgil, though gifted in all sports, had been timid as a boy and was always being bullied by rough types: "I repeatedly told him that those fellows did not have an 'S' on their chests, and before long Virgil was able to handle them." If Virgil Hill, as his trainer claimed, has "the best legs in boxing," his father could take the credit: "In football, they made him do weighted squats, and when he came out of practice, my son's legs would be exploding with bulk. I saw to it that he lived in sauna pants to thin them down a bit."

Did he have qualms about his son's becoming a fighter—with all the attendant brutality of the sport? "I would not have allowed it," he said, "except that I never did see him get hit with anything—and I still haven't."

While Hill rested between rounds, the fast-tiring Roach gave pointers to the champion's stablemate, a twenty-one-year-old sheet-metal worker from Dunseith, North Dakota, named Sonny Brennan. He was scheduled to have his first professional fight on the undercard, with all the accompanying drama of a boxing debut ("The Kid's First Fight"). Tall, handsome, painfully shy, Brennan, who is part Thai (his grandfather had been a celebrated kick boxer in Bangkok), was considered by Hill to be one of the best prospects in the country. A veteran of 350 amateur fights, he would not concede that there was anything special about his upcoming maiden effort as a professional. He knew nothing about his opponent and thought only of making sure to break a sweat and getting through the first round. At times, despite his confident words, he seemed to observers to be scared out of his wits. Still, his right hand appeared to have more snap to it in the sessions with Roach than that of the champion. "He gave me fits when we mixed it up in Arizona," said Hill, who looked on good-naturedly as his protégé went at it in the ring. The champion became vague when it was suggested that at some future date he might have to fight his young friend for the title.

. . . . .

Though the match was important in boxing terms, it was not a major fight along the lines of a Tyson defense or the Leonard-Duran match that was coming up in December in Las Vegas. Still, the stream of people entering the Kirkwood Motor Inn who were connected to the event in either an official or an unofficial capacity soon grew to the size of a small army. There was the Hill camp, which soon numbered two dozen and included a "security" man, in dark glasses and windbreaker, with the look of a lost Belushi brother. When pressed, he admitted to being Virgil Hill's cousin from Las Vegas and allowed that his "security" function consisted of going into restaurants in advance of the champion and making sure there was a table available for him. "I also see to it that girls who are after Virgil do not get out of hand," he said. (The champion is not married, although he has a two-year-old son, Virgil, Jr., who is taken to the fights from time to time.) There was also the Kinchen camp of nine people, the executive and technical staff from ESPN, assorted representatives of Top Rank, the promoters, judges appointed by the WBA (a surgeon from Mexico City, a Miami lawyer, and a Nevada chiropodist), fighters who would perform on the undercard and *their* handlers, crowds of relatives, and people whose exact duties were unclear, such as the goateed man from New York City who wore gold chains and kept announcing with pride that a fighter he had once managed had made the FBI's Most Wanted List.

Seeing to it that this unruly human mechanism functioned smoothly —and acting as something of an impresario—was the job of the fight coordinator, in this case a well-fed sixty-five-year-old referee from Naples, Florida, named Jay Edson. Employed in his current position by Top Rank for the past eleven years, Edson was quick to point out that he had officiated at forty-nine championship bouts. He described his job as being that of a buffer between the visiting fight camps and the host. "I am a combination father, mother, priest, rabbi, and diplomat," Edson said, "the one who remains calm while all others are running around like chickens with their heads cut off."

Arriving at the Kirkwood with his wife, a small, pleasant-looking woman named Georgia, Edson whose pockets were stuffed with cash (each fighter—and the members of his entourage—received thirty dollars a day for meals), immediately made for the cashier's desk to make sure that no one who was not empowered to do so had signed for any hotel services. He was quickly pressed into action by the irate Kinchen camp, which claimed that its man had been denied use of the Mandan Recreational Center, the ring having been struck and the space taken over by a wedding party. Solomonically, Edson arranged for Kinchen to train at the YMCA, dispatching four assistants to stand on wrestling mats and form a twenty-four square, each man simulating a ring post, so that the challenger would be able to get a realistic feel for the space in which the fight was to be held.

At dinner that night, in the Der Mark Dining Room of the Kirkwood, Edson deplored the current state of boxing, and particularly the rock-star-type demands made by fighters. He recalled a sunnier time when Rocky Graziano, for example, would simply show up in a promoter's office, hang his coat on a hook, and ask, "When do I fight?" The hardest puncher he had ever seen in the ring (he had refereed Hearns and Ali fights) was George Foreman, who's still active. "He made me wince when he unloaded a body shot," said Edson, who felt that Joe Louis was the most "complete" heavyweight of them all and would have been able to defeat Mike Tyson. The fighter who had given Edson the most trouble in his role as coordinator was Aaron Pryor (in his title defense against Alexis Arguello), who had asked the bellhops to carry seventy-two pieces of luggage to his Miami hotel room and then tipped them a total of three dollars. "No one ever helped *me*," Pryor explained to Edson, who had to make amends on behalf of the promoters.

Edson had made international news in Madrid when an unpopular decision against a local fighter prompted an irate fan to hurl a metal chair into the ring. This knocked the referee unconscious. When Edson came to in the dressing room, he asked interviewers rhetorically if Spanish boxing fans were animals. Expecting to be supported by the Spanish press, he awoke the next morning to banner headlines saying, "No, It Is *You* Who Are an Animal, Mr. Edson," and to accompanying stories citing Vietnam as an example of American barbarism. Edson felt that boxing had taken a step backward when the National Association of Boxing Federations ruled that referees were no longer permitted to judge fights. (They continue to do so in Europe.) "The man who is an arm's length away knows what is happening in that ring," he claimed, with Georgia nodding her head in agreement. It was Edson's feeling that fans are totally unaware of the grueling physical demands that are made on referees. In Thailand, a pedometer had been attached to the sole of one of Edson's feet before a fight. It recorded that during the fifteen-round match he had traveled a distance of three and a half miles. Edson is no longer called upon to be a referee and is clearly sensitive about this. When the possibility arose that the referee for the Hill-Kinchen fight might not be able to make it to Bismarck on time, Edson volunteered his services, an offer that caused a WBA executive to look off in another direction. "Oh well," Edson said. "I guess my having refereed forty-nine championship fights doesn't count, does it?"

. . . . .

If small towns roll up their sidewalks on Sunday, Bismarck does so with a vengeance. A visitor downtown at noon on the Sunday before the fight would have found only a single individual on the street. George, an eighty-four-year-old retired farmer from Flasher, North Dakota, had left his birthplace to take up residence at a Bismarck nursing home. Squinting his eyes toward the sun in the manner of a Plains Indian, he expressed disappointment that his decades on the land had come to a spare and lonely end. But he brightened up suddenly and recalled that his father had taught Lawrence Welk to play the accordion. When the bandleader was at the height of his fame, George decided to pay him a visit, half expecting to be ignored: "But Welk broke away from his many fans and cried out, 'George, George, your father put me where I am today,' and pretty much shook my hand off in the bargain."

On a path at a nearby park, the champion, who appeared to have drawn closer to his trainer, did a series of carefully timed wind sprints. "May I take off my sweatshirt?" he asked, stopping for a moment. "Yes, you may," said Roach. Hill then went waddling off in a ducklike gait, perhaps to amuse two men who had just arrived and who would round out the unit in his corner at ringside. One was Thell Torrance, a fifty-eight-year-old trainer from Los Angeles, who was thought by Roach to be the second shrewdest man in boxing (the first being Torrance's mentor, the legendary Eddie Futch, who trained Joe Frazier and Ken Norton). A former fighter himself, Torrance punctuated his comments with illustrative combination punches in the air and seemed spry enough to step into the ring after a thirty-year absence. "I am here," he said, "to add a little gray hair and see to it that we have a quiet corner. You don't need someone shouting at the fighter between rounds that he has been hit. He *knows* that. I will also see to it that Virgil's punches are level, and work on what he *has*, not throw him a curve at the last minute. He will never be a one-punch knockout artist, but the accumulation of the type of punches that he *does* throw can take out a lot of folks." Though Torrance was qualified to act as a cut man, Roach had thought it best to bring in a specialist in this area—since the champion is thin-skinned and might, in a dark situation, require expert attention. The man chosen for this assignment was Mike Hall, a genial New Jersey resident. Liberally passing out business cards in the style of a Japanese executive, Hall said that he had not been trained in any formal sense but had picked up expertise from paramedics and ambulance workers. When he entered the ring, he planned to have on hand several coagulants (thrombin, avitene, and adrenaline chloride), sterile swabs, end swells (pieces of metal kept in ice and applied to the face to keep swelling down), and plenty of four-by-four gauze pads.

His finest hour as a cut man, he said, was the night that he had ministered to the wounds of Willy "Sandman" Edwards in a 1985 bout with Anthony Witherspoon in Atlantic City. In the first round of the fight, Edwards suffered gashes over one eye that would later require thirty-eight stitches. Improvising as he worked and making clever use of his thumbs, Hall folded three cuts into one and was able to stanch the flow of blood, thus enabling Edwards to continue the fight and win the decision. "Everyone bleeds differently," Hall said. "You must know your man's style."

Though Hill and Kinchen were clearly the stars of the drama, there were lesser players to whom the fight was of great importance as well. One such individual was Chris Van Ess, a shapely twenty-two-year-old waitress who worked at the surprisingly trendy Peacock Alley Restaurant and Lounge. (Herbert Hoover had once dined there.) She had been chosen by Ora C. Robinson, marketing director of the Civic Center, to be one of the two "card girls" for the fight. This meant that between rounds she would be called upon to circle the ring in a skimpy costume, holding aloft a placard that indicated to the crowd at the arena (and also to the large television audience) the number of the round that was about to begin. Though she had done some local modeling and had been a contestant in the World of Wheels Legs Contest, Van Ess saw the upcoming assignment as the most important of her life: "It just might get me out of this town," she confided. Though she would be alternating rounds with Vita K. Azure, a veteran card girl, her nervousness was such that she could barely concentrate on her tables.

"Are you afraid you'll hold up the wrong number?" a friend asked.

"That's not it," said the slender, perfectly proportioned Van Ess. "I'm worried that my belly's too big and my butt's even bigger."

. . . . .

At the weigh-in on the day before the fight, the champion, wearing only black spandex tights, stepped on the official scale at the Rhinehalle banquet room of the Kirkwood and drew applause from assembled officials of the Nevada State Boxing Commission (North Dakota does not have a commission of its own) for his weight of 174 pounds. Kinchen, too, was hailed by the group for weighing one pound more. "It's what he always should have fought at," said the testy Wes Wambold. Though the main-event fighters were held to strict accountability on the scales, standards dropped off quickly when it was the turn of the undercard fighters to be weighed. "Don't bother to take off your pants," one of them was told by an official. "And we'll subtract two pounds for those alligator shoes."

When their weights had been recorded, Hill and Kinchen were led off to a private room and given physical examinations by Flip Homansky, a thirty-nine-year-old physician who is the director of the Valley Hospital emergency department in Las Vegas and has been a Nevada state fight doctor for ten years. Though he treats athletes of every kind, the boyish and unsmiling Homansky has always been drawn to boxers, who are, in his view, the last true gentlemen in the sporting world ("Tennis players are obnoxious"). The examination he gave Hill and Kinchen was fairly basic, covering eyes, ears, nose, throat, heart, lungs, and hands, and any recent history of having been knocked out either in or out of the ring. If a fighter had not competed in the past six months, Homansky would want to know why. Drug testing for marijuana, cocaine, and heroin would be done immediately after the fight, although Homansky conceded that the last thing a bruised and battered fighter wanted to do was deliver a urine specimen. "Still," he said, "it makes no sense to do it at the weigh-in, since the results would not be back for thirty-six hours. And if you test two days before the fight—and a boxer checks out clean—he still has time to load up before the fight."

In determining whether to stop a fight, Homansky does not rely on exotic techniques, such as asking a seemingly incapacitated man to count backward, but takes a commonsense "gestalt" approach. As an experienced fight doctor (he had officiated at more than a hundred title fights), he felt capable of determining a boxer's physical condition by direct observation and his mental state by observing the way in which he responded to his cornermen between rounds. Had he ever let a fight go on too long? "I was criticized," he said, "for not stopping the Bobby Chacon-Cornelia Boza-Edwards fight, one of the bloodiest brawls of the decade. Cosmetically, it looked awful, but since I knew the past histories of both fighters, I was able to see beyond the blood. I felt they were capable of continuing the fight—and I was right."

. . . . .

On the night before the fight, Virgil Hill expanded his menu to include a slice of fish (walleye) and once again slept fitfully in a stifling room, bothered throughout the night by noise from the Kirkwood parking lot. His opponent ate salad and spareribs; before retiring, he entertained his cornermen with imitations of Paul Lynde and Crazy Guggenheim.

Among the first to arrive at the Civic Center on Tuesday, the day of the fight, were the technicians of ESPN, the cable network that was to televise the event to an anticipated audience of 1,600,000 viewers. If there has been a resurgence of interest in boxing (it's the fourth most watched sport on television), some of the credit must go to this sports network, which for the past ten years has broadcast programs from "backwater" sites previously thought to be commercially unviable, such as Davenport, Iowa; Lake Charles, Louisiana; Corpus Christi, Texas; and Jacksonville, Florida. One of the ESPN shows was held on a riverboat in St. Louis, a city that had not seen a championship fight in forty years. Promoters have begun to favor such outlying sites because the enthusiasm of the crowds is evident on the television screen and is infectious; it is certainly preferable to the sleepy casino players who turn up for the programs in Atlantic City and Las Vegas. Though the sport continues to be a brutal one, and sophisticated camera angles make it seem all the more so, ESPN has managed to give its shows an almost clean-cut look. This effect is helped along by the "stars" it has created, including the crisp and analytical commentator Al Bernstein and the ring announcer Michael Buffer, whose all-American good looks (and trademark "Let's get ready to rumble" introductions) have made him a favorite of the fans, many of them female. Then, too, there are the appealing new graphics. For each match, viewers are shown a "Tale of the Tape," which lists the precise physical measurements of each fighter, right down to wrist size, and presented with a chart detailing preferred strategies for each corner ("What Virgil Hill Must Do to Win"). Between rounds, there is a computerized chart ("The Punchboard") of the number of blows each fighter has thrown and the percentage landed. According to Robert Canobbio, who invented the system, the fighter with the best ratio is the winner ninety-five percent of the time. Boxing, as presented in the fresh ESPN format, comes across more than ever as a "sport" rather than a ritualized bloodletting. The shows are a far cry from those of the days when ringside announcers would drone on about a left to the body and a right to the head, inevitably describing one of the fighters as being "game," a sure sign that it was all over for him.

While the Civic Center audience watched the first of the undercard fights, cable viewers saw WBC champion Jeff Harding win a curious decision over the Englishman Tom Collins in Australia. Collins had appeared to be doing nicely, and then simply refused to come out of his corner for the third round. This caused promoter Bob Arum to leap into the ring and insist that Collins' purse of $25,000 be withheld, a demand that was supported by WBC supervisor Edward Thangarajah of Thailand. Though the result may have been unsatisfying to cable viewers, it raised the stakes for the fight to come in Bismarck. A Hill victory would inevitably lead to a call for a million-dollar unification fight with Harding at an arena in Brisbane. Sensing that this might happen, and that he would be the odd man out, "Prince" Charles Williams, who had haunted the prefight activities like a shade, warned several ranchers in the row behind him that it would be a grave mistake for him to be passed over.

While the results of the Australian fight were being sorted out, the Civic Center audience gave a rousing reception to another of its favorites, Bruce "the Mouse" Strauss, a junior welterweight and self-described "tomato can" who had decided to have his retirement fight in Bismarck after achieving the undistinguished record of eighty-five victories and fifty-one losses. As a "tomato can," Strauss, throughout his career, had been called upon to fatten other fighters' records and to bolster the confidence of up-and-coming prospects by being knocked out by them. He claimed to have been KO'd on every continent ("If you haven't seen me knocked out, you're nobody"), but improved recordkeeping and medical techniques had made it impossible for him to be knocked senseless as often as three times a week, which had happened in the past. An acting offer from Disney's Touchstone Pictures had come along, and Strauss had decided to "hang them up." At a press conference before the fight, he admitted to being undecided as to how best to cap off his career—with a victory or a defeat. As it happened, he won a decision over a Canadian Mick Jagger look-alike in a fight whose wrestling-style theatrics, though entertaining to a crowd, made boxing purists at ringside turn their heads away. After the decision was announced, Strauss was presented with a farewell rocking chair, pipe, and slippers.

While Hill and Kinchen were having their hands taped in their dressing rooms (as champion, Hill got to select the first two pairs of ten-ounce boxing gloves from the four available), Michael Buffer, the ESPN ring announcer, warmed up the crowd with calls for a stiffer punishment for Zsa Zsa Gabor, a satirical barb that appeared to puzzle the audience of ruddy outdoorsmen. Kinchen and his cornermen then made a low-key entrance, and were followed by the champion and his people, whose approach was more flamboyant. The odds for the fight had begun in the champion's favor, but the smart money in Las Vegas had begun to come in for the challenger, dropping the odds to almost even. Giving the event some additional edge was an ESPN poll which indicated that a majority of viewers thought Kinchen would be the winner. After the governor had been introduced and booed lustily (presumably for favoring four tax initiatives), a local businessman-comedian sang "The Star Spangled Banner" in falsetto. The fighters were then introduced: Hill predictably received tremendous applause, while the crowd once again unsuccessfully tried to work up some disapproval for the challenger, whose look was menacing but who unfailingly came across as genial.

The fight then began and followed an unsurprising scenario, the first few minutes a model of the "feeling out" process that takes place in most matches where a great deal is at stake. True to form, Hill circled the ring, throwing out probing and tentative jabs, while Kinchen pursued him, attempting to nullify his speed by cutting off the ring and connecting with a series of body shots that made Hill supporters wince as much as the champion did. What followed in the last minute of the first round, however, was anything *but* predictable. Each camp, while obviously hoping for its man to win, had felt assured that the fight would go at least eight rounds and probably the full twelve, ending in a decision. With forty seconds to go in the first round, the challenger, gathering confidence and clearly enjoying the impact of his successful body punches, released a long, looping, and wide left hook aimed at the body ("He practically left the ground throwing it," the champion later said), missing by a slight margin and lowering his right hand in the process. This proved to be a mistake, because Hill countered with a left hook, a punch that had previously been described by a *Sports Illustrated* writer as being "as swift as a prairie wind." The effect of the blow was to stun the challenger— and the crowd as well—and send him to the canvas. He got to his feet before the count of ten. At that point, Lee Samuels, the publicist for Top Rank, who had professed to being bored by the event ("It's just another fight"), got to his feet excitedly and screamed, "My God, he's throwing *everything*." Hill did exactly that, pounding away at Kinchen, who was still dazed and unable to defend himself—and at the same time not alert enough to drop to the canvas a second time (a wiser option, which might have given him time to regroup). The referee stopped the fight before the bell sounded, giving the Bismarck hero the most glorious and significant victory of his career.

Still, the reaction from the crowd was strangely subdued. They may have found the result too good to be true. A more likely explanation was that the Dakota audience—people who liked open spaces and giant portions in restaurants—simply hadn't seen *enough* of a fight for their money (the exact complaint of most of the people who've watched Tyson fights). As Hill leapt into the arms of the joyous Freddie Roach and then was literally passed along from one exultant rancher to another at ringside, a group of former Bismarck residents who had traveled all the way from Portland, Oregon (they'd found work there in construction), assured one another that they were pleased with the outcome of the fight. "I don't care if it *did* go only one round," said one. "I enjoyed it."

Few in the crowd remained behind to see what was probably the best fight of the night, one in which the champion's protégé, Sonny Brennan, fought a war with an equally well schooled younger boxer named Shannon Lambert, and was happy to come away with a draw. (There was some question as to why Roach had chosen to put him in with a buzz saw rather than a tomato can along the lines of Bruce "The Mouse" Strauss.) Perhaps the most disappointed individual at the Civic Center was Chris Van Ess, who hadn't gotten to hold up a single card for the main event. (Cards are not displayed until the start of the second round.) "To make it worse," she said, "fans called out sexually perverted remarks to me."

"Like what?" asked a friend.

"Like 'How'd you like to decorate my Christmas tree?' " said Van Ess, shuddering at the shady proposal.

If Hill had broken a sweat for the fight, it was only because his trainer had insisted he do so in the dressing room, so there would be no chance of his being "caught cold." At a postfight press conference, the champion graciously praised his opponent's courage, saying that the challenger had fought like a tiger for the short duration of the fight, and had it not been for a small mistake the outcome might have been different. The ever-present "Prince" Charles Williams jumped to the microphone, thrust out his jaw, and said, "But I have an iron chin."

"That's what James said," Hill answered.

Following the fight, a victory party was staged at the Kirkwood Motor Inn, one in which the hors d'oeuvres disappeared almost immediately, the skimpy selection perhaps reflecting Hill's purse for the fight, which was kept a secret but reported to be meager. Not that it would make much difference in the future. "That shot he landed," said Top Rank's previously jaded Lee Samuels, "will be heard around the boxing world." As cases of beer and soda were carted off to Hill's rooms for yet another celebration, Mayor Marlan "Hawk" Haakenson rushed off to put in a call to promoter Bob Arum in Australia, reminding him not to forget Bismarck in the wake of the champion's exhilarating victory.

While the Hill group rejoiced at the Kirkwood, yet another face of boxing was revealed at a nearby Denny's restaurant, where a disheartened Kinchen camp silently picked at its food at a rear table. The defeated challenger had shown enormous bravery in making a last-minute appearance at the postfight press conference, congratulating the champion and jokingly chiding the people of Bismarck for not encouraging him to fight back when he was immobilized. But now he sat dejectedly, poking at a chicken-fried steak while his wife looked on with concern. "This is not the end of James Kinchen," said Wes Wambold, breaking the silence. "We'll let him rest for a bit, then get him three or four warmup fights and have him right back on top again." In response, the challenger left the table to stand outside in the darkness, and there wasn't the slightest evidence that James "The Heat" Kinchen, one of the most decent men ever to step into a boxing ring, believed a word of it.

lessons of the street

charge: murder

He probably had the wrong-shaped head for a life of crime. It was a juglike affair and would have been identifiable from a helicopter above Chicago's Palmer House hotel on a foggy day. He wore shades, was in his late twenties, and around the South Side he was known as "Terrible Teeth." A self-proclaimed hero with the ladies, his admitted specialty was the precarious one of hustling the young wives of servicemen who had been shipped off to Vietnam. At the moment he was a very good suspect in a murder case.

He sat in a small, spare, monastic interrogation room in a Chicago police headquarters. For the benefit of two detectives, he sketched in some details of his early life and a reasonably good alibi of his whereabouts on the day of the murder. The man who helped him along gently, almost fatherly in style, was twenty-nine-year-old Detective John L. Sullivan, a homicide man from the Second Detective Area of Chicago's South Side. His partner, Detective Pete Valesares, did no talking and sat, for some reason, with his legs wrapped around one leg of the small metal table in the interrogation room. Teeth took about fifteen minutes with his story, finished it up grandly, and then sat back, satisfied, as though he had completed an unexpectedly delightful meal.

"That all?" asked Sullivan.

"That be it," said Teeth.

"You wouldn't kid me, would you?"

"Not on your life."

"All right then," said Sullivan, his voice taking on a slightly different one. "Ever been picked up on an aggravated-battery charge?"

Originally published as "Arrested by Detectives Valesares and Sullivan," in *Saturday Evening Post*, April 22, 1967.

"Oh, well . . ."

"Ever do any cop fighting?"

"Once I might have . . ."

"Ever done any time in the workhouse?"

"Well, if you want to count . . ."

"All right," said Sullivan, leaning forward like an offensive tackle. "I've got an eyeball witness who'll swear that he saw you across the street the night of the crime. Now, let's try it again. You bullshit me this time, and you're really in big trouble."

Teeth took off his shades for the first time. He wiped his head, which had become soaked in fifteen seconds flat. "OK, then, police, let's start again. You got nothing on me. Except that maybe I did leave out a little something here and there. . . . It's just my nature. . . ."

. . . . .

I spent part of last January with the detective division in Chicago, and it took me a week to realize the things I saw weren't being taped as a dark-horse entry in NBC's new fall lineup. So profoundly have television and movies saturated the lives of men like Valesares and Sullivan that as they "hit the street" and investigate "fresh ones," you expect their work to be interrupted by an aspirin commercial.

Notified of a homicide, a relative falls back in the great tradition of television shock. "My God! Who in the world would've wanted to hurt that nice man? . . ."Me kill him?" says a suspect in another case, "why, that man was like a daddy to me." . . ."I don't talk to coppers," snarls a young South Side punk and obvious late-movie addict. . . ."Go ahead and frame us," barks his friend, a film buff. . . ."All right," the detective teases back handing them a Warner Brothers–inspired response, "I'll slap a frame on you so good you'll hang on the wall for forty years."

Yet finally, there are some big differences. There is no way to wrap up a real murder and make it go away in thirty minutes with three short breaks for a word from our sponsor. Crime and real violence have a smell to them that simply doesn't come through on prime time. There is no way to pan in on the hate-stitched mouth of a woman whose father has just been stabbed to death. No flick has ever picked up the smell of dead blood, the things people use to mop it up, the volcanic calm that comes over frightened people involved in a homicide. A bullet enters a man's head with neatness and modesty, but no video catsup capsule will ever show the insult it performs on flesh as it exits. Real violence doesn't require effects, montages, camera angles, establishing shots. Mostly it is the particular smell of violence that does not survive the trip from life to actors to camera across TV tubes and into the living room—the smell of rooms in which terrible things have happened, the smell of guilty sweat, serious gunpowder. There are still some chambers of life that can be lived, still some life that hasn't been packaged by people named Mort and Robby out on the Coast.

. . . . .

Captain Otto Kreuzer is the chief of Chicago's twelve hundred detectives, and it was his idea that before zeroing in on one or two of his men for this story, I ought to see a comfortable sampling of them—detectives who specialize in armed robbery, homicide, auto theft, sex, and aggravated assault.

In my talk with him, Kreuzer put a lot of emphasis on the social underpinning of crime; he used the word "compassion" quite often, saying it each time with enormous ceremony and conviction. I did not think that unusual until I had spent some time working in the detective division. There is much talk—all of it somehow expected—about police shackling, about the limiting powers of the Supreme Court's *Miranda* and *Escobedo* decisions. "The Fifth Amendment says a man doesn't have to convict himself," a detective sergeant said to me, "but it sure as hell used to help."

If the detectives are not exactly cheerful about the new rulings, they struck me as being more or less resigned to them and determined to go about their business in the face of them. One does not have to be a bleeding heart to see quickly that they retain awesome power. They have the guns, the intelligence, the techniques, and there is that manner they have of "dropping in" on people. I honestly don't think they realize the kind of havoc one of those little unexpected visits can produce. The hoods, of course, are used to seeing them—but anyone concerned about so-called police shackling needs only to observe the terrifying "calm" that comes over a banker or an internist when two representatives of the law decide to drop by on some little matter that happened four months ago.

To an outsider, at least, the power would seem to be enticing, almost irresistible. On several occasions, when someone did not answer a question quickly, when a suspect did not eagerly confess, suddenly there were no civil rights, and I was a completely transformed person, wanting only to be "left alone with the SOB so I could work him over a little." After all, I was with the good guys, wasn't I? With all of that power in the air, I am amazed that compassion comes into the picture at all—which is why I come back to Chief Kreuzer and the special conviction he brings to the word. He is one of those fair and single-mindedly devoted men who run large organizations in this country, who wouldn't know psychedelic art from a good cigar.

"I don't even know what a crime is anymore," he says. "When an organized gang cleans out a warehouse and knocks in a few heads along the way, that's a crime; but when a kid from a family of fourteen steals a pie from a bakery and gets caught—am I supposed to consider that a crime too?"

While my detectives were being rounded up, I took a tour of Chicago's dazzling police headquarters and communications center. It is the envy of the world, and police officials all the way from Hamburg come over to study it. Its best feature is that Chicago police can answer a call for help faster than any police in history. Crime is now "data systemed," "despatched," "regulated," "administered." You feel that a criminal might feel terribly elevated by it all, might enjoy a sense of status, as though he, too, in his own small way, were doing his bit for the IBM team. In the detective division there are scaled maps of the city in which different types of crimes are charted with multicolored pins. Voyeurs get one color pin on the sex-crime chart, indecent-exposure people another—so that detectives can tell at a glance whether a small wave is building up in a particular neighborhood. I noticed one clump of similarly colored pins that seemed to be piling up on the armed-robbery chart. The armed brigand in this case turned out to be a man who had been calling restaurants, asking that pizza be sent to a certain address, then lying in wait for the delivery man, hitting him over the head and stealing his money (also, presumably, the pizza). He had pulled half a dozen jobs, but now he was being "data systemed" and "processed" and before long would be snatched from the ranks of underworld specialists.

Physically, the detectives I saw were a mixed bag. Some looked like detectives, others did not, and one was from Central Casting. One soft, terribly calm man blushed a great deal, wore what the youngsters call "fat slacks," and reminded me of my old junior-high-school friend Stan Pelter, who knew entire Fred Allen radio shows by heart and went into accounting. The man's specialty was that of working alone and of being able to walk calmly into the middle of armed robberies where he would "lay out" groups of stickup men.

A brilliant Negro detective looked like a celebrated jazz musician, and indeed threw back his head on one occasion and nostalgically tossed off names of great police officers he had known as a youth—as though they were greats of the jazz world. One detective was a school-principal type, and another could have been a stand-in for Vittorio Gassman. They ran a lot to broken noses, although I never found out why. Their teeth weren't so great either. Some could meet your eyes, some could not; others would occasionally, and then you would wish they hadn't.

Most had used their guns on occasion—the Smith & Wesson .38 being the most popular—and several had "stopped a few" with their bodies. The general view was that big trouble invariably cropped up just as a man was about to go off duty, or to start out on a vacation. One fellow had been shot almost to pieces just after he had won a new pistol for starring in a department softball game. "We hope you never have to use it," they had said.

It generally gets known around the department exactly how many men each detective has killed—and it is no secret when a man "moves into the teens." The group tended to agree that fear rarely entered the picture *during* a shooting situation. If it came up at all, it would be during the buildup, the stakeout, and, of course, once it was over. I noticed that detectives, around the division, had a way of stealing up on one another, poking out a finger and saying, "Stick 'em up."

Each man made a strong case for his particular specialty. The armed-robbery people liked it because they were professionals pitted against other professionals, their adversaries often seasoned groups of known criminals, each of whom presented a separate challenge. They liked the relationship they had with criminals, the "marriage." The auto-theft detectives enjoyed their work because it had a mid-sixties tang to it, and, after all, autos figured one way or another in almost every contemporary crime. The homicide people (sex and aggravated assault are thrown into this category) were almost snobbish about their section. They were the Marines, the Green Berets to the rest of the department's infantry. Homicide was where the action was. Each case involved the taking of a human life. Can you name a greater crime? In one brutal moment a man goes from no record at all—a clean sheet—to become the darkest of all criminals. Most felt that if they could not work homicide, there would be little point in even continuing in the police department.

The department sex specialist was terribly wan and unsensational in style, almost whipped in manner. His partner, I learned a bit later, is a man who is known to be a great needler. The sex specialist smiled only once, when he mentioned the annual Second Area social in which the invitations would come in saying "Homicide and Sex Party." His wife would tease him about that. Each of the detectives I interviewed seemed anxious to be chosen as a subject for this story, to represent the department. Some fell into dramatic styles—"This then is the situation that confronted me and the other police officers." . . . "I reach around and casually slip out my gun." I had just finished auditioning actors for a stage play, and the experiences were remarkably similar.

Finally, I picked Pete Valesares and John L. Sullivan, two young homicide detectives who work Chicago's South Side and whose call letters are 7206, the "7" for detective car, the "2" for second area and the "06" for their particular number. I was cautioned not to refer to them as a "team," since a detective, finally, is to consider himself a single unit and never rely on another man as a crutch. Nevertheless, they had more or less found each other some four or five months back and had begun riding around together ever since.

Pete is of Greek descent and is teased about it by John and the rest of the department. His father runs a delicatessen, and there are no other police in his family. His father did not take kindly to his becoming a detective, but Pete says his chest now swells noticeably each time Pete is listed in the newspaper as being in on a homicide arrest.

John is of Irish and Lithuanian stock; his father was a police officer in the days of "bull dicks" and fedoras and pinky rings and Capone. The thought of John going into another line of work would have been considered heretical. You might say quickly that John and Pete are perfect opposites, that they complement each other, each filling in the other's lack. But it doesn't work quite that way. John appears to be the worrier, the plodder, the one who loses sleep and takes each homicide as a personal insult. Yet Pete, who is at first glance more happy-go-lucky, is more likely to be pessimistic about the chances of cracking a case, to show up first thing in the morning in a bad mood.

They have their separate strengths. Pete is a slightly better shot and is more successful at expressing himself on paper. He is a smoother car driver. John is a stronger man, more likely to get "physical" if the job requires it. He works out regularly on a bag and, according to Pete, can hit like a mule. He is also better at charming information out of juveniles. Both are college educated, but play this down and are much prouder of being streetwise, having grown up close to the district they patrol. There is much teasing about how they see each other more than they see their wives. In appearance, Pete is dark, tall, gracefully hooked over in the style of the great stickball players from my old neighborhood. John is brown haired, thick through the shoulders, and has some trouble with his feet. They are both terribly proud of being "homicide dicks." Each has the ambition of spending twenty-five years in the department, of getting to be known as "a good copper," and of eventually sitting around with the other on a back porch, kicking around their favorite cases.

After detectives' roll call at their headquarters, they picked me up at my hotel one morning at 0900 (military time is used in the Chicago Police Department). A newsstand clerk had advised me to remain in the hotel for my entire stay, that I was crazy to go out into the Chicago streets. "Big as you are, they'll leap on your back, snatch your glasses, and grab your wallet. They work in teams."

While waiting in the lobby, I stood with my newspaper up over my face, Alfred Hitchcock movie style, just to get into the swing of things. Their car, or "squad," on this day was a Plymouth '66, equipped with radio gear but not particularly souped up. Neither felt any particular craving for a James Bond tire slasher of a vehicle. I sat in the back next to John's attaché case, which is marked "John L. Sullivan—Crime Detection." He calls it his "clue box." At the roll call both men had checked to see whether any new homicides or "fresh ones" had come in the night before and, having found the well dry, were now going to work on their unsolved murders of the near past. John's favorite was a four-month-old gang shooting of a youth whom the killers had mistaken for someone else. A new lead had tumbled in from a "friend," as a spin-off from another case, and we were off to track it down. "You hate to forget a juvenile murder," said John, "since there are at least two hundred kids out on the street who know your man." Sooner or later, someone would start to brag about it, to say "Guess who I shot?" at some pool hall—since that was really the only reason to do it in the first place.

I had always felt the sets for Harold Pinter plays were the ultimate in grayness until I saw the South Side of Chicago in January. It is a grim, thickly populated area, made up of working-class Negroes, Italians, Lithuanians, Poles, who live in beat-up single-family homes and three-story apartment houses. Pete and John took me on a cruise of their district, and our excursion had much the same flavor as a Marine reconnaissance mission into Cong country. The area is gang inhabited, each of the warring factions staking out its boundaries on the sides of stores and buildings with giant scrawls that said, "Blackstone Rangers, "Devil's Disciples," "Apache Rangers." Pete said it was virtually impossible to survive in this part of Chicago if you did not belong to one of the gangs, but that gang activity slowed down in cold weather. Both men said they liked working the 0830 to 1700 daytime shift. Although most of the fresh cases came in at night, Saturday night in particular, real investigative work could only be done in the daylight hours. Weekends, particularly, were good for corralling witnesses and making pinches since—quite simply—everyone was home then. John and Pete agreed that the night shift was hell on a man's stomach; you wound up drinking cold beer and eating spaghetti and meatballs for breakfast.

"It was a dark and dreary day as I swung my unmarked car down State Street," said Pete, who enjoys mimicking TV detective shows. 'This looks like a dangerous one,' I told my partner John."

Pete then went on to say that his first homicide turned up when he was a patrolman. It was a "domestic altercation" ending in a fatal shooing. He was a little disappointed by the look of the bullet wound. "I'd expected much more," he said.

John had worked as a lifeguard on the Chicago beaches and had seen plenty of dead bodies. His first homicide involved a man whose head had been split with an ax over a two-dollar poker-game bet. When John arrived, the man was still alive, split head and all, but there was no way to stop the bleeding.

Both men remembered two detectives-to-be fainting during their first autopsy, and they are fond of quoting a Polish detective friend who says that to be a homicide detective "you got to wade through them bodies." Pete said he is now the most careful body inspector in the department, since he goofed badly once, failing to find a bullet hole in a victim's mouth and reporting the case as a suicide. "If a guy's been run over by a train now," he said with a grin, "first place I look is his mouth—for a bullet hole."

We ran through the area—Emma's Eat Shop, Bob's Recreation, Upper Room Healing Center, First Pentecostal Church of Christ Inc., Bush's Soul Bar-B-Que, Al's Action Lounge—until Pete suggested a coffee break, and John reluctantly said all right. He had figured you wasted three hundred hours a year on those "breaks" and imagine how much digging you could do in that time. We took seats in the rear of a restaurant, John drinking ice-cold Diet Pepsi, which he orders regularly through the day, often along with banana-cream pie. Pete said that detectives would generally sit in the rear of public places or at least with their backs to the wall. He felt that he could generally spot a detective by the way he walked into a room, looked around, took his time being seated, by the way he carried himself. He felt that a detective was somewhat more poised than the average man.

Both men said they were more or less unaware of their weapons, that guns became simply "tools," much like a carpenter's hammer. You missed it, of course, when you didn't have it. Both men said they carried their guns at all times, even when walking outside with the garbage. This was "company policy." Both men were especially gun conscious each night when driving into their garages. If a vengeful hood were to seek out a detective, he would generally try to ambush him in this spot. Pete said he took out his gun and placed it on the seat whenever he slipped into the driveway.

We left the restaurant and drove over to see the young man who might have some new information on the four-month-old gang slaying. Inadvertently, we turned up at the wrong address, and Pete said, "It's a wonder I find my way to the office every morning." I got my first inkling that 90 percent of their job is knocking on the wrong doors, or knocking on the right ones and finding nobody home. We found our man at a place on South Vernon; a low-echelon gambler and ladies' man in his early twenties with a kind of boneless, easygoing calypso style. He wore a bandanna and did not take his eyes off the television set once during the interrogation. We sat there easily, comfortably, four fellows having a midday chat. It seemed a fruitless interview, but Pete and John had put in a good word for the fellow after a recent street rumble and had a feeling there might be a little return dividend rolling in.

As we prepared to leave, our man, eyes still fixed on daytime TV, mentioned a certain "mean, ugly dude who was shooting his mouth off down at the pool hall, about a month back." John didn't respond, but in the car he said he felt a four-month-old slaying was about to be solved. "He knows who did it," John said, "but he has to figure out a way of telling us roundabout." That way, no one would ever be able to say the informant was a stool pigeon.

Pete was pessimistic, however, and like the Hollywood writer who doesn't believe he has been paid until he has not only cashed the check but spent the money, he felt that no case was anywhere until the report said, "Arrested by Detective Valesares and Sullivan. Charge: Murder." That, of course, is what it was all about, and when you had brought a case like that home you saw how trivial it was to make a burglary arrest—or any other arrest, for that matter.

Around 1300 we dropped over to lunch at Tony's Snack Shop, where a circle of small-time hoods gathered around Pete and John, testing, needling, as though to see how close they could come to the fire without being burned. "Here come the Greek Police," said one. Another tried to place me and said, finally, "You look like a fellow who keeps trying to sell furniture to my wife."

"He's new," said John. "He's working sex."

During lunch Pete and John told me about the test they had to pass in order to become detectives. In the psychological part they had tied themselves up in knots trying to figure out the questions, particularly those aimed at weeding out homosexuals. Which President do you prefer,

Washington or Lincoln? Would you rather be a ballplayer or a florist? "Well, hell," said Pete, "maybe I *would* rather be a florist, but how in the hell am I supposed to tell them that?" "It's a pattern they're looking for," said John. "If you put down florist, ballet and that you love Chanel No. 5, they're going to start wondering. . . ." John said that come to think of it he didn't want to be walking down an alley and have his partner turn suddenly and say, "John, I've known you a long time. Kiss me."

. . . . .

The following morning the two detectives seemed almost relieved to have come up with a "nice little murder" for me. The night shift had answered the call and reported the details to Pete and John. The victim was a somewhat elderly gentleman who had been stabbed to death in the kitchen of his South Side apartment. The wounds in this case had been neat, almost "polite." John said it was amazing how many homicides were the result of a single stab wound that went straight through the aorta. Later, however, the coroner would say that the lungs had been punctured, but that the actual cause of death was strangulation.

On the way to the slum area, John fortified himself with another Diet Pepsi and said, "There's no point in even going over there, because the bullet did it."

As with most homicides, this one had a single unusual feature. When the body was found, it was covered from head to toe with a blanket—almost as though the murderer was too squeamish to look at a dead face. The trick—and here any Agatha Christie buff would feel right at home—was to fix the victim's last moments and to establish a motive.

The victim, a West Indian contractor, had occasion to employ many itinerant painters. A key part of the investigation would be the interrogation of these workers to see if one of them had a grudge against the victim. It had been his practice to pay his employees in his home. A possibility was that one of them had come to get paid, began to argue with the contractor, and wound up killing him.

Relatives and friends had gathered at the scene, bowed over and respectful in their grief, but also a little keyed up about being in on a homicide. Some used stray television lines—"It had to be someone who knew him *very very* well." Later, Pete and John were to tell the next shift of detectives they had walked into a "hostile" environment, but all I could see was a numbness, a suffocation, a stopping of time, and an inchoate wailing of shock and grief.

The body had been identified by the victim's daughter and swept off to the morgue by the night-shift team of detectives for an inquest. For a "polite little murder" there seemed to be an awful lot of blood in evidence. Rags, kitchen towels, old clothing had been used to mop it down, to soak up the last traces of a man's life.

John spent a great deal of time on locks, means of entry, doors, windows—the kind of thing that would bore me if I were a detective. I would have spent all my time looking for guilt in people's faces. The victim's room had been ransacked, and Pete spent some time going through the physical trappings of his life. A basement door had been heavily padlocked; John caressed it lightly with a penknife, and it sprang open wondrously, to the complete delight of three onlooking mourners. A little later, John found a knife in the cutlery drawer and asked me to look it over. I studied it until my head ached. Nothing.

"It's the murder weapon," he said.

Pete took a quick look at it, too, and shrugged it off; John put it in a handkerchief and popped it into his pocket. John was working on a hunch, but later the microanalysis department would confirm that indeed there was human blood on the knife.

We spent the rest of the day running down suspects, all of them painters whose names had been supplied by the first detective team on the scene. None of them panned out. Pete said he was sorry he didn't work the Gold Coast—the wealthy area of Chicago—where gorgeous upper-crust girls would be lying around all day, ready to say, "C'mon in, make yourself cozy." At a restaurant one of John's fans, a small-time burglar, spotted the kitchen-knife-possible-murder-weapon in John's pocket and said, "Hey, New Breed, what are you doing now, stealing silverware?" John tucked the knife deeper into his pocket, slightly embarrassed. I noticed that jacket linings of detectives are torn in the place where their shoulder holsters rub against the linings, and, indeed, that might very well be a good way to spot a detective.

Later, returning to the station, both men got heated up about the new Supreme Court restrictions. John told of a detective who always identified himself as "Slim" when trying to break into closed-door crap games. "Everybody knows a Slim, and the door would usually open," said John. If that didn't work, explained John, this detective would pour water on the door, to give the impression that he was urinating on it. Were these tricks to fail, he would light up a newspaper and blow smoke under the door, to make the gamblers think there was a fire.

"But we're sophisticated now," said John. "If someone doesn't open the door, we say, 'Gosh, sorry, we'll return another day.' "

Pete and John worked overtime that night, and at the station I noticed that the typewriters were labeled Sex and Homicide. A sign asked, Does Your Appearance Command Respect? Pete said down to type his report on the painter murder and looked very much like a newspaper reporter until the radiator gave off a spurt of steam and he pretended to yank out his gun to take a shot at it. A detective friend named Frank came by, and Pete asked him if he had shot anyone lately.

"Yes," he said, "and I'm sorry it wasn't a Greek."

Much of the kidding around the detective bureau has violent overtones. A favorite remark is: "If you don't do (something or other) I will hunt you down and shoot you like a dog." Occasionally John asks Pete how he would like to have his rib cage pulled out.

In the time I'd spent with them, one murder case in particular seemed to be hanging over the detectives like a pall. It would come up, then quickly be dropped, and it was the only piece of business that made them behave in an odd way. It seemed to arouse a comingling of anger, sorrow, fear, disbelief. I knew they wanted to talk about it and would, sooner or later. A night-shift man came by to say he had cracked up a "squad," and "now they won't even let me drive a typewriter." Pete chuckled, and out of the clear blue tossed the complete report of the "sensitive" case in my lap, telling me that if I lost it he would "hunt me down and shoot me like a dog." It was marvelously flat, relentless reading and, of course, halfway along, when the name of a certain patrolman came into the picture, I saw what made the case so "touchy." John and Pete had worked on it for thirty straight days, and when the net had started to close in on their fellow police officer, both had gotten sick and begun to go without sleep for nights at a time. They had finally had to make the arrest, but they had not yet gotten the case out of their systems. The accused was alternately "ignorant," a "poor slob," an sob." They couldn't say it, of course, but they must have seen in this man a small part of themselves gone uncontrollably bad.

. . . . .

I went out to dinner with John and Pete and their wives. You would think that detectives' wives would feel doubly safe and protected, but that didn't seem to be the case at all. Both women seemed acutely aware of all the terrible things that could happen in the streets, and often slept with the sheets over their heads. After an evening on the town, neither Pete nor John would dream of allowing his wife to be first through the door. Nor would they permit their wives to walk more than fifteen yards unescorted at night.

Generally speaking, other women, at parties, tended to find John and Pete fascinating, because of their work, and this seemed pleasing, by and large. Both couples played Monopoly a lot and also a game called Life, in which the idea was to fall in love, grow up, buy houses, and get mortgages. John said his wife never failed to beat him at any game. It is an oversimplification, of course, but one key to a marriage is the unguarded look on a woman's face when her husband is telling a story. In this situation, both wives had a fine way of looking at their detective husbands.

John, who had never eaten clams in his life, tried them that night. It was the first time he had ever looked frightened, but he got them down and seemed to enjoy them.

. . . . .

I saw the team the following day, and they had come up with a likely suspect in the "nice little stabbing," someone who had called the painting contractor's house twice on the night of the murder and spoken to the first team of detectives without knowing it. A painter, occasionally employed by the victim, had an "interesting record," including some aggravated batteries.

The night-shift detectives had reported the suspect had no permanent home, but cited one address at which he stayed occasionally. Pete and John said there would be a sort of stakeout, but that they were short one gun, and that I might have to use my pen, which, of course, was mightier than the sword. An old-timer of a detective joined us, saying he had been all over the "United Snakes," had been a character in Jack Lait and Lee Mortimer's *Chicago Confidential*, and if I wrote that he was a dirty old man he would go all over the world and smoke me out. He said the bureau would let Pete and John, the two young kids, work on the case for about a week. "Then they'll call me in to wrap it up." He said he had worked everything from patrol to stationhouse dick to paddy wagons. "I've been shot at, I have shot, I have killed," he said. "When I wanted to go through a door, I would just stick my big thirteen through it, and that door went.

"But let's face it," he said. "These young fellows are wiry, and they think faster. I've got three years to go, and I want to go out alive." He seemed to make Pete and John uncomfortable; I found him quite touching.

We had breakfast, and fortified by eggs and sausages, we zipped off, passing the University of Chicago's great Billings Hospital. John said that if he were ever shot he hoped they would take him there, even if it meant passing sixteen other hospitals on the way. "They take bullets out of brains . . . and they don't put Band-Aids on gunshot wounds. . . ."

We (note the way it's become "we") all realized that the suspect we were looking for had plenty of time to prepare for us. He was capable of flying off the handle and mutilating people—the rap sheet said he had stomped the face of a store owner and beaten another man to a pulp over the theft of a radio.

We missed him at the first address and at several others, too; it seemed obvious he had been tipped and was staying a few jumps ahead of us. Several small-time criminals who knew him misled us on his whereabouts or "blew smoke up our tails," as John liked to put it. Some of the petty criminals showed a great deal of interest in the upcoming police exams, wanting to know whether a few burglaries, a stray knife fight here and there, and a year or so in the can might hurt them in their applications for the police force. John told me that you could be taking a man in on a murder charge, and he would turn to you in the squad car and ask what his chances were to make the police department.

Finally, a man who had been with the suspect the previous night gave us an address where he would "definitely" be found. When we got there, John parked the "squad" around the corner, safely out of view. The house, the neighborhood, and the whole world seemed very still as we rang the doorbell. There were no jokes this time, and John and Pete had their hands in their pockets. Later they told me that in this situation they would often have their guns concealed, but unholstered. During "nervous" interviews John would often shift his holster to his midbelt for easy access.

A grim landlady invited us in and said we were in the wrong house and she had never heard of our man. We started to go off, somewhat frustrated, but then a fellow in painting clothes, who had been in the house, waved us back to the front porch and said, yes, he knew our man quite well and would tell him to get in touch with the police department.

John and Pete invited the painter to sit in the "squad." On both sides of the criminal scene there is a lot of emphasis on getting a man on your own turf. Pete said the fight would go out of the world's toughest hood "when we get him in *our* playground."

Inside the detective car the painter demonstrated that sense of "territorial imperative." He said his nickname was Terrible Teeth, that he was a holy terror with women, and that he always made sure to take them to motels. That way, if an irate husband were to break in, Teeth would be able to "beat his tail, call the police, keep his woman, and get her to testify against her own husband." John casually asked Teeth about his whereabouts on the day of the crime—on the alert for a story that sounded too good. An honest man simply doesn't know what he was doing last Thursday at 5:00 P.M. Teeth seemed to have his movements pretty well covered—a little gambling, a bout with the ladies, plenty of witnesses.

We let Teeth go. Some seven hours and twelve false leads later, a fellow in a bar gave us a new address, absolutely the right one. We moved in on it, and there we found Teeth again, calmly watching television with a friend; without once taking his eyes from the set, he admitted this time that he was the "aggravated battery" man we had been looking for all the while. He couldn't admit it earlier in the day, because he had to find out exactly what the detectives were after, to make sure it wasn't an old alimony rap. Once he discovered he was being sought on a murder charge, he felt it was OK to come out in the open, since he knew he was clean. John and Pete admitted to being "faked out of our jocks." I thought it had been a brilliant piece of stage acting, too, and Pete said it was just a matter of Teeth having been a little more streetwise than the detectives. "That's the kind of guy who's going to lay me out some day," said Pete. He told me about a celebrated detective who had dropped his guard once, been lured around a corner by a streetwise punk, and "took three shells in the head."

At detective headquarters John conducted the interrogation of Teeth, concealing his knowledge of Teeth's past scrapes with the law, working him gently as though he were a fisherman luring a Minnesota muskie. When Teeth was finished, John jumped on his neck, confronted him with "discrepancies" in his story and told him he'd better get the story straight the second time. Teeth seemed flustered for the first time, but when he retold the story, he stuck pretty close to his original version, at least insofar as his connection with the murder went. At one point he said he'd even be willing to take the lie detector. "You'll bust the damned fuse," said John.

John asked Teeth for a look at his wallet, checking through for a recent dry-cleaning ticket that might mean blood-stained clothing, but all that popped out were dozens of pictures of women, all pledging undying devotion to the wallet's owner. John told Teeth that a murder rap meant only twenty-five years, but the suspect said no thanks and besides, what would all the girls do in his absence? John and Pete took a short break, leaving Teeth in the interrogation room. John said quietly that Teeth seemed to be clean on the murder charge. There were a few warrants out for him on other charges, but the statute of limitations had run out on them. "When you get the right man in there," John said, "you *know* it, even if you can't prove it."

Then, outside the questioning room, an argument broke out between two detectives over the use of a certain squad car. One of them wore revolvers in twin shoulder holsters and seemed angry enough to whip at least one of them out, but the hassle was broken up. The night-shift detectives then lined up for roll call, and the auto-theft section brought in two young car thieves for an introduction. The word was they were real "comers" in the field, and it would be good for all the detectives to get used to seeing their faces. They stood before the lineup like shy high-school actors and then were carted off to the lockup. A new detective came over and said he thought I might have a yen to see some of the pictures in the sex-crime file. It took him awhile, but he finally fished out the worst he had in stock, one involving a Mexican migrant and his adulterous bride. I thanked him, saying it certainly was a winner.

Eventually, Pete and John went back to the interrogation room, and Teeth agreed to take the lie box as soon as it was available later that week. John dismissed him, but not before teasing him about his reputation as a lover.

"I talked to one of your broadies," said John. "She said you're not enough of a man for her."

Teeth took this very hard for a moment, but then caught on and ripped off his first big smile of the day. "You know what she'll say if you ask her about Teeth? She'll say, 'That old Teeth's a fine, fine man.'"

. . . . .

Criminal investigations have a way of spilling over into one another. Making his rounds on one stubborn case, a detective will stumble across evidence that can help him clear up half a dozen others. Teeth, for example, turned out to be a dud as a suspect in the one stabbing, but during his subsequent lie-box test, he threw some light on a truck hijacking. Weeks later, Pete told me that Teeth hung around with a crowd that had known the victim in his favorite unsolved case. Pete said he was certain Teeth knew the name of the murderer and eventually would come across with it.

In the weeks that followed, Pete and John were to clear up a handful of homicides one-two-three, but the case of the old gentleman with the blanket over his head turned out to be much more tangled than they had thought. John remained optimistic, but Pete admitted that if their suspects didn't pan out, there was a chance they might eventually have to forget it. Sort of a contradiction, really, since unsolved homicides technically are never closed.

I felt young and adventurous as an unofficial third member of the team, as though I were back at college or at least in the Air Force again, cruising around with a couple of buddies. One day, I joined Pete and John at the police pistol range. Three times each year Chicago detectives must qualify as instinctive shooters. This involves quick firing at targets without the use of sights. There is no time to line up your target carefully in an actual shoot-out.

Pete's style turned out to be more natural, more spontaneous, and he had a born athlete's approach to guns. As a hunter, he had been nicknamed "Boom Boom" because of the speed with which he got off shots. He is a slightly better shot than John, who took his time, shot more deliberately. But I decided that if I were at the other end, I'd worry more about John and that deliberate style. I watched them shoot closeup (most gun battles take place within seven yards), both standing and squatting, and then longer range. I think it was later, as we examined their targets, that I first became a little numb and depressed and realized that we weren't back in college or the Air Force anymore than we were out on location for Warner Bros.

I think it was the targets that did it. Each one had an outline of a man with a bowling-pin-shaped area in his middle—the heart, head, lungs representing kill areas, and peripheral places such as shoulders, wrists, genitals, counting as disabling shots. The disabling wounds, on that faceless black-and-white target, seemed for the moment as terrifying as the kill. With just a slight shift in the wind of fate, the target might have been someone like Teeth himself; if I was not exactly crazy about him, I certainly didn't want to see him filled with great clusters of disabling wounds. Seventy is a qualifying score. John rang up ninety-five, and Pete nosed him out by one point, winning a dollar.

They said I could keep the target as a souvenir, and later I gave it to my eldest son, but then I changed my mind and took it back. I had been working with John and Pete in an atmosphere of death and tragedy and had somehow never really absorbed the reality of what I had been observing. But on the target range, I decided I'd had enough. For all of their easygoing charm, for all of the breakfast-show comedy and the account-executive styles, they were basically tough men in a bleak world the color of gunmetal where grief and human misery make up the day's workload.

. . . . .

We kept in touch. When I last talked to Pete and John, they were in the middle of Chicago's worst blizzard in many years. I asked them how they were fighting crime, and they said they were doing it by phone. The jokes again. They had always dreamed of getting a real neat extradition assignment, one that would take them to the Caribbean, Tokyo, Paris. On a vacation perhaps they would like to visit New York. I wondered if they would take their guns along. They would, of course. There was really no other way. Even if they left their guns behind, they would more or less have them along.

lessons of the
street

John is a New York City plainclothes detective whose clothes are not all that plain. He wears webbed belts, bell-bottom slacks, and all-in-one suede and corduroy suits of a type purchasable at what the radio commercials refer to as "in" shops. This fondness for mod outfits makes him a bit unusual in his profession, most detectives favoring baggy slacks and white anklets or what John politely refers to as "period dress." But the clothing helps John blend into the background when he is at work in certain "swinging" neighborhoods, particularly those along Manhattan's Upper East Side. He also keeps a conservative gray double-breasted suit on hand for Wall Street operations, and in a flash he can get himself up as a junkie when called upon for a narcotics caper.

John has ten years as a detective under his belt and sees the city with a certain shrewd streetwise vision; it was for this reason that a mutual friend suggested I meet and spend some time with him since I would be amazed at how different detectives' eyes are from anyone else's. Well, actually, I wasn't going to be that amazed; I'd written about detectives before: a few articles, stories, a novel called *The Dick*. But my fascination, not so much with crime as with detectives, continues to operate on a high burner—the guns, the hair-raising amount of power, their ability to keep a grip on their sanity, however razor thin. John is a lonely fellow, I was told, and would be happy to meet a new friend, particularly a literary type.

I rent an office-apartment in Manhattan's East Sixties, and it was agreed that we would get our project under way at my place. John showed

Originally published in *Harper's*, September 1971.

up punctually at eight one night, almost as though he'd been crouched at the door to make sure his arrival was right on the dot. As advertised, he turned out to be a dapper young man with a constant look of incredulity on his face, as though all his life someone had been whispering a long, amazing story in his ear. At times he seemed handsome, at other times quite snotty looking; on appearance alone, it would not be surprising if he was revealed to be yet another Kennedy relative, long hidden away in some obscure religious order.

Halfway through the door, John began to fiddle with my lock, asking if it was the original one assigned to me by the building. I had to admit it was, and John, with a sad shake of his head, said that not changing it was a bad move on my part since the contractors had doubtless sold the basic key pattern to the rackets people, making my flat a pushover for burglars.

I told John that the building seemed to have pretty good security, with squadrons of attendants guarding each of the entrances. But John said they would all be sitting ducks for Argentinian husband-and-wife teams who would cut through a building of this sort like locusts through a wheat field. "They are very fine-looking people who can walk through the front door on dignity alone. The husband breaks and enters and the wife's skirts are the stash. They have schools for these people in Argentina, training them in assorted con games."

John patted his breast pocket and said, "Here, incidentally, is the best place to carry your money." Tapping his backside, he said, "Here's the worst." Moving deeper into the apartment, John spotted the wraparound glass windows and said, " voyeur's paradise, I see. I'd like to lock up nine perverts in a place like this. What you'd wind up with is one fat man and a bag of bones." Like other detectives I've known (and many Air Force officers) John is obsessed, perhaps revealingly, with the subject of homosexuality. Given the slightest conversational opportunity—or none at all—he will work in a "fag" reference or girlish imitation of some sort.

I offered him a drink, which he declined in favor of coffee, explaining that he never imbibes while carrying a gun, which is always. The weapon is a .38, and he has mastered the art of wearing it in his mod slacks so that no bulge shows beneath his jacket. When his slacks are a bit too tight, the gun is difficult to draw, and on one occasion, a West Village man interpreted his wriggling about to get the weapon as an overture. A .38 is the only weapon John carries, although several months before he had been assigned a backup man who wore a pair of guns at the waist, one attached to his back, another in the crotch, and a long, saberlike knife tucked into his boots. John wears his one gun both on and off duty and on occasion has been criticized by dates who've run across it during amorous encounters. He has killed two men he knows of and a vague number of others in shoot-outs when all hell broke loose and exactly who did the killing was unclear. As to the drinking, John tries to stay away from bars where he is known. "They will slide ninety-six free drinks my way and then, invariably, there will be a six-foot-nine goon pushing people around, and I will be expected to deposit him outside on his ass."

Moving across to the windows, John was reminded of his work with "leapers"—suicidal jumpers from high buildings. As he told it, the one thing such dry-divers forget is that at some point they are going to hit the ground. "They just think about the flying-through-the-air part. And if you've ever heard the sound of a leaper coming in for a landing, you'll never forget it. It's like two tons of wet laundry dropped from a plane."

Still, John would rather deal with a leaper any day of the week than be assigned to a "roast-toastie"—a rackets victim who is burned up in a building or car. There is a requirement that little plastic tags be affixed to each section of the victim's body, a particular problem when "toasties" are involved. "You'll be standing there with an ear in one hand and a foot in the other, and the supervisor will be hollering, 'All right you men, get those ninety-five tags on.'" A standard procedure for a detective who is tagging bodies is to put a rag in his mouth to keep himself from throwing up.

"All right, " said John, leaping to his feet, "time to go out and harass the public."

. . . . .

On the way downstairs, John proudly filled me in on the fact that he had made detective after only three years on the beat, and without the help of a "rabbi"—a friend in city government. Further upward movement, however, was going to be rocky without influence. "The police commissioner can expose himself in the middle of Forty-Second Street and no one'll pay attention to him. Yet all you need is one dumdum in the mayor's office pointing to a cop and saying, 'I like that boy,' and the next day he's got a promotion." Despite this beef, John felt the department was a virtual playpen now, compared to a period in recent memory when police internal security men had more power than the Gestapo. "If they knocked on your door at three in the morning and said you were out, that's exactly what you were—out. It didn't matter if you were Cardinal Spellman's nephew. No phone calls, no hearing, no nothing. It's still a department run on Catholic morality—for Catholics, by Catholics, and for the benefit of Catholics." Actually, it had been a long time since I'd met anyone who was as strenuously Catholic as John was—and for a moment I thought of a time when I passed St. Angela Merici's each day on the way to public school, afraid of being whisked inside and forced to wear a parochial school uniform.

John broke my reverie as he, for some reason, next turned his anger on the FBI, which he and his fellow detectives regard with the same contempt that combat infantrymen reserve for the boys back at headquarters. "Do you know those guys actually believe the movies and TV shows. An agent with his suit and striped tie will rap on a door and say, 'Open up in the name of the FBI!' The only trouble is, the junkie inside hasn't seen the movie, so he fires a round through the door. The FBI guy feels all this blood coming out of his suit and can't believe it. 'How could he *do* that,' he says. 'I *told* him I was with the FBI.'"

By the time we reached the street, John was in a total lather over the federal agency, sticking a finger at my nose and saying, "And they'll get you, too, don't worry, if they want you for something. If they say you're a murderess, then you're a murderess if they got to dig up a corpse and stick one in your lap. If they want you for junk, they'll run into your apartment and start scaling bags of heroin off the walls, one kilo for you, one kilo for you over there, and one for the baby. And you're all under arrest for possession of dangerous drugs."

Once on the subject of drugs, John was off to the races, most of his years on the street having been spent as a "junk cop," which he regarded as a thankless, dreary job, but one possessed of a certain grubby nobility. "We're at the bottom of the toilet bowl, but for reliability, dependability, give me a junk cop any day of the week. It's the supreme mix—with everything coming down on us—rape, burglary, arson, homicide. The department can't exist without the junk cop and his fresh street information. A detective is only as good as his informants—and the junk man has the most, since every junkie is an informant."

Since I'd first met John, I'd been waiting for this kind of "commercial." Throughout my experience with the police, I'd never met a vice cop who didn't claim that vice work was the only place there was any real action, or a homicide dick who didn't insist that murder was the only aspect of crime worth bothering about.

When we reached my car, I held John off for a moment to ask if the vehicle's security was in good shape; it had door locks, an ignition lock, and a third little lock-switch of which I was particularly proud, tucked away at the base of the steering column. "You're fair against amateurs, a dead duck against a professional." Well, then, was a burglar alarm system worth installing? Not really. The only surefire path to absolute security in a city-parked car was to unscrew the rotor and take it along. "It's a bit messy," said John, "but you'd be surprised—more and more people are walking into restaurants with them."

. . . . .

Once in my car, John suggested we drive over to Manhattan's West Side, where we would be sure to see junkies in action, although he quickly apologized for its not being as heavy a dope scene as the East Bronx. "Up there, it's just one big syringe, with more glassine wrappers on the street than cigarette butts. The only man ever reported for suspicious behavior is a guy who's not a junkie."

Briefing me as he drove, John said that until five years ago and the arrival of stiff federal laws, Italians controlled the heroin market. And it wasn't all that bad, since at least the traffic was orderly and the prices firm. The dons would decide to import 150 keys (kilos) one year and hold it at that. But now that the Cubans are in command, all bets are off and the traffic in junk is wild. The footloose South Americans are independent operators, with no controlling network, and you might have as much as 800,000 keys a year coming into the country. As we moved along upper Broadway and then turned onto a bleak and sourly cast section of Columbus and then Amsterdam, John said he would soon be pointing out some junkies "on the set." Rolling down the window to wink at an effeminate young man, John said, "Hi there, Holly Golightly," and when a car up ahead blocked our path momentarily, John quickly marked its driver down as an out-of-towner on the hunt for an assignation. "Look at him, so horny he can hardly turn the wheel. If the radio cars spent as much time prowling as he does, there'd be no crime in the city. He'll pick up a little guppy, contract a dose and bring it home as a present for his family in Topeka. They'll spend all their lives looking for a cure."

We passed another corner which John described as a notorious nesting place for transvestites, most of them Puerto Rican, the ex-islanders being especially philosophical about this aberration. "They'll say, 'Poor José, what a shame, but that is the way it goes.' Amazingly, these people make as much money off tourists as regular pross [prostitutes]. The guy goes back to his hotel dreaming happy dreams and it never occurs to him that he's been worked over by a Puerto Rican third baseman in drag."

On a particularly forlorn corner of Columbus Avenue, John double-parked, dug a finger in my ribs, and pointed to what he described as a group of junkies "on the set." I turned to look and he said, "Don't just wheel around that way. If they see two of us staring, it's all over. Pretend you're talking to me and use the car mirror." Feeling very Sam Spade, I did so and saw a group of stooped-over people not having very much to do with one another. "A junkie 'hanging' that way means either one, he's had his shot; two, he's steering people to a connection; or three, he's actually holding something. Watch, and you'll see some shit go down." After a moment or so, one of the men ambled over to another. "Closer," said John, "closer, closer—." The two men exchanged a "take five" slap of hands and John said, "That was it."

"That was it?"

"That was it," he repeated.

"I don't really think I saw anything."

"Of course you didn't," said John. "Neither would a radio car, circling the corner for hours. It takes a trained junk dick to see a hit like that."

Feeling as though I'd slowed the march of justice, I asked John if, under normal circumstances, he would have made an arrest in a case like that. He said no—the department doesn't have enough personnel to bother with one-bag transactions. "What you're after is your half-load and full-load twenty-five bags of heroin collar. When you get one, you immediately turn the man into a confidential informer. 'You give us X number of collars and we'll write a letter to the DA to get you a suspended sentence.' The trick, though, is always to work up, getting a half-load man to lead you to a one-key man.

"And then one day, "he said, swallowing hard, "you make that fifteen-key collar."

The thought of pulling off a coup of such proportions put John in a jovial mood. Doubling back to Amsterdam, we came across a parked car with a man leaning in, talking to the driver and slipping him a package. As far as I was concerned, it might have been two fellows discussing a recent Mets game. John slowed up, then stepped on the gas, and with genuine anger, said, "Damn! Of all nights not to be traveling with my partner. There goes one of the top collars of my career."

I told John I wasn't sure I was following him and he said, "What do you think was in that box—Fanny Farmer chocolates? That was at least a two-key pinch. We'll circle 'round and five gets you ten they'll be gone. The driver took one look at my face and did you see him turn white? He knew I was the Man, all right." In total honesty, I hadn't seen any of this, but we circled the block and sure enough, the street-corner talkers had disappeared. "That was what we call a telephone delivery: swift, punctual, every half hour on the hour. Check your watch." I did and had to admit it was 10:30 on the dot. "No offense about before," said John, tapping me on the knee, "but I really did need at least one more gun."

"How come?" I asked.

"Because there were four more sitting in the back that you didn't see. On a two-key pinch, it's going to be guns and knives, D'Artagnan and the OK Corral.

"Oh, Jesus!" he said. "What a collar that would have been!"

"Well," he said with a sign, "till we meet again." He then rattled off a detailed description of the car, its color, year, condition, plate number, and a precise physical rundown on the two men we'd observed, right down to a small scar over the left eye of the one he felt was Cuban. This struck me as amazing since we'd sailed past them in a matter of seconds.

"Training," said John. "Getting used to surprise, vibrations, the rhythm of the street. Besides," he said, "the Cuban is a dead ringer for the chef in a restaurant I love to eat at."

·····

Traveling about with a detective, it strikes me, is like being in a mild accident or a fistfight. You feel fine while it's going on, even elated, and the shock of what has happened—or worse, what might have happened—doesn't set in until a bit later. I enjoyed John's company, and since writers are actors too, mimics, role players of a kind, I felt a little detectivelike myself for the next few days, looking people over more carefully and attributing the very worst possible motives to their behavior. As for John himself, I was able somehow to block out the fact that he carried a loaded gun at all times and indeed was paid, when the circumstances called for it, to blow people's heads off with it.

We kicked off our next meeting at Frankie and Johnny's, a favorite steak restaurant of mine, John dapper as ever but still grumbling about the fabulous collar he'd missed. A medium-rare sirloin distracted him somewhat, and two attractive women sitting alone helped things along even more. There was a hint that John fancied himself to be a ladies' man. I asked if women were fascinated by men in police work. "There's an old saying," said John. "Put a uniform on a hanger and it'll get laid by itself."

John expressed a certain sympathy for women who lived alone in the city; just in case I had a ladylove in this circumstance, he advised that she never allow a man to follow her at night at less than a five-foot margin. And if she ever got into an elevator with a male tenant, it was wise to let him push his floor button first—even if she knew the fellow. "And for God's sakes," said John, "tell her to make sure she locks her door each time she leaves the apartment, even if it's just to take the garbage to the incinerator. That brief moment with the door open is the worst—Freaksville Time."

Feeling a bit overdressed, John suggested we go back to his bachelor apartment on the West Side, where he could change his clothes, and I could look at his scrapbook. He lived in a small building on a quiet street. Because there had been some indiscreet passage of junk in the halls, he had let it be known that he was a detective. "Now, there's a guy six foot nine who bows down to me every morning on the way to work."

The first thing to greet the visitor to John's pad is a large, comic drawing of what used to be known as a "yegg," pointing a pistol straight at the door. This is a police target, and John said he has to qualify in marksmanship twice each year. Was he a good shot? He wasn't sure, since most shoot-outs are held at less than ten feet and the winner tends to be the one who gets his gun out fastest. The apartment was glum, temporary—the lighting faded in the style of some of the West Side street corners we'd surveyed. John never stopped apologizing for it. I leafed through his scrapbook, on the first page of which was an empty shell, secured with Scotch tape and proudly inscribed, "My First Round—With Many More to Come." John sneaked up alongside me, aimed a .45 at my eyes and pulled the trigger, shouting, "Bang! Bang!" The gun turned out to be an almost perfect replica of the real thing, complete with gun clip. John had taken it from a junkie stickup man whose victims, presumably, would actually be able to hear the clip being inserted in case they had doubts about the weapon's authenticity. I asked John if he would mind not doing that again and he said, "Okay, okay."

An hour later, driving along the East River, I was prompted to ask about the relationship between crime and the city's rivers. John said that most "floaters" were a signal from the organized crime people that they were still in business and not to mess around with them. The particular style of the killing was always significant. "We find a drowning victim with his tongue cut out, it's not because he's skipped confession." Thus, a body found in the river was generally meant to be discovered. If there was a need to dispose of a body totally, the syndicate would use either car-crushing machinery or lime pits.

"Now there's something wrong," said John, as we bounced along the quiet and seemingly crime-free upper East Side, my new friend having promised to give me further examples of his instinct for smoking out breaks in the rhythm of the streets. All I saw was a moving van parked in front of a luxurious seven-story building. "Fine," said John, "except when was the last time you've heard of someone in this neighborhood moving at eleven at night? If it was over on the West Side, it would be perfectly natural, you'd know it was a 'Midnight Mover,' some Puerto Rican guy ducking out on the rent." In other words, what was normal behavior in one section of the city was a dead giveaway to wrongdoing in another. A group of men—even one man—parked in a car at night on the East Side was suspicious. Something, someone was probably being cased. The same group parked on the rundown West Side meant someone had probably said, "Let's go sit in John's car," the vehicle being much more comfortable than the apartment of anyone in the crowd.

As we headed downtown to the East Village, John flipped his gun into a new position, between his legs, whipping it out quickly to demonstrate how he'd be able to gain an extra second in case he had to fire off a round through the windshield. As we got into the Twenties, on Second Avenue, two young men sprinted by and John asked me what I saw. "Two fellows running," I said.

"Without jackets?" he said. "In this weather? Here's where my eyes are different from yours. What I saw was two pair of hands looking for a purse to snatch." The two young men disappeared into what seemed like a small dance hall. "They've got their coats in there and, if questioned, can say they've been there all along. It's not much of an alibi, but it's something." Suddenly, everyone on the street looked a little fishy to me. I pointed to a man carrying a stick and said, "How about him? He doesn't look right to me."

"Nice going," said John. "You're getting the hang of it. The stick is a tip-off that the fellow's a junkie. Also the stooped walk. To avoid being taken off, junkies always carry something, a stick, umbrella, or a rolled-up newspaper. Not for the editorials. It's got a knife inside."

John said that most people were under the false impression that the majority of junkie crime was committed against the public. "Negative," he said. "It's committed on one another, strong junkies smelling out weak ones and sticking it to them."

. . . . .

Before long, we were double-parked on St. Mark's Place in a colorful swirl of head shops and ice cream stores, advertising such flavors as Acapulco Gold and Panama Red. A pretty young girl skipped out of a clothing store and approached a late-model car with a group of men inside. "Where'd you get the car, boys?" we heard her ask. "You gonna help me cut that bitch?" Seemingly intrigued by the proposal, one of the men opened the car door, and she hopped inside. "We're in luck," said John. "That's one of the toughest little broads on the Eastern seaboard. Pisses icewater. She's obviously jumped bail and the car she got into is a stolen job. Let's give them a light tail and see what happens."

Since I'm always at one of a half-dozen bars and restaurants and keep seeing the same people, I'd always had the feeling that the colossus-of-New-York was a myth—and that the city was actually quite small in size. But John, who rarely passed a corner without seeing something or someone he recognized, made it seem even smaller.

He waited until the car had turned a corner, then zipped off in pursuit, explaining that on a tail it was always a good idea to keep two cars between yours and the one you were following. "I think they've spotted us," said John, gunning the accelerator and racing off after them, going through red light after red light. That was my favorite part, a boyhood dream. I knew that detectives were underpaid, but it seemed to me that getting to go through red lights and park in front of fireplugs was worth at least five grand a year in salary. Before long a radio car, with sirens howling and a cigar-smoking sergeant at the wheel, pulled up alongside and cut us off. The cigar was against regulations.

"Where you off to, chaps?" asked the driver.

"Nowhere, now," said John, flashing his tin. "You just caused us to lose our tail."

"Sorry, brother," said the driver.

"Enjoying the smoke?" John asked.

"Just fine," said the driver, considering whether to dump the cigar in the ashtray and then deciding to risk a grandiose puff to show he trusted John not to turn him in.

"Dum-dum," said John, driving off. He apologized for our losing the bail jumper, but assured me that before the night was gone we'd come up with something.

A block from the police academy, true to his word, John spotted two bearded men in their twenties, pacing up and back on a street corner and shooting suspicious glances over their shoulders. "They're going to try to boost that little Volks on the corner," said John. "I'm going after them. Observe my walk as I make my approach. It will be a street-style movement, so as not to put them on the alert." Before he left, John explained that he was a student of walks and could tell exactly what New York neighborhood a man was from by the nature of his walk, even pinning it down to an Italian kid who grew up in a black neighborhood or a black youth who grew up in a Jewish one. "You are what you walk," said

John, leaving the car and moving toward his prey with a jaunty, turkeylike stride that reminded me of Ray Bolger's movements in a forties musical called *By Jupiter*. I followed behind, trying to do a Bolger myself, but giving it up quickly—no one could truly imitate the great dancing star— and going back to my normal slouching style. In a flash, John had both men against a wall, frisking them for weapons, finding only a "roach" in one man's cigarette pack. "A roach, eh?" said John. "Don't do that again."

Driving back uptown, John said, "Maybe now you're getting some idea of what this job means to me. The hunt. The defense reading the offense, constantly moving your linebackers around. When I'm doing work like this, I'm as hooked as any junkie."

. . . . .

As a special and final indoctrination, John called and said he was going to take me on a nighttime tour of Harlem. At the same time, he cautioned me that it might get a little hairy, and that we would have to stay on the alert and keep our doors and windows locked. "We are not visiting the College of Cardinals," he said.

Several nights later, doors and windows battened down, we made our way uptown, John a bit sorry I was going to miss Harlem's nine o'clock Sunday morning "Bryn Mawr Show." All up and down Lenox Avenue, according to John, you'd see pretty little blond finishing-school girls staggering out of Harlem tenements, dazed, their stockings rolled down around their ankles. The previous night, on the West Side, or in the Village, someone had invited them to a party. "What the guy neglected to tell them is they were the party."

We slipped into Harlem through its side door, a small, tidy Upper East Side Italian section known as "Northern Mulberry Street," one I had somehow missed in my previous travels about the city. John agreed that the streets were quiet and orderly but said that most of the big-time criminal escapades were being planned inside the many "social clubs" that lined the streets.

John, who was quite democratic in his ethnic slurs, dealing them out good-naturedly to Jews, Irish, and blacks alike, now took a swipe at the Italians. "I just don't see why they're supposed to be so smart. If you have an organized crime group lit up, the idea is to find the big man, the don, right? With the Italians, they do all the work for you. You've got the binoculars on them, six guys in undershirts playing pinochle, another six doing a John Wayne bicep number in the corner. Then in comes this little old nothing-looking mozzarella head you'd ordinarily pay no attention to. Except that everybody in the place jumps to their feet and practically salutes and you know who your man is."

But John felt that was true of all criminals, the need to be caught. "A guy commits a crime in a purple shirt and orange pants and insists he's all upset about being collared. 'Why the bizarre attire?' you ask. 'I just wanted to wear something nice,' he tells you."

We drove into Harlem proper now, John crouching down behind the wheel, on the alert, for all practical purposes in enemy territory. "All right, this is it," he said. "A white man comes up here there has got to be some sort of crime committed on his person—his wallet goes, his jacket is swiped, his throat cut, something. When I see a white man get out of his car, my only interest is that he has left a next-of-kin note on the front seat and instructions on where to ship the body. If you ever come up here alone, make sure your speedometer starts at fifty. A red light is the signal for an ambush."

As we moved through the sad, bleary-eyed neighborhoods of Lenox and St. Nicholas Avenues, John went into some kind of weird inverse Lenny Bruce monologue. I'd been with detectives before, and the grim attitude toward blacks came as no great surprise to me. But I'd never before seen the revulsion-fascination machinery so clearly in operation. "All right, folks, up here it's wall-to-wall junk. Open the window you get stoned by osmosis. See that building, fifteen junkies out in front? On Park Avenue you pay $750 a month and get one doorman. Here you get fifteen. . . . It's ten o'clock at night now, that's like ten in the morning in the rest of the city. These people are just waking up to start the day. . . . There's a guy doing karate in the wind. He's trying to impress some dingbat chick in the bar and hasn't executed one movement properly. . . . There's a guy with a golfing hat. Now I ask you, did that man ever pick up a nine iron? . . . See that phone booth on the corner? It's fine except there's no floor in it. Go in to drop a dime, you wind up on a banana boat going to Panama. . . ."

What really drove John wild were the hats worn by Harlem's residents. To him, the area was just one big hat show and he couldn't seem to get over it. Hat were "toilet bowls," "inverted spittoons."

"Will you *look* at that chapeau!" John said about one particularly flamboyant topper. "He don't know his hat's goin' north and his head's goin' south. Will you look at that man dig himself. He takes a perfectly good Panama number, stomps on it, chews on it, pours on a little rib sauce, and thinks it looks groovy. The skinnier the guy the bigger the brim. The fatter the guy the smaller the brim. Maybe I'm wrong?" I decided John wanted secretly to jump out of the car and start trying on all the hats in Harlem.

Before we left the neighborhood, John pointed out a restaurant-hangout where criminals obeyed the strictest of social hierarchies, the pimps sitting in one section, disdainful of the stickup men, who are sitting in another and are in turn contemptuous of the pickpockets and small-time con men, who are also cordoned off by themselves.

As a final piece of advice, John said the time you know you are in trouble in Harlem is when someone asks you the size of your shoes. If you give the right answer, your questioner will undoubtedly say, "Hey man. That's my size, too. Put your hands in the air." And you're on your way back home, barefoot.

Driving downtown once again, John said that one good thing about detective work is that you get rid of your violent urges in the day's work.

But then we passed a magnificent Bentley limousine, waiting for a green light, with some almost parodically rich and social types inside.

"Just once," said John, "I'd like to sail into a car like that, going around eighty miles an hour. Get 'em right in the grill."

. . . . .

"Maybe I'm wrong." This phrase had the slightest trace of poignance each time John used it. After I'd left him, I had to wonder what it would be like to grow up as a nice Catholic boy in a nice Catholic New York neighborhood, taught to honor God, home, and country. Everything neat. Mother cooks the stew, the corner cop's your friend, Jews are sissies, the flag makes your eyes water, and only mentally retarded girls put out. And then suddenly absolutely nothing fits; every step you take, another sacred vessel explodes in your face like a flashbulb—the flag is used to roll joints, veterans fling their medals at the White House, star pass receivers get arrested for indecent exposure, blacks get elected mayor all over the place, even appointed admiral, for Christ's sake.

It was enough to make a man go out and . . . well, write a book or something, which, as it turns out, is what John was doing the last time I talked to him on the phone. I thanked him for the glimpse he'd given me of the city through a detective's eyes, and much to my surprise he thanked me for the glimpse I'd given him of the same city through a writer's eyes. Then, with the tentative clack of a typewriter in the background, he excused himself and said he had to get back to his first chapter. And besides, the phone was probably bugged.

who's watching
the border?

It is a sad, weary-looking affair—ancient Buick, schoolteacher-ish lady behind the wheel, chewed-up muffler not helping to purify the California air. But considering some of the hard cases and the junk heaps that wash across the San Ysidro border checkpoint each day, it is a fairly routine-looking tableau. Customs inspector Tom Hardin thinks otherwise. It all looks a little "wrong" to him. He has been "on the line" at the Mexico-California entryway to the States for twenty minutes; in another minute or so, a colleague will come along and take his place, "bumping" him over to another of the nineteen lanes that service the most heavily trafficked entry point in the country. (Some thirty million people, in the year 1972, enter and leave the United States via San Ysidro.)

The schoolmarm type chugging up to lane 15 is no Ma Barker in appearance. What I'd learned, however, after several weeks at the border, is that you never know who is going to do what to whom. They had caught an eighty-year-old grandma with an ounce of heroin in each bra cup; a priest was nailed with "wheat" (marijuana) in his cassock; and they had put the cuffs on a cocaine-toting rabbi (a "Jewish rabbi," as Hardin put it). There's a picture in Customs headquarters of an inspector frisking Santa Claus, which sums up the amount of trust Customs people have in their fellow man. Dope comes across the line packed into the abdomens of corpses (Americans who died in Tijuana, say, and are being carted back to the states for burial), sewn into the coat linings of two-year-old girls with baby blue eyes, at the bottom of dirty diaper pails.

Originally published in *True*, May 1972.

One ring sent a flock of carrier pigeons across the border with junk attached to their necks; Border Patrolmen, alerted by an informer in Mexico, lined up with shotguns in the hills of Chula Vista to deal with this "threat."

Tom Hardin had filled me in on some of the more obvious tip-offs to border dope smuggling. A car that is low slung in the rear is worth a careful look. Often an extra spare tire accounts for the heavy-butt profile, but sometimes the spare is filled with kilos of hashish. You would think the old, beat-up cars would be the "dirty" ones, but smugglers tend to prefer late-model rental cars.

The driver's attitude has much to do with whether or not he will be searched. Some seem overly anxious to get across. Others will not meet the Customs inspector's eyes. There are the overly polite types who will practically jump out of the car with a "Yessirree, it sure is good to set foot in the good old USA again." Others won't roll their windows all the way down. On occasion, Hardin will reach in and put his hand over a man's heart. Don't bother to write your congressman. If there are reasonable grounds for suspicion of dope smuggling, Customs can turn you inside out in a search for drugs; even if you come up empty, there isn't a legal move you can make to get satisfaction.

What about the schoolmarm? Her car isn't exactly a Grand Prix entry, but apart from that she seems clean. The first thing that bothers Hardin is the clutter of candy wrappers on the front seats. Also a coke in a holder attached to the dashboard for convenient sipping. Heroin junkies on the way down or between shoot-up sessions are always thirsty and have an endless craving for sweets.

"What's your citizenship, ma'am?" An innocent enough question, but many Americans tend to hit the ceiling when they hear it. They're sure they look American. What do you *think* I am, some kind of gook or something? Most of the traffic at San Ysidro is straight American, naturalized Mexican-American, resident Mexican with a green card and a legal right to work in the United States, or Mexican with a white card enabling the bearer to stay in the States for seventy-two hours provided there is no travel farther than twenty-five miles from the border. (San Diego is only fifteen miles away.) But Nicaraguans and Costa Ricans have started to come in through San Ysidro, too. Illegally. Also Frenchmen, Germans, Japanese, what have you, landing in Mexico City and driving over—with phony documents—to the border checkpoint. The man from Tulsa who explodes and insists you can tell an American by looking at him is invited by Hardin to go up to Montreal and see if he can separate the Americans from the Canadians.

"United States," the driver answers calmly. Then Hardin wants to know if she is taking anything back from Mexico. Americans are allowed to bring along a maximum of one hundred dollars worth of purchases, but this aspect of Customs work doesn't particularly interest Hardin. As a result, it is generally the other inspectors who turn up illegal bottles of guava, six-pack gallon jugs of tequila (one fifth of liquor is the limit) and "pregnant" ladies with hepatitis-carrying parrots strapped to their bellies. His heart is in dope smuggling, and at the border checkpoint he is known as a "bird-dog," one of the best.

"I'm not bringing back anything," says the lady. If she were Mexican, she would have said "Nada," and if she *looked* Mexican, Hardin would have conducted the conversation in Spanish (all San Ysidro Customs men are fluent in that language), thereby heading off the possibility that a smuggler might later insist he didn't understand Hardin's question.

"Do you think I might see your driver's license, ma'am?" Some unschoolteacherly muttering here while she rummages in her purse. I know Hardin isn't especially interested in her license either—California licenses are easy enough to falsify. But it would give him a chance to study her hands, see how steady she holds them. Meanwhile, a quick poke inside with a flashlight at some of the more obvious hiding places for dope—under the seats, glove compartment, side storage pockets; had any of the screws been freshly loosened in some of the rear panels? On the outside of the car, a little tap at the tires with the heel of a flashlight to make sure they give off a hollow *thunking* sound, a feel around at the underpaneling. Check the taillights, favorite new hiding place for stuff. Have they been monkeyed with lately?

The photograph on her license makes her look like Raquel Welch, and I'm sure she's an impostor, but Hardin thinks it's a take-your-pick bet. With men, you can always tell. You don't even look at the face, just the shape of the ears. Even if a man has put on fifty pounds, ten years, and a beard, the ear shape never changes. With female styles switching every twenty minutes, it's almost impossible to check out a woman by her photograph.

"All right?" she asks.

"All right," he says, but doesn't hand back her license, so she has to reach for it and now he gets a better look at her hands. (Even when a Customs man asks a driver to open the trunk, it's not necessarily because he's suspicious about the contents. It gives him one more chance to study the driver's behavior. Lined up for two or three hours at a border checkpoint, the smuggler has a lot of time to think about fifteen-year penalties for the importation of hard narcotics. This waiting period has a tendency to stimulate the sweat glands. (While inserting the key to his car trunk, one hardened border smuggler dropped his bowels.)

Hardin spots something on the veins around the schoolteacher's wrists. Would she mind rolling up her sleeves? By this time she is into sailor talk, but she rolls one up and even I can see the trace marks. Mmmmm, interesting, says Hardin, what are these? Ever shot any smack? Well, no; uh, actually I did a little speed many years ago. How about lately? Well, actually I'm on the methadone program in L. A. And then the spool starts to unravel—never been married, two kids, welfare, heavy heroin addiction, little hooker experience here and there—not a pretty story. The fact that she is a junkie is not an arrestable offense, and it doesn't mean she's smuggling either; but most smugglers are also users, and Hardin feels she's a pretty good candidate for a skin search. A little yellow slip gets stuck beneath the windshield wipers. She'll move over to the "secondary area" where her car will be searched. A matron will be summoned to check out her body cavities. Nine times out of ten a female smuggler, traveling alone, will hide dope on her person and not in her car. When dope-carriers work in man-woman teams, the male generally is able to talk his lady friend into carrying the dope on her body—perhaps following some naïve notion that she is not likely to be searched. That goes for weapons, too. It's usually the lady member of the team who packs the "heat"—a loaded .45—under her skirt.

Most Customs men will stick on the yellow slip and turn the case over to another man in secondary, but Hardin prefers to walk the car up himself so there will be no break in the line of investigation. He guides her along slowly, his .357 magnum visible at his waist. One of the ironies of Customs work is that the government doesn't consider it hazardous duty. A short while ago, an agent named Nolan was kidnaped right off the line by three smugglers. A mile from the border, one of them put the barrel of Nolan's own gun against his temple and told him to get out of the car and start walking. He made a leap for a ditch and is still among the living. Another agent was dragged along the ground a quarter of a mile from the line by a drug dealer, the agent's arm caught in the door of the car. It is not unusual for an inspector to pry loose a cache of cocaine from the trunk of a station wagon and look up to find a .38 staring him in the face. Customs men don't mind missing out on the additional pay that goes with officially hazardous duty, but the thirty years they have to log before retirement is irritating; government people who do jobs classified as hazardous get to retire after twenty years.

The lady, meanwhile, turns out to be no lady at all. "Just my luck to run into an asshole," she says, as Hardin leads her into Customs headquarters.

"I see she's calling you by your second name," says one of Hardin's buddies.

Headquarters is about the size of a small movie lobby, with several benches for people waiting to be questioned, a few "slammers," or detention cells, and a couple of rooms for making skin searches.

A Mexican lad with heavily packed shoulders, a smuggling suspect, is calling everyone in sight "pig," threatening to tear the walls down. Some of this is for the benefit of his friends. If he can say it took five Customs men to subdue him, he's made something of a reputation. The immediate aim of the Customs officer is to see that he doesn't harm himself or some innocent party. One tactic is to let him cool off in the "slammer." The door to this little penitential cell is open. "Chico was here" and "Drugs mean peace" are written on the walls in blood. Supervising Inspector Bob Lasher, lean, flat bellied, a twenty-five-year Customs veteran and the king of nonviolent tongue lashing, has a whack at the fellow, telling him he ought to be ashamed of himself, there are suspected murderers, psychopaths crossing the border, the Customs man is only doing his job, the fellow has no right using abusive language. Suddenly cowed, the Mexican lowers his head. He is ashamed. Given the slightest chance he reverts to his essential style, which is gentle, cheerful. There is a fondness on the part of the Customs men for these people—much more so than for the Yankee tourist, a loser at El Caliente racetrack, who's been backed up at the border for three hours and comes up to the line in a rage. "I'd have an easier time getting through here if I were a commie, wouldn't I?"

Dottie Nigh, one of the two San Ysidro matrons, is on the premises, having just performed a skin search on a lovely, long-haired, college-girl drug suspect. "She gave me the modesty bit," says Dottie, chipper, bouncy, full of the World War II WAC lieutenant style. "If she's so modest, how come she was wearing her boyfriend's jockey shorts?"

The wife of an ex–Customs man, Dottie gets teased as part of her day's work. "Hey, Dot," says one desk man, "How about searching me?"

"You wouldn't like her searches," says another. "She'd make you scream."

"Yeah, with ectasy."

Dottie says she's been responsible for some two hundred body cavity drug seizures and that roughly one out of three women put in for search turns up with drugs on her person. I assume she's going to be a bit edgy about discussing her job, but curiously enough I can't get her to stop talking. A key part of her job is making sure that suspects don't suddenly swallow the evidence, flush it, or dispense with it in some other manner. Much heroin comes across in condoms that have been rolled into a ball and tied, with the excess rubber clipped off. (That is another tip-off to drug carrying at the line, clipped-off pieces of rubber, also Vaseline jars and Vaseline-marked handkerchiefs used to ease rectal drug insertions.) Suspects on their way to a search have been known to wolf down as many as a dozen of these heroin "golf balls." It's important for Dottie to get across to me that she doesn't really enjoy her work that much ("Most of the girls we search are pretty grungy") and would I please point out that apart from running her hand through teased hair and checking an occasional pulse, she doesn't actually touch the girls so much as instruct them on what to do during the internal checks. Hardin pitches in with the information that the record for bringing in drugs in a body cavity is held by a woman who took eight ounces of uncut cocaine across in her vagina.

Though hardly an old-timer, Dot has reached the unsurprisable stage of Customs work. She's searched women who've turned out to be men in drag, hermaphrodites, and an old, old lady carrying fireworks for the grandchildren in her girdle. Some of the lady smugglers, the old-timers, are quite artful in concealing drugs on their bodies; if Dot remains unsatisfied after a skin search, she is empowered to call in a physician for a more complete inspection. If a suspect has swallowed material, it may call for a stomach pumping.

Hadin's suspect is taken into a search room by Dot for a twenty-minute examination. Hardin and I go outside to the yard in secondary where cars with a hint of being dirty are checked out while their owners are being frisked and, if the evidence calls for it, skin searched. Sometimes drivers of cars assigned to secondary will suddenly bolt away, making a dash for San Diego. Customs men will not use their weapons in this circumstance—the San Diego Highway Patrol, with a booth on the line, usually catches up with the runaways. Many drivers show up at the border high on pills, unstable, this being their last chance to pop their pills before reaching the line. Other times, a man caught on the line with drugs will abandon his jalopy and make a wild dash back into Mexico to escape prosecution. This is NFL cornerback time and many a Customs man has had to take "embarrassment leave" for an injury suffered in tackling a runaway.

Hardin makes a thorough yet somehow perfunctory search of his suspect's car. It's his view that if she's carrying, it's going to turn up in the skin search and not in the car. He's looking for heroin. Otherwise he would use one of the eight San Ysidro "grass dogs," one of which, a small German shepherd, is happily prancing through a nearby camper, attempting to sniff out marijuana. The dogs are first rate at this work, playing in their off-duty time with a "bone" made of Acapulco Gold. Even camphor, used to neutralize the smell of marijuana, won't throw them off. The dogs are more than useful; so are the special jacks used to hoist the housing of drug-suspect family campers from their underpinnings to check for false floors.

On occasion, tip-offs on drug operations come from informants on both sides of the border. But I soon learn, working with Hardin, that 90 percent of Customs work rests on the inspector's instincts. Hardin is not quite so physically precision-fit as some of the other inspectors, but his eyes are an important clue to his ability. At thirty-seven, his eyes, lined and wise, make him seem ten years older—he's done an awful lot of careful looking at things. Born in San Diego, he spent five years on the Highway Patrol until a car edged him off a bridge, breaking his ribs, pelvis, and back. A year of no walking and then some work as an insurance investigator, private eye—and finally Customs work, which he does with a great deal of shrewdness and love. Unlike police people, many of whom tend to see their adversaries as "the enemy," Hardin, along with other men who work in Immigration and Border Patrol, has a certain easiness and generosity to his style. Even if the schoolteacher turns up with a bundle of heroin in her armpit, she is, after all, some kind of social problem and not a criminal one. The same goes for what they still refer to as a "wet," one who's worked his way from central Mexico to Tijuana, paid two hundred dollars and the family goat for phony credentials, and crossed the border on cow hooves so he can earn ten dollars a day working for a crooked American rather than the dollar a day he was grinding out at home. Is he a criminal? Hardin doesn't think so. On the other hand, he doesn't share the feeling of many Americans, frustrated for hours while trying to get through the Tijuana border, that Customs men should be tin soldiers who salute each car and say, " "Welcome to America, sir."

The schoolmarm's car comes up clean. Or seems to. The more you look at cars around Customs, the more it seems they are designed to aid drug smugglers. You would have to grind them to powder to make sure they're clean. Once drugs are found on a car, the vehicle becomes U.S. government property—to be sold later at auction. But if the car comes up drug free, it has to be returned to its owner in the original condition. Any scratches, it's the government's liability. I'm told of one Customs man who took apart a Datsun, convinced there was a load of cocaine in it. He couldn't find it and as he ripped away he started to sweat. Finally, when the thing was a bucket of nuts and bolts, he discovered the package he was looking for. "Thank God," he said, and fainted.

Hardin shows me a giant load of confiscated gasoline tanks that had been used to bring in "wheat." Room would be allowed in the tank for a gallon of gas—just enough to get across the border—and the rest of the tank filled with grass. Each smuggler who thought of it felt it was an original idea. The same was true of college kids who, for a while, were concealing their stuff in surfboards. It goes in trends. The only trouble with the gas tank device is that the gas gauge behaves in a funny way—an easy signal for a Customs man to pick up.

Wearily, almost fatalistically, Hardin gives up on the junkie-school-marm's wreck of a car and goes back to see what Dottie Nigh has come up with, if anything. *Nada,* and the teach goes muttering off to her sad and bleary-eyed existence with only one certainty in her life—that she'll be searched again another day. Hardin seems disappointed, perhaps because Customs men are aware of exactly who has made the most recent big seizure, exactly how much stuff each man has apprehended. They say it's good-natured competition, a way to build pride. In homicide bureaus, there's that same awareness of how many "kills" each man has on his record. In his heart, each man wants to win the MVP award.

We go back to the "line" where Hardin will bump Sol Harris, an ex–delicatessen owner, now a Customs man in charge, as a side duty, of providing questionably chewable pastrami for the boys on the graveyard shift. The car exhaust fumes are overpowering. "They say it's possible for a man to live as long as five years on the line," says Hardin with only half a grin.

Hardin feels a need to tell me about his toughest decision as a Customs man. A combat vet from Nam came across one day, not exactly a stump of a man, but a charred and disfigured one from head to toe. "The whole record of his life, past, present, and future, was on his body." A load of smack in the car. The arrangement was for this man's buddy to "fix" him every six hours. Hardin came within a hair of "flushing" the drug, but decided not to. He's wondered whether he made the right decision ever since.

. . . . .

It's late now, time for Hardin to go off and the graveyard shift to come on. People are coming across the line with *piñatas,* doodads, single bottles of tequila, but no junk to speak of. Some of them, in the Customs phraseology, "look like shit, but check out okay."

Before he leaves, Hardin takes me over to an entry lane that is manned by Art Holohan, an Immigration man, someone he obviously respects considerably. In general, the Immigration people are older than those assigned to Customs, a bit slack and gone to seed. Not so with Holohan, a lean, twenty-year veteran at the job of smoking out illegals.

He makes it clear that he is not in the least angered by the aliens trying to get across. They earn a buck a day in central Mexico and there's no welfare arrangement south of the border. Slaving away in a tuna factory, at a below-the-minimum-wage level, they can improve their situation ten times over by working in the States. On the border they say every Mexican dreams of dying in Los Angeles, and it's small wonder. If Holohan has it in for anyone, it's the farmers and factory owners who employ illegal aliens at below-the-line salaries (two are sometimes listed on one paycard), holding an obvious sword over the Mexican peasant's head. If he squawks, the owner will shout out the dread word: *Immigration.*

Holohan walks me over to the secondary Immigration building. Talk about your tired, poor, huddled masses. A beautiful Guatemalan girl, a baby sucking at her breast, claims to be Chicago born. A Tijuana man swears he's going up to Canada for a little hunting, but he's got six bucks in his pocket and the inspector happens to know that hunting licenses alone cost seventy-five dollars. Next case. A man from Veracruz insists he's a Mexican lawyer; if so, what are those huge farmhand callouses doing on his hand? A well-dressed American woman is "upset" because three illegals have been found huddled together in the trunk of her new Eldorado and she hasn't the faintest idea how they got there. Oh yes, she stopped off momentarily at the racetrack, and the parking lot attendant must have slipped the three aliens into her trunk then. The chances are she's gotten two hundred bucks a head for them; she'll go to court on a smuggling rap. A Cuernavaca businessman is incensed because he can't get papers that'll let him bring his thirteen-year-old "daughter" across to see her grandmother. She's licking on a lollipop, but she has bazooms out to here; she's thirteen going on thirty. It's Holohan's guess that she spent her formative years in a Panama whorehouse.

Much of Holohan's work has to do with checking out phony documents. As Immigrations men become more sharp eyed, the counterfeiters become more sophisticated. From the window of the Immigrations office you can look out on the Mexican side and see deals being made. A seventy-two-hour, twenty-five-mile pass goes for two hundred dollars; the more sought-after green card, enabling an alien to work in the States, might bring five hundred dollars, the life savings of a central Mexican farmhand. Not much fun when he gets picked off the line in five seconds flat and sent back to his shack in Ensenada. That's all that will happen to him usually; the courts would sink under the load if each of the illegals had to be tried. If he's actually altered documents himself, he's in somewhat hotter water. And if he's a big leaguer, a "coyote" who actually heads up a smuggling ring, they'll throw the book at him. Except that the "coyotes" stay safely behind the lines and don't get caught.

A well-dressed kid from Guanajuato State has been nailed with a phony social security card that looks like it goes for a dime in the toy department at Woolworth's. Where did he get it? He found it on the street in Tijuana. Everyone finds their phony papers on the street in Tijuana. If this were true, you'd have to hack your way through the city with a paper cutter. Under gentle pressure, he "confesses" he bought the card for two hundred dollars; it was guaranteed to fool the authorities. He'll be sent back and if he ever catches up with the salesman who stuck him for his life's savings, it's going to be no more Mr. Nice Guy.

Holohan goes back to the "line" (there are one or two Immigration lanes, seventeen for Customs) and tells me about the ones who don't bother with documents. A young girl comes across under the hood of a station wagon, wrapped around the motor. They find her with yard-long blisters on her belly. Another Mexican is taken across under a car's hood. The Border Patrol spots the operation, his two buddies panic when the hood latch won't work and leave him under there. Immigration finds him dead, his groin burned off. A Mexican comes across chained to the rear axle of a wagon; one bump on the highway and he's a headless horseman. They find forty-two illegals packed into a vinegar truck, involuntarily stoned on vinegar. Half a dozen more show up in the rear compartment of a station wagon, covered over with a ton of broken glass. Another fellow, admittedly small, is found curled up in a gas tank. You'd think they'd give some of the more adventurous ones an *e* for effort and let them stay, but they don't.

Holohan stops one driver who strikes him as being a little fishy. (He's equipped to deal with drug cases, just as Customs men are checked out on illegals.) If the fellow was born in Florida, as he says he was, how come he doesn't know the name of one of the Florida senators? And shouldn't he know that the last three letters of the alphabet are x, y, z? He gets a yellow slip and Holohan sighs. He thinks his group does a good job, but for all he knows they may nail only one out of six illegals.

So much for the official entry point at San Ysidro. What about that small matter of the 1,945-mile U.S.-Mexican border that stretches from San Ysidro to Brownsville, Texas? Can't an alien simply step across the border and be in the United States? The answer is, he can, but you can also gain a yard against the Dallas Cowboys' defensive line. A first down is another story. Some of this boundary line has a ferociously fenced-up look to it; alongside these sections, almost ridiculously, are sections with a couple of pathetic-looking strands of wire that wouldn't bother a blind man. So actually setting foot in the U.S.A. is the easy part.

But for the illegal arriving in Smuggler's Gulch with a sack of salt around his neck and a Mason jar of water in his kick, actually getting somewhere is another story. The terrain, which in some sections looks like wartime Anzio, doesn't help things along much. But his main problem is that group of fourteen hundred "defensive linebackers," the U.S. Border Patrol. Few in number, they know the area the way a trained internist knows Gray's *Anatomy*. They work out of four-wheel-drive vehicles, on foot, and they can sign-cut or track a man from an overhead Super Cub. They use walkie-talkies and even though I'm pledged not to get into this, they work with "sensors" developed in Vietnam that can electronically detect "intrusion" (human heat, metal, or ground movement) in the dark. (I'm breaking "security" on this because I read about it in a San Diego newspaper.) I bounced around some of this border territory in a jeeplike conveyance with Georgia-born Al Chapman, a good-natured navy retiree at forty-two, fullback type, Border Patrolman. What he is proudest of is that the Border Patrol is the only *uniformed* federal enforcement agency. FBI? No uniforms. Texas Rangers? Not federal. I couldn't figure out why this was so important to him, especially since most people couldn't decide what he was, some taking him for a game warden and asking if the fish were biting.

With all the sensors and Super Cubs and zone-defense techniques (helicopters, surprisingly, haven't worked out: they're too expensive for the good they do), much of the work comes down to how good the individual Border Patrolman is at sign-cutting. You'd think a farm boy would be more effective as a tracker, but they had a kid from New York who could leave the farmers in the dust. You never know. One man can look at a footprint and see a footprint. Another can look at it and see that there are bugs inside, which means it has been there for so many hours. Up ahead, there'd be another print with fewer bugs, a fresher track. Some patrolmen can work this out so precisely that all they have to do is sit under a bush and wait for the illegals to walk right into their arms. There has been a certain step-up in violence upon capture, but by and large the illegals come quietly. Chapman feels it has to do with how authoritatively a Border man carries himself. If he acts shaky, he might wind up having to use his gun. If the Customs men are fit, the Border men are fitter. They have to qualify four times a year with their revolvers. They win their share of national marksmanship awards, too.

The alien's objective once across the border is to move as fast and as far as possible, attempting to reach Los Angeles or even Seattle. One of his problems is covering his tracks. In darkness, using binoculars, Chapman says he can tell the color of a man's shirt at one hundred yards. For the most part, the alien travels at night. Some strap on cow hooves, forgetting that a four-legged animal has a gait different from a man with two legs wearing the hooves. Some walk backwards to give the impression that they're entering Mexico rather than leaving it. Others use the Sir Walter Raleigh technique, spreading their coats and taking one step at a time. They come across barefoot, in ski harnesses, often using wild spongelike contraptions. Some will change shoes four times, carrying the spares in a sack. The toughest to track, oddly enough, is the man who walks on cardboard, which leaves hardly any trace at all. He spreads a few squares ahead, steps on them, reaches behind and picks up the ones he's already stepped on—slow going, but effective.

The stray illegal, unconnected, penniless, with little or no English to work with, has about as much chance of getting anywhere as a nun in Caesar's Palace. But organized smuggling of aliens across the border is big business. Some of it is done by Americans down on their luck, who at the going rate of $250 a pop aren't so down on their luck anymore. Chapman fills me in on the system. The would-be border crosser arrives in Tijuana and is immediately conspicuous, a country bumpkin on Fifth Avenue. The "coyote" has his agents on the street who quickly pick off the potential customer, find out how much money he has, and does he have relatives in LA? For the going price, he'll guarantee him safe passage across the border, food, perhaps a job. Once half a dozen or so prospects are gathered up, a "guide" takes them across to some mountain hideout, then leads them to a highway where a car will be waiting. Perhaps one of the aliens can drive. The keys are hidden in a bush on the side of the road. If there are no drivers in the group, a "mule" will drive them, perhaps holing them up in a motel until a fog settles and they have a better chance of slipping through the deeper checkpoints at Temacula or Clemente. You'd think it would be easy to get up to Los Angeles from Tijuana, but the alien is pretty much corralled into an ever-tightening bottleneck. There are only so many ways to go. The bus terminals are covered. So are the airports. There are only a couple of highways, entry points, and these are well manned. And it's a pretty long walk.

We bounce along a while longer, Chapman telling me that if I see any rattlers, not to pay any attention to them. There were close to sixty thousand apprehensions last year in Chapman's Chula Vista Border Patrol Sector. Some say that means they nailed five out of six, others says one out of six. Those statistics again. Whatever the case, the smugglers have an effective intelligence network, constantly changing their offense to counteract the shifting Border Patrol zone defense.

Chapman isn't getting rich on the job, but he enjoys his work more than anyone I've ever run across, which has got to make him pretty rich after all. This feeling leads to an enormous sympathy for the hungry, shivering, proud men who practically crawled to the border from the mud shacks of Ojocaliente, trying to find a little daylight in their lives. By this time, I'm seeing double and not enjoying *my* work too much, so I say good-bye to Chapman, promising to fill out a Border Patrol application if they'll let me keep my beard and my evil ways.

By this time, I've spent a lot of time with men responsible for keeping drugs and "undesirables" out of the country. I start to wonder now about what would happen if, say, the Canadian and Mexican borders were simply thrown open. Putting the cuffs on kids carrying a few joints certainly hasn't put much of a dent in the drug trade. The major operators seem to be getting on as comfortably as ever. I've always felt that the heavy guns ought to be directed at the source of the appetite that makes people go to drugs in the first place. Barring criminals, psychopaths, smallpox carriers, etc., what if the borders were simply opened up to all those "undesirable" Mexicans? Hitler felt that America was no military threat to him because it was "mongrelized," one of his slight miscalculations. What if we let ourselves get a little more mongrelized? A little seasoning never hurt mashed potatoes. Scar tissue is tougher than normal tissue. There might be a Pablo Casals or a Dr. Denton Cooley languishing away in a Chula Vista "slammer," waiting for a bus to take him back to Orizaba. I don't know. An obvious problem is that the "illegal" is taking a livelihood away from the Mexican-American. Whatever the case, for the time being we've got a new kind of "cop" working the line at San Ysidro, patrolling the brush country of Horsethief Canyon. Very little gung ho here. Easy, generous men, none feeling particularly heroic when they make a bust. That has to count for something.

tom noguchi

espite the freakish side of California and an occasional Charles Manson-style aberration, death still seems an anachronism on the West Coast, a particular insult to the sun, the orange juice, and the sweet and lazy pace of life along the Pacific. The seasons shift so imperceptibly, time passes with such sublety, that people on the West Coast are shocked to find themselves old and thoroughly embarrassed to learn they are dying. Yet Californians, golden haired, bronzed, spilling over with health, do die just as other people do, some sixty thousand of them slipping off each year in Los Angeles alone. Of this group, twenty thousand or so expire under something of a cloud, thereby coming to the attention of the coroner's office, which sifts through them, turning back some six thousand and agreeing to investigate the others. (The coroner would tend to come in on suicides, homicides, deaths from scuba diving, abortions, industrial accidents, traffic deaths, ones in which the deceased had not been seen by a doctor within ten days of expiring—in short, "any death by trauma.") If the bodies are discovered within a ten-mile radius of downtown Los Angeles, they are taken to the morgue at the Hall of Justice. Beyond that zone, they are seen to by one of the outlying morgues in a rotating—are you ready for this—"morgue of the month" plan.

Each year, the county in question being Los Angeles, there are at least a handful of cases it is difficult to avoid categorizing as "juicy." Because of their bizarre nature, the celebrity of the deceased, and the potential for a foul-up before a global audience—in these blue-ribbon cases it is generally the head coroner himself who seizes the reins. Thelma Todd, Carole Landis, Maria Montez, William Desmond Taylor—the Los Angeles morgue has turned up some all-stars. Since 1967, in a weird

Originally published as "The Art of Autopsy" in *Esquire*, December 1971.

piece of casting, Hollywood's "celebrity coroner" has been a brilliant, bouncy, fun-loving Japanese-American named Thomas T. (Tsunetomi) Noguchi, whose grisly but imposing "credits" include autopsies on Inger Stevens, Janis Joplin, Sharon Tate, and Bobby Kennedy ("one of the most brilliant of all time" according to fellow pathologists). Brilliance, autopsy-wise, does not refer to superb craftsmanship with the surgical knife so much as skill at management and organization. There had been worldwide criticism of the John F. Kennedy autopsy, the renowned Dr. William Eckert of Kansas coming away with the view that it represented "a black eye for forensic medicine." Both the late senator's family and the Los Angeles Coroner's Department were anxious to avoid the Dallas confusion and to have the Bobby Kennedy autopsy come off without a hitch. A veteran of four thousand personally administered autopsies (tack on, if you like, another five-thousand-odd reviews of other people's work) Noguchi was nevertheless put to the test by the late Senator Kennedy. He does not exactly sail into an autopsy with a song on his lips, but by the same token he has trained himself to be unemotional and to see a corpse not as a person but as the "physical evidence of someone's existence." He feels that "it would not do for a coroner to break down and weep bitterly over each case." Still, for all of his objectivity, the doctor has limits and makes it a practice to avoid doing friends or relatives. Not exactly a mover among the Hollywood film colony, Noguchi nevertheless does know Ernest Borgnine and Donald O'Connor casually, and it is assumed that if either of their numbers came up, he would fob the work off on assistants. In the case of Senator Kennedy, Noguchi's feelings were deep and personal and he would have been only too glad to pass the work on to a subordinate. "But there was no way," says the Los Angeles coroner. "For fifteen minutes, at the scene, I was stunned. Fortunately, there were so many people at work. What I did to fend off shock was to compile data. Mr. So and So, ask Dr. So and So to do so and so. In our work, for technical reasons, we cover the face of the deceased. I was so happy about that. I did not want to be alone with Senator Kennedy."

As to the others in his star-studded file, Janis Joplin was just another day's work to the coroner, her Big Brother and the Holding Company style light years away from the "boogie woogie" that so charmed Noguchi as a boy in Yokosuka and which his Chopin-minded mother declared out of bounds because of its "sexy connotation." At the time of the Joplin OD, Noguchi's thoughts happened to be on Judy Garland, "because I loved *A Star Is Born*," and he was later to invite the London coroner who supervised the Garland autopsy to come over and lend a hand with the Joplin case. "I did not do Dorothy Dandrige," he points out with some modesty, but as an assistant coroner in 1962, he was called to investigate the death by suspected suicide of a girl named Marilyn Monroe. "How odd," the deputy coroner thought to himself, "that this girl should have the same name as the famed international film star." As to the Manson/Sharon Tate case, Noguchi, who calmly ticked off precise descriptions to a jury of Voityck Frykowski's fifty-one stab wounds, Sharon Tate's sixteen, and Abigail Folger's twenty-eight, calls it the most bizarre in his experience but will add nothing more, understandably, since the case is in litigation.

As a boy in Japan, Noguchi recalls a penchant for "benign mischief," one which took the form of chalking up teacher's trousers, seeing to it that their desk drawers would not open, and rigging up red bulbs that popped on when he felt they were passing on ridiculous information. He owns up to being put in closets a lot, as a punishment. Another of his rascalities was the setting of booby traps for the postman, Noguchi himself falling into the first one and almost shearing off his chin. "I vowed," the coroner says, a bit ominously, "that I would never fall into my own booby trap again." The mischief-making style continued on through his teens, and when Japan went under in 1945, his comment was, "Oh, well, win some, lose some," and off he went to California to practice medicine in the winner's camp. To keep their sanity in a joyless profession, American coroners are known to practice among themselves a grisly form of graveside humor, referring jocularly to corpses as "stiffs" and to "floaters" (bodies taken from the water) as "job security," since ordinary doctors prefer to avoid working on them at all costs. The japing coroner is to be taken as seriously as the newspaperman on a sluggish day who wishes for a good rape or a nice healthy industrial fire. Dr. Noguchi, the Yokosuka prankster, who refers to his work as "horizontal medicine," had a style that was tailor made for the American Coroners' Laugh Academy. Several years ago, Dr. Noguchi was dismissed from his post and became the center of a wild and hair-raising investigation before the Los Angeles County Civil Service Commission, a case that charged him with "doing a gleeful death dance" at the prospect of performing an autopsy on the dying Senator Kennedy, praying for a loaded Boeing 727 to crash into the International Hotel so that he would become famous, and standing at the door of the LA morgue, crowded two deep with flu victims, and with outstretched arms saying, "You're mine, all mine." Though the hearing left Noguchi penniless, it firmed up the spine of the Japanese community in LA and eventually sent the coroner back to his old post, clean as a whistle and with full back pay. It also turned up some hints of a vendetta against the doctor by the universities and medical schools that didn't want him hired in the first place. But somewhere in the picture was an echo of those benign graveside chuckles, badly misunderstood this time and perhaps shoving the boy from Yokosuka back into one of his own booby traps again, this time with near-fatal results.

At first it appeared that Noguchi would not fight his dismissal; the seventy-seven-count indictment by powerful L. S. Hollinger, the county's administrative chief, seemed so massive, so thunderous, so outrageous and all-encompassing that no man could possibly survive its onslaught. Like a good West Coast Oriental, Dr. Noguchi was expected to cower in shame and silence and meekly slip away. Not unlike the hundred thousand World War II American-Japanese who allowed themselves to be trundled off to internment camps after Pearl Harbor. But someone had failed to count on a certain "heavy" lady, to use the current parlance, who (1) teaches immunology, serology, and electron miscroscopy at California State College, (2) had been yanked out of UCLA in 1941 and tossed into one of those wartime internment camps, (3) was now Mrs. Tom Noguchi, and (4) was not about to do a repeat shuffle off to Amachi Detention Center. Though it was considered very "un-Japanese" of them, the Noguchi's prepared to do battle with city hall. At first, many in the usually timid Japanese community had winced at the charges, especially the ones proposing that Noguchi was off his rocker, mental illness carrying a special stigma in all of Asia; they hated him for even being accused of it. But as the hearings moved along, and the county's case began to smack of a World War II fear campaign, local Japanese began to rally round and finally to support Noguchi to the hilt with a defense fund called JUST (Japanese United in the Search for Truth). It's a lucky thing someone was backing him, because the charges began to come at the little coroner like a missile attack: He had prayed for Mayor Sam Yorty's helicopter to crash with press people around; he was a notorious Cloud Nine pill popper; he referred to Asians as "yellow submarines," threw his shoes at one employee and called him a black bastard; he kept saying to a certain Indian-born Dr. Gupta, "Never trust an American"; on occasion, he would yank out his coroner's knife and threaten to do autopsies on live county officials; he wanted to start a "forensic mafia" and lock up all coroner work west of the Mississippi; he would from time to time jump up from his desk, slap a wall map and cry "This is my jurisdiction"; he had actually (this one really hurt) mucked up the Kennedy autopsy. One by one the charges were picked off, neatly fielded, and discredited by Godfrey Isaacs, Dr. Noguchi's brilliant defense attorney, who produced ten witnesses who swore they never heard Noguchi pray for major disasters; expert pathologists who practically wept when they observed the completeness of the Kennedy autopsy; secretaries who said he was a fine boss, put fresh flowers on their desks each Monday, and paid for the coroners' Christmas office party out of his own pocket; and still more experts who pointed out that it was no big thing for a Japanese to stand around looking elated during a disaster since "they smile no matter what happens. . . ." Some three thousand pages of testimony and ninety-three witnesses later, the hearings wheezed to a halt and Noguchi emerged, totally exonerated and permitted to go back to his old job. Indeed, the ball ended up bring thrown back in the court of his accuser, whose own competence was questioned and whose job seemed a bit shaky for a time. The local Japanese were thrilled, the nisei saying what a terrific country it was and loving the Bill of Rights and the *sensei* saying come off it, the way to get it on is with Japanese Power and why should we leave the field to the Panthers and the Brown Berets. Plopping down in his old coroner's chair, Noguchi, surrounded by admiring assistant coroners and coronerettes, said, "Oh, I feel great, I feel good," and Mrs. Elizabeth Palmer, a secretary who had backed Noguchi at the hearing, seemed to speak for the entire team when she said, "I feel it was a victory for a great boss, one I did not wish to say sayonara to."

As a boy in Yokosuka, Tom Noguchi was fascinated by the fighter planes at the nearby military base, spending long, futile hours trying to shape strips of bamboo into working Zero-like wingspreads. Later, when the American P-38s came over on raids, he was even more impressed by them. "We'd gotten all this encouraging news about how well Japan was doing and then I'd look up at the P-38s and say, 'Hey, wait a minute, if we're doing so hot, what are *they* doing *here!*'" But it was the B-29s that really got him. "The first time they came over, I looked up and estimated some five hundred of them in three waves. I was so impressed by the magnificence of the formations that I forgot how dangerous it all was and almost got blown to bits." The raids hammered Noguchi's medical school into rubble, on one occasion causing him to lose a silk umbrella, but the next day it was class as usual, right in the ruins, the students wearing helmets and shoulder pads, the professor handing out exam papers, then scooping them up at the sound of enemy raiders and leaping into a foxhole. "You had to learn to cover the entire exam in the shortest time possible because the professor would sit in the foxhole and score you whether you had finished or not." The grim time for Noguchi was the end of the war, with the coroner-to-be in his first year of medical school, his mother heading up the Japanese Red Cross (a position normally held by the empress) and the country having its territory sliced away. After four years of hearing the Americans described as "apes with lots of hair and tails," suddenly there they were with their candy and their height and their smiles and their directness and undeviousness, qualities Noguchi, who had honorable professor'd his way through school and honorable sir'd his way through life, had never dreamed existed. All this American stuff really knocked him out, and he bought the whole frank, hand-shaking, open-faced, I'm-from-Seattle package right on the spot. Now, twenty-six years later, he is almost parodically American. To come upon the nation's number one coroner now, handsome, wavy haired, beaming with fitness (skiing, scuba diving, skydiving any day now), brazenly frank ("You're here because I'm controversial, right?"), cheerfully ambitious (he envisions a U.S. Coroner's Office and could probably be persuaded to head it up), is to feel you've met a posterish, big-screen, slightly stylized, living version of all those frank, outspoken, cards-on-the-table American Virtues, swallowed without a second thought by the adoring young medical student greeting the GIs in the rubble of Tokyo. You would think his dismissal and those six anguished weeks in the dock might have made him a little suspicious of the open-faced Yank style. He does appear that way for a while, dressed neatly for the interview, ushering you into the "smoking section" of his office (little laugh here) and introducing his wife, the Noguchis at home around the coroner's office, very folksy, ABC-TV family stuff. It is the "Bobby Kennedy Death Dance" hearing that has been the touchiest part of his administration, and you suggest that perhaps he would prefer to pass over this sensitive area. But before the suggestion is out of your mouth, he becomes frank, ballsy, undevious, never-duck-an-issue GI-Tom Noguchi again. "Oh no, no, not at all, I insist on talking about the hearing, no problem." He then tells you that for years the LA County Medical Association and the deans of the UCLA and Southern Cal medical schools were accustomed to having a sort of "control" over the corner's office and more or less naming the coroner. This would work out especially well if one of their people, tired of the university life, wanted a cushy two-year stint in the coroner's office. "But what if one of their surgeons made a little mis-take on an incision," Noguchi asked himself, "and what if he suddenly had a little death-by-negligence on his hands." Noguchi decided it just would not do for the coroner to be a captive of the medical schools— or of the police for that matter, who often had to be investigated in questionable shootings. Considered too young, too inexperienced, and a bit too independent, he nevertheless got the job for six months, on a probationary basis, with the feeling in the air that they would watch him carefully and shoot him down on the slightest technicality. "Within the six months," says Noguchi, "suddenly there was the Kennedy case and the helicopter crash case and I got commendations from all over the world and that took the wind out of their sails. When the hearings finally came up, they never dreamed I would stand up. But you see I just didn't *feel* like an oppressed minority fellow. I didn't *feel* like a humble little Japanese. There wasn't any question I would fight the charges." As to the support from Japanese groups, Noguchi seems a bit uncomfortable about it; indeed, after meeting him awhile, it is as easy to imagine him marching shoulder to shoulder with Asian solidarity groups as it is to picture Philip Roth hosting a Hadassah convention. "Japanese food once in awhile in Little Tokyo and that's about it. Of course I didn't want to be the first Asian-American, our new term, like Black-American, to resign under a cloud."

But enough of the recent past; he would much rather talk about his Yokosuka boyhood, the prankish gadgeteering side of which came to an abrupt ending one day when his younger brother Kazuo developed cerebral palsy and young Tom (then Tsunetomi) told his Honorable Father, a busy eye, ear, nose, and throat man, that he would take full responsibility for the sickly fourth-grader. For two years, he carted his brother three miles back and forth to school on a specially constructed bike with the crippled Kazuo strapped to it. One day, the school had a showing of movies and Tom, who had returned home, forgot that he had left his brother behind to watch them. He found him hours later, looking at an empty screen in a bare auditorium, and since Kazuo couldn't go to the bathroom unaided, he had soiled himself. "I went over and smacked him," says Noguchi, "and then I felt terrible about it." As he tells the story, he lowers his head in mixed rage and shame and he is right back in that Yokosuka movie auditorium, and you feel he might go out a window, even though the forty-year-old Kazuo is doing fine, as owner of a busy coffee shop in Tokyo. The bike story is revealing in that it points up Noguchi's natural flair for responsibility, but it doesn't really indicate how he got interested in forensic medicine and the coroner game. He is ready for you on that one, telling of a day he happened to be sitting in his father's office when the old man was swabbing the throat of a young sore throat victim with iodine. Suddenly, the patient keeled over backward, went into a coma, and died. Well, it looked like a clear-cut case of negligence, the newspapers and prosecutor insisting that Dr. Noguchi was a careless user of loose cotton and that the patient had choked to death. That's three years behind bars under Section 211 of the Japanese Penal Code if he's convicted. But the elder Noguchi took the unusual step—in Japan—of ordering an immediate autopsy, which showed that the cotton had stayed lodged in the young man's teeth and that he had probably died of some weird allergy to iodine. Case dismissed, except that Tom Noguchi, torn at the time between law and medicine, decided it would probably be a good idea to take on both of them—forensic medicine, learning not only the causes of death but the legal aspects of medicine. People don't usually make lifetime career decisions on the spot, but it makes a fine "At that moment I realized that the trombone was for me" type of anecdote. In any case, that was 1945, the year of those magnificent B-29 formations and the candy-carrying GIs, and Noguchi began to keep a secret eye on the United States ("a country that could beat the hell out of us") wisely disregarding Japanese nomenclature in the medical texts and asking his honorable professor if he could take his medical exams in English. After that, it was Orange County General Hospital's maternity ward (two hundred babies delivered the first month), hours and hours in the student nurses' ward "just practicing my English"; Barlow Sanitorium to recover from pneumonia and meet Miss Right, Hisako Nishihara, who won his heart by shipping ozoni and mochi into the ward instead of the traditional "rabbit food"; and finally, on to become head medical examiner in a county of more than seven million potential coroner cases.

Where does a man go after winning the Tate-Joplin-Kennedy Coroner's Triple Crown? It's a tough act to follow, but it doesn't matter, because to Noguchi, every death, even a nonfamous one, "has a little twist to it." A compulsive reader of mysteries (Erle Stanley Gardner, a friend, once called him and said, "A man finds a petrified finger. Go with it"), Noguchi feels that most doctors are too conservative in their outlook and ought to read "crazy stuff" because sometimes a murderer will get an idea from it. To illustrate, Noguchi, in his new suit, suddenly falls to the floor, eyes rolling, tongue protruding, to demonstrate a recent "crazy" case in which a man was found by his roommate, screaming for help, a towel around his neck. He choked to death and the police were convinced the roommate had helped things along. Clear-cut homicide, right? Guess again. Noguchi's autopsy turned up cancer of the stomach; the towel man had indeed choked to death on blood and vomit, but it was strangulation, and certain towel tests showed there hadn't been any pressure applied by the roomie. Score one more for the coroner's office.

Noguchi insists that whether the deceased is a high-ranked exec at Warner Brothers or a fellow in children's ready-to-wear makes no difference at all, autopsy-wise, and that the basic approach is the same. Each one takes from four to six hours, although a heavyweight case, since it involves press conferences and elaborate on-the-scene investigations, will often tie up the coroner for ten days. Noguchi can still recall his first autopsy, back at Tokyo Medical School. "The professor opened the plastic bag and frankly, I didn't feel so good." After that, it was business as usual, although with little difficulty he can think of a forensic gaffe or two. One involved a fifty-year-old baby-sitter who died, according to the fledgling coroner's autopsy, from a "coronary narrowing." Soon afterward, the concerned parents of a baby that had been under the sitter's care called and said their child had meningitis and did the baby-sitter by any chance suffer from the same disease? With red face, Noguchi realized that he had not done an examination of the baby-sitter's brain and that he had committed what turned out to be one of his rare coroner-type boners.

As to the general Noguchi style around the morgue, the man who once tried to make Zeroes and P-38s out of bamboo is still a relentless gadgeteer, proud, for example, of his department's use of the postmortem angiogram, normally used to locate brain tumors in the living and now, under Noguchi's influence, set to ferreting them out in the dead. Drugs remain an ever-mounting, frustrating, subtle, and very often undetected cause of death. "It's easy to bump off a junkie," says Noguchi, "just give him something a little stronger." The coroner is inching ever closer to "an instrument that will deliver precise drugprints, much the same as fingerprints and voiceprints."

"We don't really understand drug deaths at the moment," the coroner feels. "LSD, for example, is not detectable in the blood under present methods." New York heroin is generally "cut" with quinine (which attacks the heart), and Los Angeles heroin by procaine (which anesthetizes the brain), and what happens is that many deaths result from the "cut" stuff and not from pure heroin. If the medical examiner isn't looking for one of the contaminants, he won't find it and the death (which might have been someone murdering a junkie by giving him an overdose) will go down on the certificate as heart failure.

A question you're compelled to ask is what's the toughest kind of homicide to solve, and once again, Noguchi feels it's in the drug department, "the millionaire suffering from heart disease whose heir is a faithful butler giving him medicine and perhaps an extra pinch of digitalis which does the trick." A favorite case of Noguchi's is *People v. Ashi*, involving a man who had enormous success pulling off "insulin quickies," disposing of three wives and four relatives in this manner and scooping up their insurance before he was brought to bay. "With all of our science," says Noguchi, a bit mournfully, "insulin in the blood is still very difficult to detect."

Another passion of Dr. Noguchi's is organ transplantation. You need the consent of kin to have an organ donated in California and Noguchi would like to have the whole process speeded up. Kidneys make fine transplants if you can get them going within half an hour after the patient dies. They can be stored in refrigerators for more than thirty hours and flown across the world in that period for use in remote areas of the globe. But it's difficult to get the consent within that half an hour, and as far as Noguchi is concerned, he would just as soon go with the kidneys now and get the consent later. The LA Coroners' Department, with Noguchi's encouragement, will lend a hand to anyone who needs a kidney, liver, or heart.

Any day now, Los Angeles will open a new $3.5-million coroner's building, and you would think this would keep Tom Noguchi happy down at the morgue; but sooner or later he begins to speculate dreamily about a United States center for forensic science, perhaps based in Washington, one which would bring together experts in medical engineering, psychiatry, pathology, toxicology: all those skills the coroner has to bring in on his own initiative now and that most small-town coroners obviously don't have at their disposal. "After all, you do want to trust the death certificate, and at the moment, you really can't. If a person in a small town dies after a minor accident, his relations are entitled to know if the accident contributed to the death. That would make them candidates for double indemnity. But very often, it goes down as natural causes, because of a lack of expertise in the coroner's office. The same goes for death by rifle wound. The sheriff says suicide and the family has that trauma to contend with. But it may have been an accident that only a medical engineer would be able to discover." And you can't find a medical engineer in Nowheresville, Wyoming.

As to an overall philosophy of death, the busy Noguchi ("This human computer reviews one thousand deaths a year") has not actually had time to cook one up; he does feel that the hang-up about death is that people associate it with pain while in actualilty, "the person who dies doesn't suffer a fraction as much as we think." He does not take the Eastern view and see himself coming back for another go-round as an insect. "I'd be delighted, however, to turn up as a fellow who finally gets to finish law school." Noguchi's own dad, the "loose cotton" man, is still alive, still practicing at eighty-three, and recently toured thirty-three states ("There was no holding him back") in a first trip to America. One man Noguchi admired tremendously was John Foster Dulles, who, dying of cancer, worked quietly at his desk until the day he went under; Noguchi, too, would like to live until 110 or so and die with his scalpels on.

Unless he gets a bit too daring as a middle-aged sky diver, the chances are strong that he is going to be top dog at the LA morgue for quite some time to come. Thus, the next Hollywood superstar to wander fatally off life's highway can be assured the personal attentions of the smiling gentleman from Yokosuka, who aside from a graveyard chuckle or two, which won't be heard anyway, will minister to the celebrity with an expertise borne of thousands of trips down the autopsical pike. And as further and perhaps ultimate testimony to the courtesy extended at the LA morgue, Noguchi, unable to resist a final macabre rib tickler, points out that he himself has reserved a slab "upstairs."

"So that I can be assured of absolutely first-rate service."

PART FOUR

elsewhere

my life among
the stars

I wasn't getting along with a Hollywood producer. He was trying to figure out a way to put me in my place. He thought and thought and finally he said: "You know your trouble? You will always be one of those hundred-thousand-dollar guys."

. . . . .

In the late sixties, I was summoned to the offices of "Jolly Joe" Levine, the legendary producer of *The Graduate*, who had admired my play *Scuba Duba*.

"You will never again have to worry about money," he said to me.

I felt wonderful when I left his office. What a feeling—never again to have to worry about money. But he was wrong. Not a single day since has passed without my having to worry about money.

. . . . .

The nearest thing to a star we had in our Bronx neighborhood was the younger brother of Jules Munshin, a nightclub comic. I played football with this fellow. Each time I went out for one of his passes, I would say to myself: "I am now going out for a pass that will be thrown by Jules Munshin's younger brother." This made it difficult to hold on to the ball.

. . . . .

Originally published as "Hi, This Is Bruce Friedman, Reporting from Hollywood . . ." in *Esquire*, August 1976.

The only movie star I ever danced with was Jean Seberg. It was on the set of *Lilith*.

"You're Jean Seberg," I said, "and I'm dancing with you." Half of this was sincere and the other half was an attempt at boyish charm. I may have said it too many times.

. . . . .

Years later, I met Jacqueline Bisset at a party and talked to her for a while, not realizing she was Jacqueline Bisset. She seemed to be a nice person and she made some great comedic faces. Then I found out who she was, the most beautiful woman on the screen at the time, and I made an adjustment in my style. I got heartier or something. Since then, I have kicked myself for getting heartier.

. . . . .

I probably married my first wife because of her Cyd Charisse imitation.

. . . . .

My favorite nightclub comic was Jackie Miles. I memorized all his routines and went around doing them for girls who lived in Westchester. I thought of myself as a funny person, and it was amazing how long it took for me to realize that *he* was the funny one, not me.

. . . . .

I wanted to be a stand-up comic and tried being one in front of five hundred sorority women at the University of Missouri. They were crossing and uncrossing their legs and the mike went dead. I couldn't get anyone to quiet down and I fainted. An economics major I hated took over for me. Before I went under, I had apparently gotten off half a dozen jokes. Standing close to me was a fellow named Schapiro who had heard them. As I was being revived, he said: "What'd you have to faint for? You were terrific."

. . . . .

The director Jacques Levy and I collaborated on a play that starred Tony Curtis and was produced by David Merrick. It closed out of town.

Everyone kept asking me about Tony Curtis, but I could not come up with much. He would only wear a special kind of underwear, and when he told a story, say about someone who dropped a veal cutlet on the floor, he would actually drop a veal cutlet on the floor. To illustrate his point. He had a ravishing daughter who kept showing up, and he advised me to get started on hair transplants. ("This is the perfect time for you.") But that's all that I had, and I felt I was disappointing all those people who wanted to know about him. I got a lot of David Merrick stories out of the experience, but very little on Curtis, and I felt this was a failure on my part.

. . . . .

When the above show closed, what I worried about most was Joe Allen's wall. He is a saloonkeeper who keeps posters of flop shows on his back wall in Manhattan, and I had one up there already. Could you be put up there twice? From my hotel room in Philadelphia, I called a friend who got in touch with Joe Allen. Allen said not to worry, the most you could be put there was once. That was a big relief.

. . . . .

I had the briefest encounter with Steve McQueen. I'm sure he didn't remember it, but I did. I was rushing out of the Beverly Hills Hotel and he was coming up the walk. My suitcase broke and a whole bunch of hair spray cans came rolling out. He did one of those little Southwest shrugs and kept on moving, but I think he saw the cans. Only time I run into Steve McQueen and he has to go find out I use all that hair spray. I don't even use it anymore, but was McQueen told about that? Highly doubtful.

. . . . .

I keep wondering if Cybill Shepherd can say *tochis*. After all her contact with the Jews. It's not some weird Dostoyevskian obsession, but it does cross my mind. I don't mean *tokis*. I know she can say that. I mean with the *ccchhh* sound. Hell, a lot of Jews can't even say it—or pretend they can't—so why should I expect her to get it right? Poor Cybill. First they want Uta Hagen, and now she has to say *tochis* correctly. Maybe if she studied with Lee Strasberg. He's probably the only one who could have gotten a nice clear *tochis* out of her.

I still can't get over seeing certain movie stars in person. Kirk Douglas, for example. I spotted him in the lobby of a Broadway theater. He was wearing a nice suit and appeared to have a modest style; he wasn't snarling out against injustice or anything. He was scaled down in size, of course, but it was him alright, with the teeth and the jaws and the chin. Jesus, I thought, he's got to go around being Kirk Douglas every second of his life, with no letup. First thing in the morning, Kirk Douglas. Afternoon. Kirk Douglas. He gets up one day and says: "Today I don't feel like being Kirk Douglas." Too bad. He's got to continue being Douglas whether he's in the mood or not. Even if there's a sharply different individual inside, crying to get out.

I find all of this disturbing.

. . . . .

Last summer, I inherited a new Hollywood agent. "I know all about you," he said. "You're one of those cult writers." I had to correct him quickly. At one time I would have loved that label, but I knew now that if I let it stick it was going to cost me a lot of money.

. . . . .

In my capacity as an editor at the Magazine Management Company, I got to interview several movie stars. The most beautiful one I ever saw was Tina Louise, at eighteen or so. She had just come in from the sun and was so paralyzingly beautiful that I literally could not speak to her. She noticed something was wrong, and I got it across that I had just had some root canal work done. I probably forgot a few, but another most beautiful one was Groucho Marx's cook, in his final years. The three nurses weren't too shabby either.

. . . . .

I wrote a screen version of *The Owl and the Pussycat* and complained to the producer, Ray Stark, about the secretaries he was sending over. It isn't that they were homely. I wasn't looking for great beauties. But he was sending over tornado victims. I knew what was on his mind. He didn't want me to be distracted while I was doing the work. But he was going too far. I was distracted the wrong way. One day he announced, "Your secretary is here," and in walked Natalie Wood with a pad and a pencil. "Very cute," I said, in appreciation of the joke. Except that she really *was* my secretary. And she was good, too. After we got past one difficult word, and she spelled it correctly on her own, she was fine.

My definition of a great producer is someone who sends over Natalie Wood to be your secretary.

. . . . .

I have never been able to adjust to the idea of Thomas Mann spending all those years in Hollywood. Also Brecht and Mrs. Mahler. The idea of someone stopping Mann and asking him if he knew the best way to get to Doheny. I can't deal with that.

. . . . .

I had to reprimand an agent for introducing me as a fellow who wrote whimsy.

. . . . .

There were some dancers from the Royal Ballet at a swimming pool in Hollywood. No one was paying attention to a frail one in the corner. So, being a notorious "wounded bird" man, I went over and said hello. I told her I would go see the ballet and pick her up afterward and buy her a hamburger. She turned out to be the prima ballerina, Antoinette Sibley. Seven thousand people got to their feet and applauded when she appeared onstage. Then there was trying to get to her dressing room. You had to fight your way through dukes. I asked her why she hadn't told me how famous she was, and she said she didn't think it was terribly important. So I got her the hamburger and, since I was driving a Dodge Dart or something in the middle of all the Mercedes and Rolls, I got to feel like one of those fumbling, good-natured filling-station kind of guys. Now, this is not my favorite kind of story, but it happened, so I thought I'd throw it in. In my kind of story, she continues to be frail and unfamous and ultimately boring and I'm wrong to buy her the hamburger.

. . . . .

For a long time, I have been going around saying the saddest Hollywood story I know took place a few years ago when I was the sidekick of a Famous Actor for a month or so. It was my first shot at being a sidekick and I didn't mind it. It takes a lot of pressure off a person. A beautiful young girl saw the Famous Actor and made it clear she wanted to be with him. He said fine and then left her with me while he went off to get rid of his date. That was my job as sidekick, to kind of keep an eye on her until he was available. So I stood with her in the rain outside a discotheque. She was around eighteen and had just gotten back from Vegas. She said she had once had twins with a lounge singer and they were put on a farm in the northern part of the state. (Sometimes a woman will open up to a sidekick in a way that she won't to a leading man.) She started to cry because she missed her twins so much. I hugged her and she had the trembling shoulders and everything and all of a sudden she drew herself up and said she wasn't going to sleep with the Famous Actor. It was some kind of moral decision that tied in with her twins. After a long reflective pause, she said: "I *will* give him head. Because, after all, he is a movie star." But in the words of the immortal Terry Southern, there would be no vag—pen. I thought all of this was touching, but on retelling it, I can see that it's not that touching. Maybe it's only slightly touching. I probably like the story because I get to be a sidekick in it.

. . . . .

I think everyone should be a sidekick at least once. It's like going to an ashram. I think even Warren or Redford himself should try it. Let Dusty do the leading man and him be the sidekick. Cleans out the spiritual passages. And not a bad little career move.

. . . . .

I keep thinking of last summer as the best one I ever had. The Summer of '75 is the way I think of it. But the details are fading fast. I passed up an apartment on Sunset on the grounds of seediness. I don't mind seedy, but this was overseedy. In a last-ditch effort to get me to rent the place, the landlord told me that Gig Young picked out the carpeting. I spent most of the summer on a stretch of beach just short of the famous Malibu colony. I said I was living in the Bronx of Malibu. I ran into Burt Lancaster's niece, who looked eerily like Lancaster. I got to meet a certain type of actor that I had missed on previous trips—David Janssen, Stuart

Whitman, Robert Stack, that type of actor. John Dean, the Watergate man, seemed to be trying to blend in with these fellows at Hollywood parties, but I think he stood out. The nicest one of this type of actor was Vince Edwards, who turned out to be an expert on freezing people, cryogenics, and can talk for hours on the subject. There seemed to be a Gatsby contest going on. Fellows with Belgian copper fortunes took over Hollywood mansions and gave sumptuous Gatsby-like parties. While the parties were going on, these fellows stood off to the side in kimonos and talked about power. The philosophy of it. They discussed this in loud voices—with British directors. There was naked swimming the instant you got to these affairs. No hors d'oeuvres; ring-a-ding-ding, into the pool. The thing no one points out about sex in swimming pools is that it hurts. I've heard women complain about this, and I think it hits them the hardest. Maybe it's the chlorine level. A starlet described what she did in pools as "light screwing."

.....

The most attractive women last summer were with hairdressers, a few of whom went on to become famous producers. Some of the women were outrageously thin, beyond skinny. I though this was going to start a terrible trend, a kind of Auschwitz look that would work its way east in the way of so many Los Angeles movements, but it hasn't seemed to catch fire.

.....

I think I caught the beginning of the S and M wave that did sweep across the country months later. One night, at Dino's Lodge, I ran into a woman with a lovely pornographic face and I discovered that I had some of it in me, too, if the right button were pushed. I hung around in rib joints with Jerry Lieber, who had kicked his preoccupation with Thomas Mann and gone back to the more appealing Lieber of *Hound Dog* and *Kansas City* fame. Toward the end of the summer, I visited the producer Sy Litvinoff at a house high above Trancas that made my heart pound in the way that hearts once pounded in Thomas Wolfe novels. When characters were confronted with vastness. The house itself was not distinguished but it was on a hill with a sheer drop to the beach, and the Pacific was tremendous—hot and crazy blue lace. The orange juice was better than ever. I bought giant vats of it at Malibu supermarkets and drank them right down. Practically took baths in that orange juice. They almost got the veal right in certain LA restaurants. My favorite dish became anything at all at Sneeky Pete's on Sunset. But, much as I loved it all, on September 14, I packed up and went back to teach "Fantasy and Prophecy" at York College on Jamaica Avenue in Queens.

It was a close call.

my jerusalem

 f I forget thee, O Jerusalem, let my right hand forget her cunning. But I haven't forgotten thee. I just haven't gotten around to thee. And that's about to change.

It's my first trip to Israel. For years, I've lived apart from Jews. Now I'll be among millions. How will I do? As the day of my departure approaches, my voice takes on a talmudic lilt. I become a cross between Yitzhak Shamir and Jackie Mason. All day long, I hum selections from *Fiddler on the Roof*.

"Getting ready to leave, eh?" says my wife.

She has seen me become rangy and laconic before trips to Fort Worth, turn into Charles Aznavour on my way to Paris.

Suddenly, Hurricane Bob devastates my area and I'm clearing tree trunks off the back roads with Foster, Robbins, and McNee. Can I become Jewish again in time for my trip? I leave my house without power, water, or light, clearly a Biblical prophecy. (I'll find light in the land of Israel?)

On the El Al flight, I ask the stewardess, Zipporah ("Zippy to you"), if she knows of a pub in Jerusalem for writers and artists.

"That's funny," she says. "Neil Simon asked me the same thing."

The captain, whose vocal coach clearly was Shimon Peres, announces the in-flight film, *Misery*.

"And for her performance, the actress Kathy Bates received an Academy Award."

I go into a coma (clearing all those tree trunks); when I wake up, we're over the Greek islands. I look out the window, marveling at the terrain, convinced I can make out the Bacchae in a Dionysian frolic.

Originally published in *Playboy*, December 1991.

"So this is Greece."

"No, you're looking at clouds," says Zippy. She points to the other side of the aircraft. "That's Greece over there."

Soon I'm lined up at the exit door, along with yeshiva students, touring groups of the hearing impaired, and bearded rabbis who smell of candy. The doors fly open, the man behind me starts to daven. "Sh'ma, Yisroeyl, Adonoy Eloheynu. . . ."

I join him in prayer and become a Jew again, in the nick of time.

.....

The cab drivers look like Jewish gangsters of the Prohibition period. The car of choice is Mercedes. And here I'd agonized for months over whether to lease one. I'm assigned to Bugsy Siegel. Quickly, on the road to Jerusalem, I see that Israelis can hold their heads up high among the crazy drivers of the world. The terrain is harsh and scruffy. It begins to sink in that this is the Middle East, not Santa Barbara. The desert hasn't been made to bloom so fast. But the air is sweet and spicy and altogether intoxicating (fertilizer? The land of milk and honey?). After forty-five minutes, we roll up to the doors of the celebrated King David Hotel. The manager points to Meg Ryan and Dennis Quaid at the checkout desk and tells me they had a wonderful stay.

I take my first bath in a week—in the Holy Land.

.....

Everyone at the hotel seems to be from New Jersey. A woman complains to her husband that a clerk ignored her ("Should I make a stink?"). My spacious and somber room looks out on the walled Old City of Jerusalem, rebuilt by Suleiman the Magnificent in the sixteenth century, thought by some to be the site of the Garden of Eden. It's felt by Orthodox Jews that here the Messiah will return in three centuries or less. The King David appears to be a jolly Catskills hotel flung back in time to the land of Abraham and Jesus and Mohammed. The room furnishings are faded deco. The peach-colored bathroom tile, the orange bath mat, the forties shower fixtures—it's as if the Federmann family, owners of the hotel, have produced a replica of my childhood apartment in the Bronx.

.....

With questionable timing, I've arrived on the night of the Shabbath. Jerusalem is wrapped up tight as a drum, or a scroll, as it were. I decide to have dinner in the formal dining room of the King David and order— what else?—gefilte fish. If I can't trust it here. . . . Also chicken stuffed with pine nuts, from a kibbutz in Galilee. The captain asks if I'd mind another single at my table. I tell him, Why not? This is the Holy Land. I'm joined by a dour, middle-aged Frenchman who owns a condo in Tel Aviv. Thanks to Hurricane Bob and and a week of eating out of cans, I'm famished and prepare to dig in. Jean-Claude asks if I'd mind if he said a kiddush. Of course I don't mind. How can I mind: He rises, I rise with him, holding a cloth napkin over my head in place of a kippe. His kiddush is a long one—and when he's finished, the hotel presents a cantor with a beautiful voice to do another, more formal kiddush for the entire dining room. Soon, rival kiddushes break out around the room. I'm still on my feet and I haven't eaten. Finally, the ceremonies end and I attack my dinner, which, since it's kosher, is on the bland side but has the saving grace of being authentic. Jean-Claude says he is from Morocco and that at the age of twelve, he saw arm patches being prepared for the Jews as Rommel took Tunisia. "Then the Americans came," he says, smiling, giving me credit for their appearance. I order a bottle of wine, take a sip and pronounce it excellent. The captain says it's from the Golan.

"Really? In that case, you should never, under any circumstances, give up the Golan Heights." There's a silence. I look at the captain's name tag—Mahmoud, an Arab—and see I've made my first blunder in the Holy Land. ("You *didn't*," my wife will say.)

. . . . .

My guide arrives, Ami of Galilee Tours. Fresh from steering twenty-seven Indiana charismatics through the Old City, he appears happy to see me but asks why I've never been to Israel before.

"I'm here now."

"But what took you so long?"

This is a refrain that follows me throughout my stay. It's not enough that I'm here. I didn't get here fast enough.

Tall, confident, a thirty-eight-year-old paratrooper and veteran of three wars, Ami carries a backpack and has the long stride of an antelope. I picture him bounding zestfully over archaeological ruins in Masada while I struggle to keep up with him.

"Not to worry," he says, sensing my discomfort. "I'm tired all the time."

We set out for the Old City in ninety-degree heat, but *dry* heat, which is supposed to make a difference. Ami points to an abandoned trunk road beside a two-lane highway.

"This," he says, "is Jerusalem."

The road was designed to alleviate traffic congestion. But when construction began, the Jews decided the site concealed a Maccabean fortress. The Moslems insisted it lay above an ancient mosque, and the Greek Orthodox Christians were confident it was the site of a twelfth-century Byzantine church.

The result? Endless, contentious, Jerusalem-style arbitration—and, as yet, no road.

We approach the Jaffa Gate, most heavily trafficked of the seven open entrances to the city (least used is the Dung Gate in the back.) The effect is dizzying, stupendous, a cascade of history pouring down on my head. We enter the Old City itself, and within minutes, I've sidestepped a camel, leaped over a goat, brushed against Bedouin women, collided with a Druse, and shaken hands with a former Greek Orthodox monk who has become one of Jerusalem's top archaeologists. One of Ami's charismatics comes by and, assuming I'm a native, congratulates me on my English; I'm high-fived by a black fitness instructor from Harlem who has toured seven countries with a backpack. Ami points out graffiti scribbled on a wall by bored soldiers in Rome's Tenth Legion. I almost fall into a tomb—supposedly used to seal up, and punish, two engineers who helped build the wall and forgot to include David's tomb, which still lies outside. Turks, Armenians, Arabs in black-and-white-checked kaffiyeh, Iraqis, Yemenites, ramrod-straight Ethiopians all parade by— none of them Hollywood extras. I've heard of interesting places, but this is ridiculous. It's a feast and a headache. Why would the Israelis want to administer it?

We approach the Church of the Holy Sepulcher, where Christ is thought to have been crucified, buried, and resurrected. Six religious groups govern the church—Syrians, Catholics, Armenians, Ethiopians, Greek Orthodox, Copts. (The Copts, from Egypt, are allowed to use a small entrance in the back, but there's pressure from the Cairo government to allow them to enter in the front.) The job of controlling access falls to a Moslem—a slight, pleasant-looking man named Mr. Nusseibah whose family has been entrusted with the keys to the church for seven centuries. Mr. Nusseibah introduces himself, lets me hold the keys and confides that he also gets to vouch for Greek Orthodox miracles.

We line up behind several dozen visitors from Athens whose turn it is to visit the tomb. Half a dozen of Ami's charismatics fall in behind us, refusing to relinquish him as a guide. When it's our turn, Ami and I hunch down and wiggle through the entrance of the tomb to a slightly larger cave inside—the enclosure itself. We take perhaps a fraction more time than we should in being awe struck—and the restless charismatics pour into the tiny space behind us, blocking the entrance. I'm convinced I'm going to suffocate. How would that look to my family, if I choked to death in Christ's tomb?

Clearly, this is a passionate place, an emotional place. What happens if someone is overcome, or even, God forbid, has a stroke? Are there special medical teams on hand?

"No," says Ami. But there *are* designated Arabs who will carry stricken people out on their backs and race off to Hadassah Hospital on Mount Scopus.

We continue our walk above the street, leaping from roof to roof. This entire goulash of a city, all 220 acres of it, divided into Jewish, Moslem, Armenian, and Christian quarters—can be crossed in this manner or, as a matter of choice, on stones that are two thousand years old. We stop for a moment on the roof of the Arab marketplace and look out onto the Mount of Olives, the most exclusive cemetery in the world. It's thought that when the Messiah makes his appearance, he will approach the city through this ancient cemetery. But what good is that to the average man?

"Don't worry," says a rooftop eavesdropper, visiting from Englewood. "I can get you in for fifty thousand."

We fall in with a thick, winding column of Arab shopkeepers who have closed their stores at 1:00 P.M., out of either fear or respect for the intifada. Is there any danger? "Possibly of being stabbed," says Ami, who normally carries a weapon but honors me by leaving it at home on this occasion. He says don't worry, he'll walk in front of me. Frankly, I don't see how that will help. Shouldn't he walk in back?

We stop for lunch at the Abu Shukri Restaurant in the Moslem Quarter, where the hummus, ground by a secret process, is thought to be the finest in the Middle East. Once this was a meeting place for Arab and Jewish notables. Since the intifada, the Jews have stayed away. I scoop up the hummus on warm pita bread, dig into the spicy cucumber-and-pepper salad, and award the restaurant five stars, easily worth the risk of being gunned down.

Outside, in the *souk* (marketplace), an Arab offers me souvenir post-cards. Ami waves him off—his price is too high. The Arab comes down a little, but it's still a rip-off. Suddenly, years of rage show up in the man's face. "It's because I'm Arab," he screams. "You'll take him to buy from a Jew." We walk on. Ami says he once served as a guide for Brooke Shields and found her surprisingly nice, not stuck up. But I can hear the man shouting at us: "Don't walk alone, my friend. Don't turn your back." The refrain follows me back to the hotel.

. . . . .

. . . . .

At night, in my hotel room, as a muezzin summons the faithful to prayer, the sonic boom of an Israeli Mirage knocks a Maccabee beer out of my hand. The BBC reports that a British cricket team has trounced poor Sri Lanka.

In the lobby of the King David, there's pride in the fact that one of three young Soviets who died flinging himself onto a tank during the recent attempted putsch was a Jew. And for the first time, the Kaddish will be heard throughout the crumbling Soviet Union. There is also talk of a fight that broke out at the Hotel Jerusalem between Russian and Ethiopian immigrants—the Russians became incensed when the airlifted Ethiopians strolled out of the dining room with free grapes, while the Russians had to pay for theirs.

I take to the streets. Ami has told me I can go anywhere in safety, but I'm not so sure. There seems to be less light than in most cities. I stroll along Keren Hayesod Street, marveling, as have many before me, at the very fact of the Jewish state. In other cities, I've had the "Jewish Quarter" pointed out to me. Here everywhere is the Jewish Quarter. Jewish supermarkets (Supersol), Jewish gas stations, Jewish cereal. Every ten steps, a pair of Defense Force members walk casually along in a characteristic duck walk, cradling Uzis and longer-range Galils. Some are tall, handsome, battle-hardened sabras, others pimply postadolescents of the kind that show up at American comic-book conventions. They would be lucky to play right field in little league. But here their step is firm and confident. There's a huge burst of post-Shabbath activity on Ben-Yehuda Street, a giant collegiate mall, Santa Monica with semiautomatics. I speculate about Israeli women. The El Al stewardesses are world-class beauties but seem out of bounds, as if they're being specially groomed as the girlfriends of Hollywood executives. The IDF women are trim and appealing in olive drab; no doubt the deadly weapons they carry, like parasols, lend them spice.

I stop and chat with a leather worker who made a killing making carrying cases for gas masks and holsters for self-defense weapons during the Gulf war. On the subject of Israeli women, he becomes rhapsodic—

they're kind, intelligent, the loveliest, most caring creatures on earth, each one a true friend.

"You're very lucky," I suggest.

"Why? I married a Frenchwoman."

At a pub called Gilly's, I chat with a weary-looking British architect who has moved to Jerusalem for "the stone and the clime." (The entire city is built with a distinctive honey-colored stone—the City of Gold.) Clearly, the man has spent a lifetime worrying. His current concern is that the highly educated Russian immigrants can't be absorbed. "What can we do with so many railway engineers? We've only got one railroad."

. . . . .

I make a note to stop at Feferberg's on Jaffa Street. The menu in the window says it features *pupiks* (chicken stomachs), stuffed *miltz* (spleen), *patcha* (calve's-feet jelly), and borscht by the glass. Jewish soul food. How bad can it be?

. . . . .

The next day, I make a pit stop at Mea Shearim—a forty-acre stone compound, home of the ultraorthodox who refuse to recognize the state of Israel. The feeling is that of eastern European shtetls—or of Vilnius, Kraków, Lublin—the pages of Isaac Bashevis Singer. On almost every wall, a poster warns women to dress and behave modestly—and it cautions men against giving them attention-getting jewelry. A tourist in an orange dress with exposed elbows is dangerously close to the edge. It's disconcerting to see swastikas slashed across the Star of David. Only when the Messiah comes will the people of Mea Shearim recognize a land of Israel. Young Israeli men have to throw over three years to the armed forces; young women, too. These ultraorthodox are exempt, the theory being that their prayers are responsible for Israeli victories on the battefield. Doesn't that produce resentment on the part of those who serve? I ask.

"No," says Ami. "Hatred."

. . . . .

I stand among gentle, newly arrived Ethiopians at the Knesset, seat of government, while an interpreter points out Shamir's seat and explains that Israeli representatives are not chosen by geography but by party. The

Ethiopians look on uncomprehendingly. Desert nomads, for the most part, many still don't know how to work a toilet. Suddenly, there's an alarm, and we're all led off to a safe area while a bomb squad rolls up to the building and pays out a 150-foot line, so that a suspicious object can be examined at a distance. No one breathes. To break the tension, an Iranian-Jewish woman from Beverly Hills tells the increasingly perplexed Ethiopians she met Mike Tyson in West Hollywood.

It's a false alarm—half a sandwich discarded in a bus shelter.

Ami says Israel is the only place in the world where you can put one million dollars in a suitcase and leave it on the street for safekeeping. Everyone will run away from it, assuming it's a bomb.

. . . . .

The building opposite the King David Hotel fascinates me. It's a YMCA but unlike any other—an architectural miracle, built by Turks during the British mandate, filled with Byzantine wonders. I put my head in. A movie, *American Samurai*, is being wrapped in the lobby, and I introduce myself to the director. He says the budget is 2.5 million dollars, but with the sale of ancillary rights, the company should do all right. With the Old City visible, there in the shadow of two thousand years of history, Sam Firstenberg and I discuss the merits of Creative Arts Agency.

. . . . .

That night, after dinner at a Yemenite restaurant, I confront disaster. Chills, fever, shooting pains, the fires of hell, the whole package arriving at four in the morning. Unquestionably, this is the work of the Almighty, now that He has me cornered in Israel, scolding me for not being Jewish enough, and also, of course, for taking my time about getting there. But there's a silver lining. Secretly, I'm delighted at my good fortune in getting sick in the land of Jewish doctors. I get one out of bed, and within the hour, an Orthodox doctor, formerly of Chicago, is at the door. After a thorough examination, he lays out all the possible things it might be.

"But what *is* it?"

"Who knows?"

He produces a variety of pills and describes the negative features of each one. My best bet, frankly, is to do nothing.

"Can't you tell me anything specific?"

"Yes. My fee is eighty dollars, preferably in *shkolim*."

I soldier on and make a solitary pilgrimage to Yad Vashem, the Holocaust memorial, easily the quietest place I've ever been. The silence is broken by the voice of a girl from Long Island.

"Oh, my God, this is unreal."

The photographs of Jews stacked like cordwood represent a new phenomenon to her, not to me. I'm taken by a series of doomsday woodcuts by Moshe Hoffman (1938–83) and its ironic title, 6,000,001. And I take note of an SS document consigning 358 persons to heavy prison sentences for having sex with Jews. Oddly, it's a display of books ordered to be burned that unsettles me the most—the works of Stefan Zweig, Thomas Mann, Albert Einsten, Heinrich Heine—and Heine's words: "Wherever books are burned, human beings are destined to be burned, too."

An elderly man holds his grandson by the hand and points out a mistake in a painting that depicts life in the infamous Theresienstadt camp.

"That was a toilet, not a water cistern."

"How do you know, Grandpa?"

"I was there."

I ask the attendant if the Germans visit and, if so, how they react.

"They look."

"That's all?"

"That's all."

. . . . .

I'm still in the grip of a mysterious illness. Half the hotel claims to have it, too. Some say it's the fruit—the figs, in particular, which are cheap, but you have to wash them. A man from England tells me I'm a fool to have used ice cubes. "Why do you think Britain was able to become a colonial power?" he asks.

"By not using ice cubes."

"Exactly."

Still, I'm in Jerusalem. How can I not pay a visit to the Western (formerly Wailing) Wall? Ami and I make the pilgrimage. He and I—both secular—have our pictures taken with *t'filin* (phylacteries), which I haven't worn for decades. Maybe now that I've worn them—with the wall as a witness—I'm not so secular anymore. A man approaches and says that for a fee, he'll pray for me and my loved ones for forty days and nights. During the period, we will all be protected from evil.

"And after that?"

"You're on your own."

. . . . .

In the days that follow, I continue to prowl the city. I sit in one of
the four adjoining synagogues of Yochanan Ben-Zakkai, once the center
of Sephardic life in old Jerusalem. Exquisite examples of camelback
Moorish architecture, the synagogues were gutted in 1948, used as stables
by Jordanians, and lovingly repaired by the Jews in 1967.

I kick off my shoes and pay a balancing visit to the Dome of the
Rock, third holiest Moslem site (after Mecca and Medina). From here,
it's believed, Mohammed rode his horse, el-Buraq, to heaven. When I
come out, my shoes have been moved by a Holy Land wise guy, but I find
them in front of another mosque.

At the Israel Museum, I examine, under glass, the eight Dead Sea
scrolls of leather, the most important archaeological find of our time—
a long, informative love letter from the ancient world—and pay tribute
to Professor Elazar L. Sukenik, who stubbornly pursued them, to his
son Yigael Yadin of Israeli intelligence, who continued the hunt after
the professor's death, and to the poor men and women who risked their
eyesight unpeeling the fragile scrolls, making sure not to scatter any
precious fragments.

I become friends with David Rakia, owner of David's Art Gallery, a
thin-chested Viennese and a lover of Kafka who escaped the Nazis in
1938. He points to the site of his first home in Israel, which sits on the
old border with Jordan. "It was bombed into rubble by terrorists.

"But I didn't care," he says, drawing himself up tall. "We had ten
thousand rifles against seven Arab armies. I lived history. We built a
country."

For seven days and seven nights, my mysterious illness continues.
Then, just when it's time to leave, with celestial irony, the sun comes
out (the metaphorical sun; the real sun has been out all along). Gorgeous
Sephardic gift-shop owners, who'd avoided my eyes, suddenly shower me
with attention. A Morocan beauty says I look "fresh." The hotel manager
says I can check out at midnight—he won't charge me for an extra day. A
Turk in the marketplace hands me a huge slab of halvah, on the house.
But what good is it? I'm on my way.

For my last meal in Jerusalem, I choose Fink's, the oldest restaurant
in the city, a twenty-two-seater and a favorite, it's quickly pointed out, of
Paul Newman. It's here that arms deals for rifles and light machine guns

were struck by the Haganah during the British mandate. I discover the combination of chopped liver on honeydew and eat a magical schnitzel made with tender Holy Land veal.

"Will you come back?" asks Muli Yehezkieli, the Israeli maître d', who has given me a table even though I didn't call for a reservation.

"Let me get over this trip first."

So I leave this stubborn, complex, riotously beautiful "city of sieges," where every stone is history and everyone is an expert, scraggly bearded young men with the experience of an unripe turnip lecturing me on life and love. But what am I complaining about? I walk away with memories, dreams, stunning moments, fast friends. I take away much more than I've given. And I wonder if that isn't true of America as well, spoken of with reverence by one and all in Jerusalem as "our one good friend."

"Did you take pictures?" the stewardess asks me on the return flight.

"Only in my head."

And the film on the flight home is, again, *Misery*.

dark watercolors from
port-au-prince

They are leading a blind Haitian toward the plane. He is the blindest man I've ever seen. The kind of blind in which the eyes remain open and staring, two giant socketed holes with dead TV screens in them. He might have been branded. Or he was *struck* blind, from seeing something terrible. There is a tiny satchel of flesh below one socket that looks as if it might contain his old sight, all folded up and tucked away. Now, they are taking him back to Haiti. Perhaps back to whatever it is that struck him blind. His blindness is enormous. Is he going to stand opposite that terrifying thing and *not* see it with that same enormity.

. . . . .

Port-au-Prince. . . . I have been away for thirteen years. The only difference I can perceive is that the welcoming band is hooked up to electronic amps. I am almost past the airport security net when an inspector spots a small Y-shaped handgrip in my carrying case. He doesn't like the looks of it. Suddenly, there are eight men with guns around me. I tell them the item is for strengthening your grip, and I demonstrate by knocking off a quick seventy-five with my right hand, sixty with my left. Not a smile in the crowd. They just don't like the looks of it. What are they thinking—that I'm going to take over the country with a handgrip? Go down to the president's palace, wave the grip at the palace guard and

Originally published in *Playboy*, January 1974.

say, "Alright, nobody make a move." They let me go, but they are still not convinced. Not really.

. . . . .

Olaffson's. . . . Giant tropical salad of a hotel with a little chocolate . . . . .
mousse on the side. A very rich brew. House of Flowers, Casablanca, House of Blue Leaves, Serendipity, and the Coney Island Fun House. If it were a cake, you could only handle a few bites a day. I once told an actor who was annoying me that he had too much charm. He told me it was the cruelest thing anyone had ever said to him. Olaffson's is just on the edge. Just a little more charm and it goes sinking into the mud. I am put in the Mick Jagger Suite. It is next to the Barry Goldwater Suite. I look at the hotel brochure and find myself wedged between Sir John Gielgud and Lord Snowden as one of the many luminaries who have been here. Since I have never stayed at the hotel, this opens up a credibility gap on Sir John and Lord Snowden. Either that, or it is the voodoo at work, calling me from the mainland. They knew I would be here some day so they simply included me in the literature.

. . . . .

A girl bounces into the hotel, full of energy, heavy with metallic jewelry. She is the entire *Village Voice* rolled into one. Interests: folk art, shell collecting, cultural bike rides, pottery. She has recently enrolled in a course called "The Changing Media" offered by the Smithsonian Institute. And she has just come from a small Haitian village where she has recorded the voices of children in a Baptist church. She whips into the lobby, plays some Bach on the piano, and switches briskly into selections from "Annie Get Your Gun." Comes back and hurls some rock specimens on a table, also a little petrified wood. There is something missing. She says she is studying pre-Colombian art on the side. That's what was missing. I don't usually do this, but I take it upon myself to suggest that she pare herself down a bit, simplify her life. She looks at me and says, "You're an attractive man."

. . . . .

I am joined at dinner by a "sugar beet CPA," an American accountant who analyzed Haitian beet production for a sugar company. We talk about

Haiti. He says he doesn't know if there has been progress. When "Baby Doc" Duvalier visited Cap Haitien to dedicate a plaque, fifty locals had to be put in jail—for the duration of the visit. I reach for the butter and he winces. He advises me not to touch the dairy products, not unless I want "the Haitian jollies." I skip to the main course and I am about to dig in to the squash when he shrugs and says, "Your funeral." Vegetables are out, too. When I reach for some cold Mango, he says, "I hope you've brought along twenty or thirty changes of underwear." I was quite ill the last time I visited Haiti, thirteen years back, so even though my appetite is savage, I wind up eating bread and drinking wine. I am about to put a little salt on the bread when he says, "Oops." Salt is out, too. I discover later that he is a fellow with a sensitive stomach who gets sick all over the world. He's just a sick fellow. The next day I dig in, salt, butter, squash, mango, mountain goat, the works. Nothing happens. I feel fine.

. . . . .

The last time I was in Haiti, I was with my wife. Now I'm alone. I notice that when you are alone and seem to be enjoying your own company, it makes people uncomfortable. Everyone wants to help you and get you to have fun. Less-than-perfect couples want to get at your secret. You can't fake this alone business. You have to want to be alone for it to work. On that last trip, people wore pistols on the hip and the hotel owner traveled around in an armored car. I saw my first serious roadblock, not the state trooper kind, but one that indicated you could get killed. Two people hanging on a hook, as a warning for the villagers. I don't know if I saw that last one, read about it, or dreamed it. Haiti is that kind of place. Poverty is a word that doesn't apply. Poverty is civilized. This is beyond poverty. It has a smell to it that coats your skin and lingers, for years. A few Haitians had whatever money there was. They were schooled in France and sent their children there. One of them whipped us through a village at a hundred miles an hour. If someone happened to get caught on the fenders . . . well . . . There aren't a million stories out there. There is just one—and a grim tale it is. All that flesh. You have the feeling you can order up a dozen teenagers through room service—six boys, six girls, two with a limp—and they will be served with a frozen daiquiri and hors d'oeuvres. I've been out there. This time I'll stay at the hotel and get some sun. That ferocious Haitian sun. I'll stay at the pool and let the island come to me. It does.

. . . . .

At the pool, the most perfectly matched couple I have ever seen. They are slender, small boned, and French. Everything they do is in sync. They swim with an immaculate rhythm and put on suntan lotion that way, too. He is the male version of her, and she is the female version of him. When they look at one another, it must be like staring into a mirror, one that adjusts for gender. Is it possible they are brother and sister? I don't think so, but I am not ruling that out. Did they find each other after a long, gruelling search or did they stumble into this arrangement? I would like to have the answer to that one. You don't want to ask them questions, somehow. It might throw them off the beat. They dry off, after a swim, and sit on a chaise longue, arranging themselves like bookends. This is what the world "couple" must mean. I have an idea of what their lovemaking must be like. I would like to see it, but I am not sure I could take too much of it. It must be pretty and also masturbatory. It would upset me a bit if I found out that either one had a lover. But I would not be surprised. There would have to be a need to get an atonal note in the picture, to break that prefect rhythm.

. . . . .

Three middle-aged ladies from Ohio. They take up a great deal of room at the pool, mostly because of their equipment. Aspirin bottles, containers of milk, headache powders. It takes me longer than it should to realize that this is drunk equipment. The ladies are on a drunk tour. They are not modestly and discreetly tipsy but plastered, ossified, blasted out of their skulls. In the broiling sun. That is the purpose of their trip to Haiti. They are sad and gentle people, but they are also desperately unattractive. It gives you a hangover just to look at them. Squinting through swollen lids, a once pretty one announces that she would love to be taken to a Bawdy House. I don't pick up on this. When I don't, she says I have "charisma." I don't pick up on that either. Instead, I concoct a story about practicing Abstinence. I think this works the wrong way. It adds to my charisma.

. . . . .

A young sales executive tries to organize a bare-ass swimming party at midnight. The ladies dig down deep and come up with some shyness. He hits the bare-ass phrase very hard. The great quantum leap forward in sexual understanding has passed him by. He is stuck in the fifties. With bare-ass. I wait for him to organize a panty raid. I'm sure that's next.

Later, I find out he has taken the Ohio ladies to Madame Evelyn's, where the whores, shaky in their geography, have serenaded the foursome with "Tennessee Waltz." On reflection, it seems a very kind thing for him to have done.

. . . . .

Late in the afternoon, a couple swim toward me; the young man has cheerful blue eyes and a gold ring in his ear. The girl is compact, Arabic. I do a quick reading and take them for a couple from a New York suburb. He is in children's wear, but would like to be known as a fellow with freaky tastes. The gold earring. It is almost fun when I find out how wrong I am. The fellow is a famed Radical of the sixties whose voice once went booming round the world. Some say that he, and others like him, mobilized the nation's conscience and ultimately closed down the war. I don't disagree. The girl is a Gestalt psychologist. She introduces herself and says she is insecure in Haiti. "My reputation usually precedes me." It's a big, slow, fat pitch, but I don't swing at it. She is likable, and I respect the Radical. The beard is gone, but the eyes remain wild, messianic. I don't like the way he swims. He seems to be restless, shifting around for a new and exciting stance. He is a bit like a rock star whose backup men have scattered, whose fame has slipped away. He says he is going down to the palace and knock on the gate and ask to see young Duvalier. I respectfully suggest that he not do that. "They don't know about guerrilla theater here. They don't know about put-ons." We shift to Watergate. "The people who hate Nixon are really having a field day," he says. Is that the way he's going to go? He's going to start loving Nixon? I pick that one right off. It's not going to work. It's not going to send his voice booming around the world a second time. He needs something else.

. . . . .

Enter the Greek. Chiseled face, magnificent beard, eyes blazing with Freedom, Liberty, Conscience. He's a walking commemorative coin. I find out quickly that much of this is Freedom to push his own welfare, taking Liberties with other men's views. The Greek says he is an artist, a citizen of the world. He tells me he once had a little trouble in Spain. At a bar, he was overheard shouting that he would like to shit in the president's mouth. They threw him out. I can see he's in the wrong country now. For his style. He lowers his voice, chuckles, and says that in Haiti, the current technique is to put you in jail and change your name and then forget about you. You have never existed. I can see that the Greek is going to be a great deal of trouble. I turn out to be right.

. . . . .

That night, the Radical and the Gestalt psychologist run into the hotel, excited. They report that a sea of Haitians has just converged on a woman who beat up her baby and now wants to eat it. Is the crowd going to eat her before she eats the baby? No one is sure. I have dinner with the Radical and his girlfriend. I tell them I'd like to read a piece telling what happened to the sixties' Radicals. What happened to the Movement. My new friend says terrific, he'll write it. I tell him that's not the one I want to read. It would have to be written by an outsider. Someone with cold eyes. The main course is pigeon. The Radical feels there is something wrong with eating a peaceful bird. "It doesn't want to be eaten." But while he is saying that, he is eating the pigeon. I don't think he ought to be doing that. What you do, I think, if you don't want to eat a pigeon is send the pigeon back and order a cheeseburger. Or you eat the pigeon and be quiet. I come to an easy and cozy conclusion and I don't like myself for it, but I am stuck with it: That's what happened to the Movement. Some of them ate the pigeon.

. . . . .

Later, the Radical rips off a *New York Times* from the casino and gives it to me. It's a nice thing for him to do—the paper is virtually impossible to find on the island—and even though it isn't much to him, he knows how important the "print media" is to me. I'm even more sorry about the pigeon hypothesis, but I believe it and I can't drop it.

. . . . .

I gamble for a while alongside some Syrians. I have a naive belief that people gamble according to their national styles. The Syrians are supercautious at the blackjack table. A Syrian has a twelve, sees the dealer's picture staring him in the face, he doesn't draw. He holds on to what he's got, afraid of what may be up ahead. This style forces me to be a little more reckless than I am normally. I pull on sixteens, start pulling to soft seventeens. Under his breath, one Syrian mumbles, each time I draw, "Ouvert, ouvert." He is rooting for me to go bust. This makes me even more reckless. I feel like drawing to eighteens and nineteens.

Maybe that's the Syrian business style. Get you infuriated so that you move away from your normal pattern. You fall apart, and the Syrian is there to pick up the pieces.

. . . . .

Coming back to the hotel, at four in the morning, I see thickets of people playing a board game under a sour light. The driver says they are "the ones who never sleep." I tell him they must sleep sometime. Never, he says. Then they must die young. No, he says, they never sleep and they die in their eighties and nineties.

The owner of the hotel and his wife arrive from Key West. I've always wondered how an American can stay in this country for long periods of time. The owners miss Chinese food and that is one reason they travel to the mainland. I watch the hotel owner in action. He has a gruff, cigar-smoking, Vegas style and his work involves dealing with an endless procession of Haitian officials, high and low, who appear before him with their hands out. Each time this happens, the hotel owner looks startled, outraged, and shouts "Pourquoi?" He fixes each solicitor with a long menacing stare, but no one gets stared down. No one goes away, and the hands remain extended. He reaches into a cigar box and, with more menace, hands over a Haitian bill as if to say, "Don't try that again." But they do try it again. All he has done is slow down the process a bit. The bills are of meager denomination, but they must add up. That's his work. Handouts all day long and Lord Snowden in the evening. He can't possibly be in this for the money.

I am told of a towering gangland figure who came through with two bodyguards. It upset him that there were no air conditioners in his room. The hotel owner said he knew of a fine hotel down the road where the visitors could have three clean suites, each with its own air conditioner, spanking new. He started to make a call and the racket leader said, "We stay here." For a week, through record-breaking heat, the bodyguards never removed their jackets. After several days, the head man said his men would prepare a sphaghetti dinner for the guests who were to assemble at the pool at six o'clock, two hours before the regular dinner hour. The owner had to roam the island, hunting down sphaghetti sauce ingredients. None of the guests assembled at the appointed hour, and the sauce did not work out. Toward the end of his stay, the racket leader put an arm around the hotel owner and said, "I have a plan to take all the goat milk in Haiti and ship it to the States to make mozzarella cheese. We will be partners." The owner wondered about the starving Haitian children who need this milk. "You don't understand," the racket man said. "I have a plan in which we take all this goat's milk and what we do is ship it to the States to make mozzarella cheese. You and I will be partners."

"Now I understand," said the owner.

. . . . .

"Bitch."

"Pig."

"Chauvinist dude."

The world's most complicated individual comes running down to the pool. He has long, flowing hair and a Maoist moustache and goatee. He is a grape-working-Maoist-Liberated-Activist-Radicalized homosexual who makes a living in show business. It's difficult to know where to start with him. He has just had a big fight with his roommate. He feels they have no business living in such luxury and wants them to stay in a thatched hut with underprivileged Haitians. The roommate appears. He is a media man who loves the sun. He has dyed black hair, heavily barbered. No way you are going to get this fellow into a thatched hut. The complicated fellow is in a constant state of pique, but I notice that they stay at the hotel. To my knowledge, they never make it to that thatched hut.

. . . . .

The Greek has been losing his friends. He seemed to have a great many at first, but they are dropping away. He looks at me with a certain longing. He holds his upper abdomen a lot and I find out he has an ulcer condition that's in high gear. He has fainted a few times and there is a woman at the hospital who gives him shots to keep it under control. It isn't really under control. He is not supposed to do this, of course, but he drinks brandy around the clock and smokes six packs of cigarettes a day. He says to me: "I have a story to tell you, but I can't tell it while I'm in this country." I tell him not to say he's got a story, but that he can't tell it. That's no use to anyone. He lets that pass. And I have a feeling I'll be hearing from him again.

. . . . .

I am in Haiti for a rest, but I am not much of a rester. As soon as I feel rested, I'm finished resting. I can't imagine doing any resting for the future. I have to get away from the hotel and look around. I buy a Haitian primitive painting and I am delighted to learn that the artist is eighty-two. I look at some cameras. There is a great to-do about a new Minolta that can take pictures around corners. They can't understand why I don't want one. "You'll get a Watergate," one says. I head for a place called Kenscoff, in the mountains, stop off for a bite and wind up having the most magnificent meal of the trip. Or any trip. It costs twenty dollars just to get to this restaurant, and I appear to be the only customer of the day. Possibly the month. It is not an ideal location for a gourmet restaurant, and I deduce that the host is a poor planner. I never get to Kenscoff. I do make it to Duvalier's grave. I've heard that ten men with submachine guns guard it night and day. It is inlaid with hundreds of thousands of dollars in gemstones. The crypt is neat, handsomely marbled, smaller than that of other dead Haitians. A little vacation home. Of the ten guards, five are military slick, the other five are sleepy and sit on chairs, dozing, with guns in their laps. I worry about these sleepy ones. There is an eternal fire in front of the crypt, and I flirt with the notion of lighting my cigar on it, but I don't proceed to do so.

On the way back, each time we stop for a light, cripples and blind people are presented to me by their children or friends as though for comment. As each one is shoved forward, the presenter steps to the side with a flourish as if to say, "What do you think of that?" We pass a square where there is a giant picture of the dead Duvalier and a banner that says, "L'idole des peuples." I recall an argument at the hotel in which a Haitian insisted that the banner said, "Duvalier, *hero* of the people." He was incorrect.

. . . . .

I've had enough. It is Thursday and I plan to leave Friday. The Greek is up to eight packs of cigarettes a day and is drinking shots of rum along with his brandy and black coffee. As I understand it, this is poor ulcer therapy. He is living under a very real cloud, but I notice that he has managed to pick off the wife of a vacationing Midwestern ecologist. He has made a loud public announcement to this effect at the pool, describing the seduction in detail. So he is not the world's most attractive fellow, but in spite of this, I don't enjoy seeing him in poor condition. He takes me aside and attempts to tell me his story. Before he begins, he gestures toward a man in an open-collared sport shirt who is sitting ten steps away, on a barstool. I realize that he goes with the Greek. Whenever the Greek moves, this fellow follows him, ten steps away. No sunglasses. No apparent weapon in his slacks. This is the new Haiti. Except that he is always there.

The Greek whispers his story to me. When he is finished, I wait to be enveloped by a sense of outrage. This does not happen. Here is his story:

A group of wealthy Haitians hired him to give "order, structure and technique" to Haitian art. His way of going about it was to start a kind of commune, bringing together ten of the country's most promising artists and, in some cases, their wives and girlfriends. They lived with the Greek, ate with him, slept at his house, and used his equipment. The arrangement was that the art produced would stay within the group, until five years had passed, at which time some thought would be given to its commercial use. And there would be a division of the profits. The Haitians turned up one day with a lawyer (someone with a badge that said "Lawyer") and said they wanted their work back, they were backing out. The Greek said, "Take it," and stepped out on the terrace, wondering how they were going to take 40 percent of each canvas. The artists took 250 canvases of theirs, slashed a painting of the Greek's, and took the supplies he had brought to the country. While they were doing this, the Greek's adopted ten-year-old Haitian son bit one of the artists on the knee and then fainted. A day later, the Greek discovered that five thousand dollars in cash, hidden in his underwear, was gone, too. He called an official in the government who told him to leave Haiti as quickly as possible. He asked the owner of the hotel what to do and received the identical advice. When he made arrangements to leave the country, he found that his papers "were not in order."

So the story does not outrage me. I have seen the Greek in action. It's possible the deal he made with the Haitians was highway robbery. Bringing your wife or girlfriend to live in the Greek's house is not intelligent. This is hardly a cause célèbre, and the Greek is not Central Casting in the hero department. Still, heroes are in short supply these days. And I don't like the biting episode. I don't think they should have taken the five thousand. Once again, it's not the Dreyfus case, but I don't like the shadow assigned to him. I don't think they should be warning him to leave the country and then not letting him out. The ulcers, the terror in his face, are unmistakable. It's not pretty to watch. The Greek says he will go the airport with me on Friday, pretending that everything is alright. I picture a scene in which I'm let through the gate and the Greek

is seized, screaming for help. What do I do them? I'm not looking forward
to it.

. . . . .

The Greek is amazing. In the middle of this squeeze play, his eyes
showing both ulcer pain and the fear of Haitian prisons, he takes time
out for a nude swimming session with the ecologist's wife. Before he
jumps in the pool, he covers his genitals. I call him on that. Generally,
he is having some trouble being sexy. He says he's been told not to go
near the airport on Friday. To stay where he is. In Haiti. So I don't have
to worry about that airport scene.

. . . . .

The Greek takes me back to his villa and shows me his paintings.
They are being put onto rolls, some of which will be handed over to
the "bare-ass" salesman, for sale in the States. The Greek is working
very quickly. He is proud of some giant, surrealist canvases; they seem
derivative to me. There is a group he did in Paris, in the early sixties,
which are exceptional, soulful, long-legged women with great exploding
thighs. The Greek has repudiated these. I take a swim at the hotel, and
when I am finished, my contact lenses are missing. I've put them in the
exact same place, six nights in a row, and now they are gone. Any other
place in the world I would dismiss the possibility that someone has been
fucking around. But we're in Haiti. The Greek is very hot. And I'm the
only one who goes near him. So I get infuriated and I am impossible to
deal with until I leave. That night, the Greek knocks on my door, puffing
at a cigarette as if it's his lifeline, and asks me if I'd like to take the Ohio
ladies to the whorehouse. I tell him I don't want to do that. And that isn't
all I tell him.

. . . . .

I am happy to be leaving. I say good-bye to a few people at the pool and
then I come to the Greek. A good question to ask is how come they are
torturing the Greek? He is not a political type. What good is it going to do?
The Greek answers this for me. He says he has used up his trump card, a
friend in high Haitian circles who has promised to come to the hotel and
square things up. But the friend never showed up. And he can't be reached
on the phone. "Maybe he got lost in traffic," I suggest. The Greek says:

"I don't understand the man. I know his wife. I know his mistress. We all made love together. I made beautiful love to his mistress." So I guess the answer lies in this area. The Greek asks me to give him a book. I hand over my copy of *The Digger's Game*, which I liked a lot and wanted to keep. He gives me a "soul" handshake and asks for my number in the States and says I should wait a few days and if I don't hear from him— blow the whistle. I'm not sure I have a whistle to blow. I try to leave, but he won't let go of my hand. I have a great deal of trouble getting away from him.

. . . . .

I go to the airport with the salesman. In the car, I wonder aloud if the Greek is going to get out. He is a Greek citizen, but I don't imagine the colonels are going to be of much use to him. The salesman taps me on the shoulder and gestures toward the driver. I get the idea and I am quiet. I am very happy when the wheels of the plane leave the ground.

. . . . .

It is Friday. I wait until the weekend goes by. Then Monday and Tuesday. Late Tuesday, I get a call from Paris. Collect. It's the Greek. He has gotten out, traveled through Guadaloupe, and then on to France. What he did was go to the airport as though everything was in order. A Haitian official lectured him there, saying, "Maybe you'll conduct yourself properly in the future," then ducking down and whispering, "It's two hundred in cash to leave." He paid up. The Greek said it was marvelous once again to be breathing the clean air of freedom and would I please talk up his surrealist canvases in art circles so that he could follow at some point and sell them for huge prices.

. . . . .

Long before the Greek calls, I decide not to go back to Haiti. It is not exactly a moral judgment. People from the land of Watergate don't get to make those for a while. It's just that I've been there twice. I know what's there. And at the moment, it's not for me.

tokyo

I t was midnight in Tokyo. Mike Halsey looked in all directions for a cab, which was not easy since he was bent over at a ninety-degree angle, the result of having bowed too enthusiastically to a Mitsubishi executive. He was late for an assignation with Yukiko, a beautiful "brain squeezer" from Todai University, whose job it was to sit down with high-ranking employees who were about to retire and extract their wisdom for deposit in a company bank. (After being "squeezed," they were free to seek work in noodle shops.)

Since his arrival in Japan a month before, Mike had worked on an assembly line, saved his hard-gambling friend Bill Atenabe from the Yakuza (Japanese mob), and become ill to the extent that he had been fitted for a death mask. Mike didn't know it at the moment, but in the next twenty-four hours he would consummate his brief affair with the lovely Yukiko, then set off on a mad dash across the city to save his friend Bill once again, this time from committing hara-kiri over the loss of his (newly) feminist wife and his failure to land a coaching job with the Hiroshima Carp baseball team.

A cab stopped for Mike. Relieved, he got in and gave the driver Yukiko's address. He was all hooked over, like a human question mark. There would be no more bowing for Mike Halsey.

. . . . .

Mike Halsey is the central character of *Tokyo Woes*, a novel I wrote in the late eighties. An American contractor, Halsey awakens one morning with a sudden and unfathomable urge to charge off to Japan. He acts on the impulse. At the airport, he calls the woman he lives with, who is

Originally published as "Tokyo—Never Too Late" in *American Way*, September 15, 1991.

understanding but thinks it rude of him to go off to the Far East without first having brought her the Sunday paper. Mike, nonetheless, flies to Tokyo and plunges into life among the Japanese; a few months later he returns to the States better equipped, presumably, to begin life anew.

The book had a decent reception. Some reviewers were enthusiastic; others less so. But not one guessed that the author had never been to Japan. Though the book jacket did not carry a disclaimer, it had never been my intention to mislead. I had always planned, as a minimum courtesy, to visit the country I was writing about. And, after all, I was writing *fiction*. But my wife became pregnant, and I could not bring myself to let her have the baby without the benefit of my expert coaching. So I decided to *begin* writing the book. A few months after the baby was born, I thought, I would head over to Tokyo and gather firsthand information about my subject. At least that was the plan.

Although I had never been there, Japan was not entirely foreign to me. I had read the novels and stories of Kawabata, Abé, and Tanizaki, enjoyed the great Kurosawa films, and boned up on books dealing with Japanese customs and culture. I had barreled through works that purported to explain the Japanese "phenomenon." Japan had become my hobby. Tokyo street maps lined the walls of my office; I kept a Yellow Pages directory of the city close at hand.

So I started Mike Halsey off on his journey. I was familiar with his state of mind, and I certainly knew enough to get him to the San Francisco airport. I had a sense of what the flight would be like, and it would be no problem to have him meet William ("Call me Bill") Atenabe, a friendly Japanese contemporary, returning from the States. Bill easily dissuaded Mike from checking into one of the fabled "mail slot" hotels, inviting him to stay instead at the Atenabe family home. I set off, in this tentative spirit, to write the novel and seemed, at every juncture, to know—or at least to *feel* that I knew—what I was doing. Mount Fuji, music of the Meiji period, the Atenabe home, Japanese assembly lines all seemed familiar to me. Feeling giddy, I pressed on and within five months had finished writing the novel. The publisher suggested a few minor revisions, and without further complications the book went to press. While *Tokyo Woes* did not quite go storming up the best-seller lists, the experience was not without its rewards; chief among them was the pleasure of pulling off something risky.

However, the question of the *real* Japan remained, as it were, a pebble in my shoe. Though Oscar Wilde (who died, I'm convinced, from the strain of having to speak in aphorisms) insisted there *was* no Japan—he suggested that the Land of the Rising Sun was merely a figment of our collective imagination—I was determined to visit this alleged country to see how it measured up to my version of it.

Last May, I made the long-delayed journey, touching down at Narita Airport and taking a shuttle bus to the strange and wonderful New Takanawa Prince Hotel, which turned out to be in the Shinagawa ward, home district of Inspector Imanishi, the low-keyed and relentless hero of Seicho Matsumoto's brilliant detective novels. The lobby of the New Takanawa Prince is stark, minimally decorated, and roughly the size of Shea Stadium, which seemed curious considering the national preoccupation with miniaturization. The room I was shown was small, but before rushing off testily to the Imperial, I made an attempt to appraise it with Far East sensibilities. My pulse soon returned to normal, and I settled in comfortably, allowing myself to enjoy the room's discreet pleasures—a lovely balcony with a view of Tokyo Tower, freshly pressed kimonos, engraved pitchers filled with hot and cold water, a selection of exotic teas, and several English-language newspapers. Before the day was out, a crow flew in through an open window for a quick visit, and a delegation from housekeeping arrived to inform me with regret bordering on shame that my jacket was unacceptable for dry cleaning; it was feared that a tiny spot in the lining might spread to the lapels. My wife, who had stayed home, had given me permission, indeed encouraged me, to have a "married man's" massage (but don't you *dare* turn over, she warned, teasingly). I ordered a massage from the front desk, and soon had a stocky little Japanese grandmother stomping up and down on my back, howling with laughter as she cracked my shoulder joints and pounded my head, no doubt to drive some sense into it—all of which caused me to sleep past dinner.

. . . . .

It was not my intention to visit Mike Halsey's haunts, since, frankly, I did not know where they were. Halsey lived in a kind of generalized Tokyo, spending most of his time at the Atenabe residence (no address given in the novel). At other times, he exercised his fictional prerogative by simply turning up at factories, private clubs, and country inns. As a character in what I thought of as a fable, he did not have to puzzle out street addresses, deal with crowds, or struggle to make himself understood to telephone operators.

His creator's experience was different.

I began each day by jogging through the immediate neighborhood, returning (awkwardly, on the run) the bows of puzzled merchants while being careful to avoid Mike Halsey's mistake of bowing too deeply and becoming imprisoned by the maneuver.

I would pull out my map and mark off a different section of the city—Ropponga, Ginza, Shinjuku, Yurakucho—and wander through its streets. Exactly where I was didn't matter. Everything was fresh and new and unusual, and the idea, during my brief stay, was to get a sense of the city. It quickly became apparent that Halsey's city—the one I had imagined—was more tranquil and serene than the city I finally visited. I was unprepared for the thunder and congestion of the real Tokyo, controlled and harmonious and orchestrated though it is. (Manhattan is congested, too, but it's *my* congestion, and I don't sense that I'm sticking out in the crowd as I get swept away in the human tide.)

I know little, virtually no, Japanese, and so, in a jam, I would cravenly cast about trying—and failing—to find an English-speaking Japanese. I did run across several bilingual Norwegians who came to my rescue, once when I was lost in the Tsukiji fish market, another time in the bewildering subway.

I cannot imagine a city better suited to the lover of curiosities. It's as if Tokyo's streets had been designed by a gifted but mischievous child. My novel hinted at the scattershot nature of the city's design (the Atenabe family home, for example, is wedged between kimono shops), but it was enlightening to experience Tokyo's actual streets, with surprises popping up out of nowhere: a tiny, tilted silver "skyscraper" (with rooms for rent) beside a noodle shop, which leaned in turn against a huge, gladed retreat for corporate executives, and a bit farther along a liquor store called an "Alcohol Station" that abuts the Center for Instruction on the Enjoyment of Recreation. Continuing my random stroll, I passed a spotless auto-repair shop (how to get a car into its tiny garage would be a story in itself), a barbershop with an old-fashioned striped pole, happily coexisting with a neighboring Buddhist shrine, and suddenly rising mightily and incongruously out of an industrial yard, a pair of giant Edo period horses. Across the street, a grizzled woman, easily in her eighties, cheerfully buffed the shoes of an executive while listening to his harried anecdotes.

I soon discovered that in Tokyo, the most mundane of objects—an exit sign, a road divider, a traffic light—is seized upon as a design opportunity. Garbage collectors, chimney sweeps, and construction workers wear handsomely designed uniforms you might find in the windows of exclusive Madison Avenue shops. Neatly dressed radicals shouting "The emperor is God" cruise through the streets in trucks that are on the cutting edge of design: sleek, dun-colored vehicles that seem to be some kind of civilian-military hybrid. Watching somberly, Tokyo's riot police wear the most uniquely designed uniforms in this fashion-conscious city; they look like futuristic hockey goalies with masked helmets and padded, elbow-high gloves that would be the pride of the NHL. The walk sharpened my appetite, and after a quick bite in a modest restaurant, I was given a beautifully inscribed check whose calligraphy was worthy of hanging in an art gallery.

. . . . .

Unlike Mike Halsey, I did not have a Bill Atenabe appear and offer to have me as his house guest. I did, however, run across Tom Tanaka, a retired UN diplomat, who guided me through a maze of department stores in Yurakucho; Ron Spotz, an American expatriate who took me to the Fukuzushi Restaurant in Ropponga, a favorite of Japanese film stars; and Robb Simpson, a Japanese-American, who, along with his lovely friend Yumi, whipped me through the mysterious transit system, then high up on a mountaintop for a three-hour traditional Japanese luncheon.

In *Tokyo Woes*, Mike Halsey experiences a bit of testiness here and there. At one point, locked in combat with a whisk-broom-wielding department-store salesman who dusted him off too vigorously (in Halsey's view), he tumbles down an escalator. My own experience was the opposite. Apart from having been passed up by a few cab drivers in favor of their countrymen, my encounters were cordial ones. On one occasion, a Japanese man not only lit my cigar in this land of smokers, but insisted that I keep his engraved lighter. I was continually stopped by Japanese who were anxious to try out their English on a *gaijin*. One woman, a sixty-year-old mother of three, asked if I would have a glass of tomato juice with her so she could toss English phrases at me. In a coffee shop she produced clippings from her local newspaper, hailing her with banner headlines, for her courage in returning to school after raising a family. Upon hearing that my sons were married (hers were not), she broke into tears.

On the street I would occasionally see an older woman trotting alone, in ceremonial dress, behind her husband, perhaps en route to a wedding. I had read a great deal about the subjugation of women in Japanese society, but the women I saw were often gathered in comfortable, convivial groups, talking and laughing among themselves. Traditional family pressures notwithstanding, they appeared to be happier than their male counterparts.

The Japanese in my novel—as represented by the Atenabe family—struggled to preserve their heritage against the encroachments of the

West. In actuality, apart from the tailored navy blue suits worn by look-alike executives, I saw very little of this encroachment. A Kentucky Fried Chicken outlet may have been thrown pathetically into the landscape, but most everything I ran across—from saltshakers to sushi bars—seemed relentlessly Japanese and, in my view, cordially but firmly sealed off to outside influences. (Japanese visitors may have a similar impression of American cities.)

So, I am left with the questions: Would I have written my novel differently had I first visited Japan? A better question might be: Would I have written the book at all? Who, after such an experience, would be audacious enough to attempt to capture the essence of Tokyo with mere words?

Let's say I *had* visited Tokyo, then sat down to write. I might have added a bit more detail here and there, gotten Mike involved with some American ex-pats, since torn and divided people are always intriguing, thrown in some street addresses, and described the landscape more accurately. The effect surely would have made a more detailed snapshot. Then again, I wouldn't have had my fable.

prague—
the gray enchantress

P rague. A gemstone in the heart of Europe. So haunting in its beauty that Hitler himself, the great *sensitif*, could not bring himself to ravage it, choosing instead to add the city, untouched, to his collection of architectural treasures. If cities can be said to have a gender, Prague falls into the feminine column and is best described in terms that are politically incorrect—languorous, coquettish, alternately sly and accommodating. Landlocked, surrounded by covetous and historically unreliable neighbors, the Gray Enchantress has had to use what once were called "feminine wiles" in order to survive.

I arrive at a time of transatlantic crisis. Ross Perot, after being presented with a $150-million TV advertising proposal, has dropped out of the race, confirming my suspicion that for all of his billions he may be a cheapskate. ("I can get on all those shows for free.") Of more immediate importance, Vaclev Havel, the great Czech playwright who took a reduction in status to become the republic's president, has resigned his position. Slovakia, bursting with ethnic pride—some say misguidedly—had made known its intention to become an independent country. I've barely checked into the Palace Hotel, and half the country I've come to visit is gone. But the mood in the lobby is philosophical. The Czechs feel that Slovakia doesn't have much to offer, and the country will be better off without it. An engineer from Seattle assures me that I'm not to worry. He's there to buy up a shipment of the fabled L-39 Albatross jet trainers and feels confident that the tiny Czech nation, with its pool of brilliant

Originally published as "My Prague" in *Playboy*, January 1993.

scientists and craftsmen, will rival Germany and France as an economic power within ten years.

"Just leave them to their own devices."

But will they be left to their own devices? All about me, hustlers and schemers from around the globe have arrived in force, Americans to buy up buildings, Canadians to swallow up farms, Germans to snatch up breweries. An Australian pulls me aside and tells me to say away from crystal and get into light manufacturing. Then he describes an advertising campaign he's concocted that will take Prague by storm: The Rainbow Man is Coming to Town.

"What product are you selling?" I ask.

"What *difference* does it make," he says snappishly. Then, retreating a bit, he adds: "In Sydney, it was bread."

For some reason, the management makes me out as someone who's there to visit the Jewish cemetery, and there's a concern that since it's Saturday and it's closed, I won't be able to do so. I suggest that the cemetery isn't necessarily a priority on my part, but they can't seem to grasp that and propose that I walk past the grounds and peer in over the fence—then make a more full-out visit on Sunday when it will be open for inspection.

I choose instead to visit Wenceslas Square—in the center of the city— whose grandeur and size hit you in the face with an almost physical force, much in the manner of the Piazza San Marco in Venice. I'm drawn into a great multinational orgy of buying and selling. Shoppers from all over the world have come to join the Czechs in snapping up imitation Seiko watches, Led Zeppelin T-shirts, and dresses that look as if they've been taken from a truck in Passaic, New Jersey. Havel has described the Velvet Revolution as being "a revolt of color, authentic history in all of its variety and human individuality against imprisonment." But here on the square, it's as if the Czechs revolted so that they could shop for discontinued jogging suits.

The shopping is eery and silent, since there is no automobile traffic on the square and the enormous cobblestoned space (half a mile long, sixty yards wide) absorbs the shouts of a thousand hawkers and the cries of victory as cagey Austrians are able to negotiate down the price of model airplane kits. There may never have been such a vast international stewpot. Icelanders and Uruguayans line up to buy American popcorn and pizza from Bosnians who've managed to escape the carnage in Sarajevo and set themselves up in stalls. Bolivian Indians serenade French teenagers as they have their hair braided with colored cotton by spike-haired Boy George look-alikes from the seventies. Black softball stars from the Netherlands, cash in hand, circle the square, asking where the ladies are; they are told to check the hotel lobbies at night. Czechs, who've been known to get on any line, no matter where it leads, queue up to pay thirty crowns for a look inside a stretch limousine at a pair of Brits who are presenting themselves as rock stars. The Japanese (few in number) stay together in shy groups and claim to see hostile Koreans in the shadows. The Germans, who have more joint ventures with the Czechs than any other nation, seem to be there at the moment to correct pronunciation. "Not Wences*laz*, a Berlin man instructs a Canadian who's asked for directions. "Wences*platz*." A Georgetown professor seems to be deranged as he looks out at the great entrepreneurial carnival and cries out: "Fine. But what about poor Bulgaria."

Kafka merchandise is in hot demand, the brooding novelist having become an unlikely pop icon. T-shirts, beer mugs, and even cuff links bearing his likeness disappear quickly from the shelves. There may be an explanation in the Prague *Baedeker* which points out that "two of his novels have been turned into movies." Close on Kafka's heels as the James Dean of Prague is Mozart, whom the Czechs have seized up as one of their own; strictly speaking, the composer spent only a short time in the city, having come there to have his operas produced when they'd received poor reviews at home. Gorbachev T-shirts fly out of the stalls along with hats left behind by Soviet military commanders (all, mysteriously, in small sizes). Mario Puzo's *Sicilian* is a strong seller in the bookstores, as are, mystifyingly, the antiquated novels of Louis Bromfield and slim biographies of Tom Cruise.

Threaded in among the crowd are young Americans (there may be as many as forty thousand living in the city), many of them with a Czech in tow, delivering paid instructions in English while on the run. Chris Scheer, a native of Santa Barbara and editor of the English-language newspaper *Prog-nosis*, has defined them as Posties, post-Viet Nam, post-Cold War, post-Reagan, posteverything, living in something of a moral vacuum with nothing to be for or against. They've come to Prague because the living is cheap (fifty-cent lunches, ten-cent subway rides) and there is not much for them at the moment in the States. But to be fair, it isn't only the economics that has drawn them to the Golden City. The overthrow of a forty-year-old Communist regime, arguably the most repressive in Eastern Europe, had a literary flavor to it, driven as it was by artists and writers and particularly Havel, who is a hero to the Americans here. Allan Levy, editor of the English-language *Prague Post*, suggests, perhaps too sweepingly, that the Americans in Prague are the equivalent of Hemingway's fabled Lost Generation in twenties Paris and that there are future Isherwoods and Audens and Fitzgeralds among them. He concedes that not a single glittering paragraph has been produced yet, but insists that many of these potential greats are holed up in garrets, "working on their novels." Many more have been taken on by government ministers as "consultants."

"What are they consulted about?" I ask a Czech journalist.

"It doesn't matter," he replies. "For many years Americans were held up as the enemy. Now it's fashionable to have one as a consultant."

.....

Though the Czechs have taken to private enterprise with a passion, the transition from the Marxist to the Western style has not been an entirely smooth one. Czech women haven't quite learned to negotiate their miniskirts, with the result that there are exquisite blunders on the trams and in the taverns. Czechs in their sixties and seventies shake their heads dolefully at the skyrocketing prices for sausage and cabbage, and there's little question many would welcome a return to the old system. On Narodni Street, a merchant, confident of becoming rich overnight, has stocked his store with fur coats and gloves and seems puzzled that they are not being snapped up in the suffocating July sun. An American grad student from the Wharton School of Business is proudly taken on a tour of a thirteen-hundred-employee factory by a thirty-year-old Czech who's replaced an old-line Communist Party figure as manager. Suddenly panicked, the Czech takes the American aside and says: "What on God's earth do I do now?"

There is a desperate need to get it right, to get it "Western," as though there is a precise mathematical formula that keeps eluding them. At privatized restaurants, bartenders, with quavering hands, carefully pour vodka as if it's a rare elixir, as supervisors, with folded arms, sternly oversee them. The waitresses and chambermaids seem frightened—as if a single incorrectly positioned saucer will cause the entire new society to crumble. And there's a holdover stiffness and rectitude that calls to mind Communist bureaucrats and the faceless clerks who show up in Kafka novels. A Czech chemical engineer presents me with an example of the new Western-imported decadence that's sweeping the land. At a border crossing near Dresden, three young women approached his car and introduced themselves as college students from Brno. He chatted with them for a bit and later found out, from a friend, that they were prostitutes.

"And?" I say, waiting to be shocked by the coming example of degradation.

"And nothing," he says, puzzled. "Isn't that enough?"

. . . . .

. . . . .

The Czechs may have engineered a glorious revolution and sent the Soviets packing, but they can't seem to believe they've pulled this off. At night, I ask a cabdriver to take me to a highly recommended jazz club on Krakovska Street. When we arrive, the streets are dark and deserted. The cabdriver is nervous about stopping, but finally does so. I knock on the door which opens slightly; I'm scrutinized and then admitted, tentatively, as if we're back in Prohibition days. Inside, several hundred— I'm sorry to report—sweating Czech jazz lovers are packed together in a cloud of smoke and haze, listening intently to a trio led by a spin-off Gerry Mulligan. The mood is clandestine, quietly defiant, as if being present at this white-bread performance is an act of defiance, a show of the irrepressibility of the human spirit. Eyes turn from time to time toward the entranceway as if at any moment the KGB will smash down the door. But this is 1992 and the KGB is long gone. Any prerevolution "informers" are happily dispersed among the crowd, moving to the music. There's nothing to rebel *against*. Yet the Czechs continue reflexively to resist a phantom regime.

An architect in the crowd tells me that during the Communist occupation, a list was circulated in the underground that cited ninety-eight bars and restaurants as being filled with Communist spies.

"We're in one of them," he says, "and quite truthfully, I'm a little uneasy about having this conversation with you."

. . . . .

After dark, the prostitutes come out in force. They are blonde, for the most part, and pretty, and no one seems to have checked to make sure they're of a correct age. "The Russians," I'm told by a journalist, "have made off with the really beautiful ones." Money changers slip out of the shadows, offering to convert dollars into what turns out to be virtually worthless Yugoslav dinars. Gypsy women, many with a single tooth, come cackling forth, one making a decoy lunge at your genitals while a confederate tries for your wallet. They seem puzzled when this is thought not to be endearing. Droves of couples cross the Old Town Square, hand in hand. It's a city for lovers, but there is also a field day to be had for the lonely if such is your persuasion. The streets are mazelike, and it takes little effort to walk for an hour only to end up at your starting point. There is an aimless quality about the city that is infectious—so that a visitor might start out with the stalwart intention of having a look at the Schwarzenburg Palace and end up spending hours inspecting antique Czech muskets at a Narodni Street gun shop. In the evening, the entire population seems to drift over to the six-hundred-year-old Charles Bridge, and the city is at its most stunning when seen from that vantage point. A strolling Englishman stops for a moment and is overcome by the massive Hradcany Castle and its surrounding fairy-tale complex of medieval palaces and chapels, all haloed in gray and gold.

"My God," he exclaims, "this is more beautiful than Venice. Why wasn't I told about it!"

The huge crowd that drifts across the bridge—and comes under the inspection of thirty-nine baroque statues of saints—seems to be a Woodstock Nation come alive again and is held together by music, both good and bad. It's irritating to listen to a guitarist from UCLA hold a section of the locals in thrall with a fraternity-level version of "Hotel California" and make them feel they are on the cutting edge of Western music. But then a mad Czech Jazz violinist lures them away and is quickly backed up by a gifted Senegalese percussionist. Still another wing of the crowd falls in behind a New Orleans Dixieland combo which pipes them off to an all-night jazz club in Mala Strana. The hope arises that this multination of twenty-somethings will never make war on one another, held together as they are by a common music. Of course Hitler wasn't deterred by his love for Alice Faye movies.

. . . . .

The city is a study in wild swings and contradictions. The Vltava River, which curls importantly through the city, is decorative, but has absolutely no commercial or navigational use. The food—with its base of cabbage and duck and dumplings—is numbingly routine, but then one is presented with a masterful and possibly life-changing goulash at Vladimir Vacek's spectacular restaurant adjacent to the Old Town Square. A Bloody Mary will cost eleven dollars at one bar and less than a dollar at a more attractive spot across the street. Caviar, prohibitively expensive at one restaurant, is virtually given away by the bucketful at another. The entire world seems to be trooping to Prague at the moment, and much of the city is under construction—yet the streets are somehow immaculately clear of litter. Czechs are tremendously polite to one another, but the result is often chaotic. A young man on a crowded tram will yield his seat to a young woman who in turn gives it up to an older man who immediately offers it to someone he insists is more decrepit than *he* is and the result is more disorder and commotion than if everyone had stayed in place. The ultimate irony is that many of the Czechs who supported the Velvet Revolution are still in hundred-dollar-a-month jobs while the "evil Communists" of the old regime are cheerfully ensconced in their old government and managerial jobs. Banned from government, the dreaded secret police functionaries have grown prosperous in private security firms. Is this the picture of a society in transition—or has Prague always been the city of irony, taking for its saints and heroes individuals who've thrown themselves from balustrades in defense of some forgotten principle?

. . . . .

I decide to stop chasing after Prague and take up shop outdoors in a *pivnice*, or beer bar, on Na Struze Street, to see if the city will come to me. Before long, I'm joined by a middle-aged Czech financial consultant. (Everyone in Prague is a consultant of some kind. Even the consultants have consultants.) He is fifty and looks seventy, a condition I've noticed in many residents of this much-traumatized city. He points toward a villa in the hills that he has been able to build by making use of the single word of advice he's given to foreign investors: wait.

"For what?" I ask, always the dogged investigator.

"For Stage Three," he says. "In Stage One, right after the Revolution, outsiders arrived with ten thousand dollars in hand, pointed to a building, and asked: How much for that one? In Stage Two, we politely showed them to the airport."

"And Stage Three?"

"The good stuff," he says, generally, then quickly calls over a textiles salesman he describes as "the most sophisticated man in Prague."

He joins us, just as a woman with a substantial bosom passes by.

The world-class sophisticate winks at me and says: "It's what's up front that counts, no?"

The two men—as do all the Czechs I meet—begin to list their grievances against the current government. Prices are too high, the man who pushed a broom under the Communists is still pushing a broom. The bureaucracy is worse than ever, one big game of musical chairs. The minute you make contact with a minister he's replaced by some new idiot. Drugs now flood the city, although, in a sense, this is a good thing, since the laboratory-produced concoctions under the Soviets caused more havoc than the now available heroin and cocaine.

A beautiful young dancer joins us and adds her own litany of complaints. Her rent has been raised, she's about to lose her apartment. Yes, she's free to travel abroad now, but where will she get the money to do so. The arts—music, ballet, theater—have shriveled up. At least under the Communists, they were state supported; there was always money.

She seems totally defeated by the current system. Yet when I ask her if there's anything she has now that she didn't have before, she looks at me with surprise, her shoulders straighten and she breathes freshness and passion into a single word I would have thought had become stale through its overuse by politicians and ninth-rate patriots.

"Freedom."

little rock

I t's the photograph that lingers, one that he was reluctant to release to the *Wall Street Journal*, as if he feared it would reveal a shameful secret. In it, Vincent Foster—a handsome man by any standard—appears to be grim, unsmiling, guarded and does not project the image of a man who is getting a great deal out of life. No question hindsight makes a contribution, but even at a sunnier time, Foster's smile, as he strolls, along with the Clintons, through the lobby of his beloved Little Rock Repertory Theatre, seems tight and controlled. "Who is Vincent Foster?" the *Journal* asked, in a critical piece that appeared last summer, a short time before the White House deputy counsel—and the president's personal lawyer—took his own life. Many speculate that it was the drumbeat of attacks from the *Journal* itself, so highly thought of in Arkansas corporate circles, that helped lead Foster to his glum decision. The attacks were certainly on his mind when he wrote his last tortured list of grievances. "*The Wall Street Journal* lies with impunity."

Months after the tragedy, there are other pieces of the tableau that continue to resonate—the uneaten M&Ms, the ride in a Toyota to Fort Marcy, the Civil War cannon at the site, the ritualistic removal of jacket and tie (a man still in control), the gun placed in the mouth (a 1913 Colt revolver, inherited from his father, who had died eighteen months before). The single shot that tore away the brain stem.

And then a fresh set of characters: the exotically named White House decorator, Kaki Hockersmith; Bernard Nussbaum, who had joked with Foster that as chief counsel, *he* ought to be getting more attention from the *Journal* (see separate folio for Friedman's Theory of Jokes); the Park

Originally published as "My Little Rock" in *Playboy*, January 1994.

Rangers, like Keystone Cops. Finally, William Safire's powerful questions in the *New York Times*, each ringing out like a gunshot, all still unanswered (Who tore up Foster's note? . . . Where is the Missing Piece? . . . Where is the middle-aged male, driving a white van, who reported finding the body to a parking lot attendant?).

. . . . .

Rock musicians are fond of pointing out that you can't judge or predict behavior on the road. Washington, D.C., was the "road" for Vincent Foster. Would he be alive if he'd stayed at home in Little Rock? We're told that he had great misgivings about going to the capital in the first place, and did so only at the urgent behest of his long-term friends, the Clintons. He was something of a Golden Boy in Little Rock, had never suffered a setback there, and was able to live in great comfort on his three-hundred-thousand-dollar-a-year income at the Rose law firm. Harry Thomason, the producer, and a player in the Travelgate mess that troubled Foster so greatly, is convinced it was Washington that killed him. Foster himself, in his anguished final note, said, "I was not meant for the job or spotlight of public life in Washington," and it's known that he suggested to his wife that they return home—a week before he died—and was encouraged by her to stay on until the end of the year. No one, of course, could know his state of mind at the time. "Men are never convinced of the seriousness of your suffering," says Camus's narrator in *The Fall*, "except by your death."

What about Little Rock? Is it the special, nurturing place it's painted out to be? As it happens, I spent some time there, in the summer, several weeks before Foster's death, drawn by a curiosity as to what it was, if anything, that made the city unique. Clinton had lived most of his life in Little Rock—as had Foster. Was there something in the makeup of the city that helped the president—and those around him—survive the long, arduous, and ultimately miraculous journey from watermelon-growing Hope to the mighty office he was to occupy?

After first glance, and even second, Little Rock is a city like so many others, with a river (the Arkansas) running through it to no particular purpose, a downtown area with pockets of life, but one that's more or less been abandoned to a few commercial interests—and the usual movement to an outlying more optimistic district, the West Side in this case, with its affluent homes, monster malls, and a spreading network of restaurants, both pricey and affordable. At every turn, the visitor is told about the rise of Systematics and the miracle of Tyson Frozen Food, but apart from food consumption, there doesn't seem to be a great deal going on. It would not seem possible for a city of 175,000 to support as many restaurants as exist in Little Rock, but support them it does, and new ones keep rolling in. There must be something in Steven Crane's beloved "piney air" that explains the city's eating habits—and the president's celebrated appetite as well.

Dutifully, I visited the state capitol (a scaled-down replica of the one in D.C.), listened to Copperhead at Juanita's, sampled the justifiably celebrated ribs at Sims, wandered through the historic Quapaw section and sat beneath the Do Not Spit sign at a livestock auction at which the farmers spoke in country music lyrics. ("You buy those hogs, your daddy be proud of you.") I showed up at Ray Winder Field to watch the last-place Travellers ("Travs" to you, bud) win a ball game from the Shreveport Captains. I'd been told it might get rowdy at these games, but I found it to be all *Field of Dreams* innocence and Bingo and "Take Me Out to the Ball Game"; the most boisterous note was an occasional frail plea to the pitcher to "strike the bum out." I'd had my doubts about the women of Little Rock—heartbreaking faces, agricultural haunches—until I saw the Travelettes with their silky hair and long lazy legs in lazy white shorts and what I took to be their languid dreams of the Big City.

None of which brought me any closer to the spiritual heart of Little Rock. It's only when I visited the huge (165,000 sq. ft.) Wal-Mart Food Emporium in Conway that I got my first clue.

A man sat alone in the luncheonette, at a table for two, smoking a cigarette and sipping a cup of coffee. At first glance, he seemed to be wearing an African mask, one that had been left out in the sun and was now bleached white and had a corner chewed off. A closer look indicated that he was not wearing a mask at all, that I was looking at his face. I circled round a few times, at whatever a discreet distance is, coming up on him from different angles, hoping that I was wrong, but I wasn't wrong. It was his face alright. I felt a need to *do* something, go up and ask him how he was getting along, but I decided not to. No one else in the Wal-Mart seemed to feel this call for action. No doubt they had concluded that the man might not *want* anything done, that he was doing just fine, sitting there, drinking his coffee, watching people who'd come from as far away as Crumrod in the east and Bloomer in the west to shop for bagel dogs, flop sticks, ribwiches, and black tip shark.

They'd accepted him. He was a neighbor in a city of 175,000 neighbors, part of a state filled with two million more. You accept your neighbor, look out for your neighbor. I could think of places where this fellow might be scorned or hidden away in attics, and others where he might even be worshiped, but none in which he would so casually be allowed to go about his business.

. . . . .

. . . . .

So perhaps that was the secret. Little Rock is our most caring city. It's been said that Foster couldn't go back, couldn't rejoin the Rose law firm. How could he pursue new clients when he'd just "failed" the most important client in the country? How could he rejoin the country club when he'd quit to protest its discriminatory policies? But the evidence is that he would have been taken back warmly by this welcoming city of friendly porches, great drinking water, Depression-level rents, and huge breakfasts. (At Wallace's Grill, the President's favorite, it's a struggle to spend more than two dollars.)

"It's the most egalitarian place you'll ever find," says Alan Leveritt, publisher of the bright and cheerfully opinionated *Arkansas Times*. "There's no rich landed aristocracy. Everyone is a step removed from the farm. You're dead if you try to put on airs. Little Rock is Don Tyson, the richest man in the state, showing up for ribs at Sims in a pickup, wearing a chicken suit like the guy who works at the filling station."

There's a darker side, too . . . the sad and forlorn neighborhoods of the East Side (you're encouraged to drive west), the street cemetery where fifty crosses mark the graves of blacks who've been killed by other blacks in local drug wars . . . a food-and-beverage man at the Capital Bar who told me not to delude myself about the city's kind heart.

"You're in a Third World country. Ninety percent of the money—and some of it is 'slave' money—is in the hands of 5 percent of the folks. They're out there in Edgehill and the Heights and if you're not part of their Old Boy network, you'll never rise above the peon level."

So maybe the city isn't quite as caring as I'd wanted it to be. At lunch, Rose Crane, the girl-next-door to Clinton when he was a boy in Hot Springs, and who served in his gubernatorial administration, summed up Little Rock this way: "It's a wonderful place to be poor."

. . . . .

It's a place to be touchy, too. Built into the character of the city—and of Arkansas in general—is a sensitivity about its past, its reputation, in Mencken's phrase, as a "miasmic jungle," one in which "the men drink moonshine whisky, the women chew and dip, the big gals go barefooted, with tobacco on their lip." For the past several decades, Little Rock has been a symbol to the world of snarling racists, Governor Faubus, and the notorious standoff at Central High. Much of that self-consciousness has been erased by having a son of Arkansas in the White House—a Kennedy look-alike at that, with a steel-trap mind—but the Arkansas skin remains thin. Hillary Clinton is said to become infuriated when someone says, self-consciously: "I'm just from Arkansas."

"For the *Wall Street Journal* to question *our* mores," a leading Little Rock businessman says to me . . . and then can't continue the sentence. . . . It's as if he's been shot in the stomach. Foster had his office just down the street from this rock-ribbed conservative. The White House deputy counsel came from a state that's touchy about its past, its politics, and its image in general. The first joke that Arkansans hear is that it's a good thing Mississippi exists—so that Arkansas doesn't have to be last in everything. In this context, it's not difficult to imagine Foster, who obviously lacked the rhino hide his friend Clinton is blessed with—becoming increasingly dispirited as the *Journal* poured it on. "The legal cronies from Little Rock." . . . "The Clinton crew." . . . "The Rose clique". . . . "Arkansas' peculiar mores." . . . "Who is Vincent Foster?" . . .

.....

Had Foster ever made it out of Washington in June, he would have returned to a city in which the mood was one of mild hurt and abandonment. Half the world had descended on Little Rock for election night and the inauguration celebration; it was not uncommon for a local resident to sip a cup of coffee opposite Peter Jennings, to trade niceties with G. Gordon Liddy, or to watch Ivana Trump sail by in a limousine. Restaurants and hotels were filled to capacity, the money flowed, and there was a feeling that Little Rock was about to become Boomtown, USA. But Wolf Blizter and the Secret Service were gone now and Richard Dreyfuss was back in Beverly Hills, and the city seemed bewildered and shell shocked.

"It's three months now," an executive said to me at the Capital Bar, "and he (Clinton) hasn't done a damned thing for us."

"What can he do?" his friend asked, with genuine curiosity.

"We've got all that rice," the first man said, then muttered something about tax credits for small businessmen, but it was all spoken without conviction.

"The real trouble with Little Rock," he continued despairingly, "is that we do not have a niche. Milwaukee's got beer, Chicago's got the Bulls, and I do not have to tell you about Orlando."

"What about hogs?"

"That's exactly my point. Hogs are not a niche."

After the Foster death, I got back in touch with some of the people
I'd spoken to in the City without a Niche. Beth Arnold, a journalist and
longtime resident, said that most of the people she knew were resigned
to the fact that Foster took his own life, plain and simple. There were
some who took seriously, however, a story circulating in Little Rock
that his death was linked to a series of "alleged" suicides in the military
that Foster was investigating—suicides that were really cover-ups for
murders related to drug smuggling, using the services as a conduit. Four of
these "suicides" were Arkansans. Alan Leveritt, whose *Arkansas Times*
covered the bizarre theory, personally discounts it. "I grew up in a right-
wing family so I'm not a stranger to conspiracy theories, but I don't
believe there's anything to it. Foster was tremendously idealistic about
the move to Washington. When Hillary made her farewell speech to the
Rose law firm and told how they were going to make a better life for
America, Vincent was the only one in the room crying. When he got to
the White House and felt he'd let down a man who was not only his
closest friend, but also the president, he shot himself and that's all there
is to it."

A man who was terribly shaken by the Foster suicide was the leading
Little Rock businessman I'd spoken to, one of the three most influential
in the city, actually. He'd been to see Clinton three times in the White
House and returned home leery of the "ozone" and the way it seemed
to be affecting the people around the president. He received the news of
the Foster suicide when he was vacationing in the Carolinas. Returning
to Little Rock, he assembled his staff, and they all concluded it was
something that could happen right there, "to any one of us." That night,
untypically, he sat out beneath the stars and drank a bottle of fine
California wine and concluded: "This is what's important, not what the
Wall Street Journal thinks of you."

There are roughly forty-thousand suicides in the United States annu-
ally (most of them forty-ish white males), yet the Vincent Foster death
lingers. Few question that Foster was the "wonderful man in every way"
that the president made him out to be, and the grief in Little Rock
and across the nation as well was no doubt genuine. But as with every
suicide there were other more complex feelings as well. This was a *White
House* suicide (the first since Secretary of the Navy James Forrestal in

the Truman administration). As such, it held out the promise of scandal and skulduggery in high places. Indeed, there were plenty of rumors—an aborted homosexual tryst in Fort Marcy, an affair with Hillary, something truly explosive in the *Washington Times*—yet none of this ever panned out. Possibly this left a cable-TV-hardened public frustrated, determined to hold on to the Foster story until given the tangier scenario it's been led to believe it deserves.

When we annoint our fellow Americans and send them off to Olympus, a.k.a. Washington, D.C., we assume they've shed their banal earthly concerns and are ready to lead—on our behalf—a gilded, trouble-free existence. When it turns out that this hasn't happened—that they've fallen victim to the same concerns that we have to deal with—loneliness, overwork, feelings of failure—there's a sense of sadness, of course, but also of betrayal.

To discover that the privileged Vincent Foster went to the White House and remained one of us is unacceptable.

That he found a way out is even more so.

Acknowledgments

The author is grateful to the following colleagues. Each has been helpful along the way. Dan Wakefield, Gordon Lish, the late Harold Hayes, Byron Dobell, Lee Eisenberg, John Rezek, Robert Brown, Geoffrey Norman, Arthur Kretchmer, Terry McDonel, the editors of *Wigwag*, William Emerson, William Ewald, Melvin Shestack, Michael Caruso, Clay Felker, Mark Horowitz, Erik Carlson and, in particular, Geoffrey Huck.

DATE DUE
